PARLIAMENTARY HISTORY: TEXTS & STUDIES

4

Knowledge and Power

Parliamentary History: Texts & Studies

Knowledge and Power

The Parliamentary Representation of Universities in Britain and the Empire

by

Joseph S. Meisel

Wiley-Blackwell

For

The Parliamentary History Yearbook Trust

Registered Office

John Wiley & Sons Ltd, The Atrium, Southern Gate, Chichester, West Sussex, PO19 8SQ, United Kingdom

Editorial Offices

350 Main Street, Malden, MA 02148-5020, USA

9600 Garsington Road, Oxford, OX4 2DQ, UK

The Atrium, Southern Gate, Chichester, West Sussex, PO19 8SQ, UK

For details of our global editorial offices, for customer services, and for information about how to apply for permission to reuse the copyright material in this book please see our website at www.wiley.com/wiley-blackwell.

Library of Congress Cataloging-in-Publication Data

Meisel, Joseph S.

Knowledge and power : the parliamentary representation of universities in Britain and the Empire / by Joseph S. Meisel.

p. cm. – (Parliamentary history texts & studies ; 4)

Includes bibliographical references and index.

ISBN 978-1-4443-5020-3 (pbk. : alk. paper)   1. Higher education and state–Great Britain–History.   2. Great Britain. Parliament–History.   3. Representative government and representation–Great Britain–History.

I. Title.

LC178.G7M45 2011

378.41–dc23

2011020691

A catalogue record for this title is available from the British Library

Set in 10/12pt Bembo

by Toppan Best-set Premedia Limited

Printed and bound in Singapore

by Hó Printing Pte Ltd

1   2011

CONTENTS

TABLE OF TABLES

ACKNOWLEDGMENTS

When I first came across the existence of university seats in the course of undergraduate research, I thought the concept fascinating but never could have imagined that I would one day undertake a substantial study of them. The origins of this book lie in a conversation with Mordechai Feingold at the California Institute of Technology about his goals for expanding the subject of the *History of Universities*, a journal he was editing. I made an offhand comment about how a study of university representation in Britain during the 19th and early 20th centuries might be interesting as a new way of connecting the history of higher education with the history of politics. In the years that followed, Moti persistently encouraged me to produce such an article, which eventually I did.[1] I discovered that university representation was a much more interesting subject than I had imagined at the outset, and a phenomenon with far greater significance than had been claimed for it in any of the very few previous and partial works about it.

In the preparation of this book, my gratitude begins with Clyve Jones who was receptive to the idea of publishing this material as part of *Parliamentary History*'s Texts & Studies series. Anne Rickard shepherded the text with exemplary care and thoughtfulness. I need to reiterate my thanks to Margot Finn, Susan Pedersen, Sheldon Rothblatt, Christopher Stray, James Thompson, James Vernon and *History of Universities*' anonymous readers for their contributions to my discussion of university representation in modern Britain, now reformulated and expanded in Chapters 2–4. For consultations on, and readings of, the book manuscript in part or in whole, I must thank Bernard Bailyn, Sugata Bose, Linda Colley, William Lubenow, Stuart Macintyre and Iain McCalman. As with all my other historical efforts, a special debt of gratitude is owed to my mentor and friend, David Cannadine.

Librarians and archivists are rarely acknowledged to the extent they deserve. This study would have been impossible without the assistance, both on site and remotely, of many custodians of research materials. In particular, thanks are owed to: Adrian Allan, University Archivist, University of Liverpool; Deepa Banerjee, South Asian Studies Librarian, University of Washington; Tricia Boyd, Senior Library Assistant, Special Collections Department, University of Edinburgh; Martin Davies, House of Commons Information Office; Ruth Gibson, Special Collections, University of Birmingham; Liza Giffen, University Archivist, University of Leeds; Barbara L. Krieger, Archivist, Dartmouth College; Hannah Lowery, Archivist, Special Collections, University of Bristol; Emma Marsh, Archives Assistant, University of Oxford; Julia Mant and Nyree Morrison, Reference Archivists, University of Sydney; John O'Brien, Archivist, India Office Records, British Library; Eva Oledzka, Special Collections Administrator, University of London; James Peters, University Archivist, University of Manchester; Mari Takayanagi, Parliamentary Archives; Richard Temple, Archivist, University of London; Katie Wood, Reference Archivist, University of Melbourne Archives; Matthew Zawadzki, Archivist and Records Manager, University of Sheffield. In a similar category are those who undertook research on my behalf in places where the time and expense of travel were prohibitive: Lana

[1] Joseph S. Meisel, 'A Magnificent Fungus on the Political Tree: The Growth of University Representation in the United Kingdom, 1832–1950', *History of Universities*, xxiii/1 (2008), 109–86.

Nadj, lawyer and research consultant, Sydney; James Waghorne, History of the University Unit, University of Melbourne; and Angela Werren, Manager of Academic Policy, New Zealand Vice-Chancellors Committee.

It is also worth noting that, while a great deal of the most important material for this study was only available in libraries and archives, the ability to uncover university representation's history and expose its deeper and broader significance was made possible by the existence of a wide range of electronic databases. Allied with the historian's traditional methods of identifying and investigating archival and library-based sources, the ability to search through vast corpora of digitalised newspapers, books, periodicals, parliamentary papers, legislative debates and other documents was critical for discovering the multiplicity of ways and numerous locations in which the topic of university representation was raised, and thereby demonstrating the case for the importance of this topic. In the imperial settings particularly, even establishing the basic facts of university representation was heavily dependent on dogged database searching. Because valuable information about university representation was typically embedded within discussions of larger issues, the neglect of the subject and the failure heretofore to recognize the extent of its significance may owe much to the obscurity of the record. This study could not have been realized, or its arguments advanced, without the power to sift out isolated particles of evidence from the vast terrain of documentation related to political representation in Britain and the empire. In these ways, then, this book is an example of scholarship made possible by mass digitisation.

I could not have written this book without the superb support of the Mellon Foundation's librarian, Susanne Pichler, and assistant librarian, Lisa Bonifacic, who were as generous with their time as they were resolute in pursuing a wide array of arcane information and source materials on my behalf. I am also grateful to Don Randel and Harriet Zuckerman for their general encouragement, and for allowing me the time and resources to carry out the research for this book. My superb former colleagues at Mellon and the extraordinary scholars I was privileged to associate with and support were my intellectual whetstones for more than a decade.

Last but hardly least, I must thank my family for constant support and generous forbearance. My father, Martin, and late mother, Martha, initiated both my love of history and my lifelong engagement with Britain. My wife, Felice, has lived indulgently with, and even enjoyed, both these characteristics for a quarter-century. This book is dedicated to my son, Luke, whose knowledge and power increase daily and wondrously before my eyes.

NOTE ON TERMINOLOGY

Throughout this book, the use of place names like 'Oxford' or 'Calcutta' will typically indicate the universities there located, unless otherwise specified.

Introduction

The representation of universities – involving not only special franchises for graduates, but also the privilege of returning their own members to sit in the legislature – was a feature of parliamentary life in Britain and beyond for around 350 years, and it has not yet vanished entirely. This book is the first attempt at a full account of this long-enduring but barely studied component of the 'Mother of Parliaments' and a number of her offspring, taking in university representation's entire chronological and geographical sweep while also examining how it functioned within the political systems of which it was a part. Originating in 17th-century England, the conception and practices of university representation were transmitted over the ensuing centuries to other places as part of the spread of English, then British, imperial control and constitutional ideas. Introduced in the vassal Irish parliament shortly after the English originals, forms of university representation subsequently came to be implemented or considered throughout the British empire – in India, North America, Australasia and the Mediterranean. In the meantime, it grew within the United Kingdom, ultimately extending across England, Scotland, Ireland and Wales.

The bases of political representation, though generally conceived of in relation to population, territory or economic interests, have historically been defined in a wide variety of ways in response to social, practical, theoretical and ideological imperatives. At the most general level, the story of university representation is that of the uneasy and at times ambiguous relationship between knowledge and power in both the modern British state and its imperial outposts. Parliament was the world of power; universities were the world of knowledge. The creation, maintenance and spread of university seats in parliament as the seeming embodiment of learning in the legislature could suggest that the two worlds were mutually reinforcing. But the history of university representation demonstrates that their interests were hardly identical, and the broader forces at work in the political world did not necessarily pull in the same direction as those acting on, and within, the universities. Like other categories of representation, university representation was not a static concept. Over time, the institution of university representation adapted to changing circumstances, and the meanings ascribed to it were correspondingly transformed, as universities evolved from clerical seminaries to secularised centres of higher learning, as the structures of politics moved in difficult and uneven steps from royal absolutism to mass democracy, and as England transformed into a multinational state and global imperium.

Although university representation was created in the 17th century, and by the early 18th century had spawned two durable overseas expansions, its major period of growth and development occurred in the late 19th and early 20th centuries. Its deeper historical roots notwithstanding, university representation was less a constitutional antique than an outcome of political modernisation. Beginning in the 1820s, and proceeding apace in the Victorian era, the establishment of new universities (and reform of the older ones in Scotland) created a substantial number of new potential constituencies to which the privilege of returning burgesses to parliament could be extended. Simultaneously, successive extensions of the franchise and redistribution of parliamentary seats in Britain between 1832 and 1928 created opportunities for universities' advocates to seek inclusion of their institutions under this special category of constituencies. The characteristics of university graduates and the nature of the MPs they would be likely to return featured prominently in debates over the kinds of people who were fit to receive the vote and the nature of parliamentary representation itself.

The 19th and early 20th centuries also witnessed rapid imperial expansion and colonial development. In many of the major imperial territories, as in Britain, the building of modern political structures also overlapped with efforts to create new higher education institutions to serve the needs of government and society. As in Britain, too, there was considerable variation in the motives and functions associated with university representation in the empire. In the settler territories, it had to be considered in relation to the emergence of colonial self-governance. In the case of India, it was understood as a means for the British administration to begin including segments of the native population in the administration of their own affairs. More generally, university representation in both Britain and the empire played a mixed and at times shifting role in relation to moves towards greater democratisation.

The remainder of this introduction attempts to set the conceptual and historiographical stage for the ensuing analytical chapters. The central fact is scholars' general neglect of university representation in both its British and imperial articulations. The interest of university representation lies not in any antiquarian appeal as a quaint eccentricity of British politics. It was an integral feature of parliament that played a unique role in Britain's modern political development. As a specialised legislative formation that theoretically united knowledge and power, university representation constitutes something like a 'strategic research site', the study of which brings to light new dimensions of the political history of Britain and the empire, and of the complex interrelationships between them.[1]

1. *University Representation in British History*

A very small number of works have taken up the history of university representation in Britain in any detail. The most substantial of these, by Millicent Barton Rex, details the origins and first 86 years of the institution at Oxford and Cambridge.[2] The contemporaneous case of the University of Dublin, not to mention subsequent university enfranchisements in England, Scotland, Ireland and Wales, are beyond the scope of Rex's analysis (she did not complete a projected follow-up volume covering the years after 1690). Another, much briefer, account by Thomas Lloyd Humberstone (a prominent member of the University of London's convocation) covers the whole history for the

---

[1] The concept of strategic research materials developed by Robert K. Merton involves 'the empirical material [i.e. research sites, objects or events] that exhibits the phenomena to be explained or interpreted to such advantage and in such accessible form that it enables the fruitful investigation of previously stubborn problems and the discovery of new problems for further inquiry'. Robert K. Merton, 'Three Fragments from a Sociologist's Notebooks: Establishing the Phenomenon, Specified Ignorance, and Strategic Research Materials', *Annual Reviews of Sociology*, xiii (1987), 10–23, quotation from 10–11.

[2] Millicent Barton Rex, *University Representation in England, 1604–1690* (1954).

United Kingdom, but is an anecdotal chronicle rather than a work of historical analysis.[3] Both works were produced around the time that university representation ceased to exist, and were thus addressing a subject at a moment of unusual topicality. In each case, the authors focus mainly on presenting a narrative of university representation as a constitutional peculiarity, and on accounting for the activities of the university members. While Rex studiously investigates university representation's record in relation to the tumultuous politics of 17th-century England, Humberstone does little to situate the growth of this special franchise within the larger history of political reform and modernisation in Britain.

For historians of British politics, the parliamentary representation of universities has sometimes attracted passing curiosity but rarely sustained investigation.[4] University representation, if mentioned at all, is generally treated as an anachronistic survival of England's *ancien régime* constitution, and therefore peripheral to the tenacious political narrative of gradual democratisation by stages. In the large literature on British political development in the 19th and 20th centuries, works sometimes mention the addition of university seats in successive reform bills and their elimination by the Attlee government. Most often, however, the university seats are passed over quickly or dismissed as mere outliers from the main action taking place in the borough and county constituencies. This is most especially true in works rooted in the study of electoral practices, because university constituencies had their own distinctive methods of selecting their MPs. Even when historians have duly taken account of university representation, they have paid scant attention to the significance attached to it in the debates surrounding virtually every proposed measure of constitutional or electoral reform.

On the biographical front, lives of notable figures who held university seats – including Isaac Newton, the younger Pitt, Lord Palmerston, Sir Robert Peel and William Gladstone – may discuss the special characteristics (and challenges) of these constituencies in relation to their subjects, but a systematic consideration of university representation falls outside the biographer's brief, even when the authors are deeply versed in the mechanics of British politics.[5] Biography also has limited value for systematic understanding of university representation because it treats the experiences of individual members in isolation. Additionally, not all who held university seats were sufficiently important in other realms to have merited intensive biographical study.

---

[3] T. Lloyd Humberstone, *University Representation* (1951). Humberstone published much of the material in his book as three articles in *Parliamentary Affairs*, i, no. 1 (1947), 67–82; no. 2 (1947), 78–93; no. 4 (1948), 78–88. See also R.B. McCallum and Alison Readman, *The British General Election of 1945* (Oxford, 1947), ch. 21. An earlier account that provides a useful overview of developments up to the beginning of the 20th century is Edward Porritt, 'Barriers against Democracy in the British Electoral System', *Political Science Quarterly*, xxvi (1911), 1–31. A provisional effort to document the archival record of university representation appears in Adrian R. Allen, *University Bodies: A Survey of Intra- and Supra-university Bodies and Their Records* (Liverpool, 1990), 81–3, 250, 273–4.

[4] Even A. Lawrence Lowell, that great explicator of the intricacies of British politics (and future president of Harvard), devotes only one small paragraph to the subject in his monumental study, *The Government of England* (2 vols, New York, 1908), i, 197.

[5] See, e.g., John Ehrman, *The Younger Pitt* (3 vols, 1969–96), i, 24–5, 57, 149–50; Kenneth Bourne, *Palmerston: The Early Years, 1784–1841* (1982), esp. 50–64, 73–8, 239–48, 506–8; Norman Gash, *Mr Secretary Peel: The Life of Sir Robert Peel to 1830* (Cambridge, MA, 1961), 211–18, 560–4; H.C.G. Matthew, *Gladstone, 1809–1874* (Oxford, 1986), 70–2, 129; Susan Pedersen, *Eleanor Rathbone and the Politics of Conscience* (New Haven, CT, 2004), 220–8.

Perhaps most surprising, the significance for universities of having direct representation in the national legislature is also little remarked upon by historians of British higher education. In histories of the educational institutions that were granted this privilege, university representation may be mentioned at appropriate junctures, but they generally focus on the internal politics of electoral contests.[6] W.R. Ward's studies of 18th- and 19th-century Oxford are notable exceptions by virtue of their extensive treatment of the local and national politics surrounding the election of the university's burgesses. But his thesis, that the importance of these burgesses at Westminster waned over the course of the 19th century as Oxford's purview with respect to church and state diminished, is inadequate for understanding the broader significance for Britain's political and educational history of university representation's growth and diversification, or the arguments and justifications that were marshalled in connection with these developments.[7]

The history of university representation's expansion in the United Kingdom challenges accounts of British democratisation that emphasize linear progress while also adding a highly revealing but overlooked dimension to scholarship, arguing that the extension of political rights was a far more contested, contingent and at times contradictory process. Looking at public political meetings between the world wars, for example, Jon Lawrence has written of the 'fundamental paradox of politics in modern Britain', in which the creation of a more formally democratic polity was accompanied by developments that made politics effectively less democratic.[8] Similarly, the history of university representation in the 19th and early 20th centuries demonstrates the strong connection and even mutual dependence between the development of new systems of political participation and the persistence of older forms. Historians' elisions of university representation belie the fact that it was precisely the increasingly anomalous character of university representation in a reforming electoral system that required politicians to grapple with it in ever more serious ways.

---

[6] See, e.g., James Bass Mullinger, *The University of Cambridge* (3 vols, Cambridge, 1911), ii, 459, 463–4; iii, 207; *A History of the University of Cambridge*, ed. Christopher N.L. Brooke (4 vols, Cambridge, 1989–2004), iii, 386–90, 421–2, 485–92; Charles Edward Malet, *A History of the University of Oxford* (3 vols, 1924), ii, 238–9; *The History of the University of Oxford, Vol. 4: Seventeenth-Century Oxford*, ed. Nicholas Tyacke (Oxford, 1997), 196–8; *The History of the University of Oxford, Vol. 6: Nineteenth-Century Oxford, Part 1*, ed. M.G. Brock and M.C. Curthoys (Oxford, 1997), 46, 54–9, 188, 202, 311–12, 322–5, 236. The University of London's successful struggle to obtain representation is not touched upon in the volume produced for its sesquicentennial anniversary: *The University of London and the World of Learning, 1836–1986*, ed. F.M.L. Thompson (1990). Even older works, which might be expected to pay more attention, provide the barest mention – e.g. John Pentland Mahaffy, *An Epoch in Irish History: Trinity College, Dublin, Its Foundation and Early Fortunes, 1591–1660* (1903), 156. Review of many histories of the 'modern' universities that made up the Combined English Universities constituency (too numerous to be cited here) turns up no mention of representation, even in works dating from the early 1950s, shortly after the constituency was eliminated.

[7] W.R. Ward, *Georgian Oxford: University Politics in the Eighteenth Century* (Oxford, 1958); W.R. Ward, *Victorian Oxford* (1965).

[8] Jon Lawrence, 'The Transformation of British Public Politics after the First World War', *Past & Present*, no. 190 (2006), 185–216. Influential studies of the complexities and contradictions of political reform include: James Vernon, *Politics and the People: A Study in English Political Culture, c.1815–1867* (Cambridge, 1993); *Re-reading the Constitution: New Narratives in the Political History of England's Long Nineteenth Century*, ed. James Vernon (Cambridge, 1996); Catherine Hall, Keith McClelland and Jane Rendall, *Defining the Victorian Nation: Class, Race, Gender and the Reform Act of 1867* (Cambridge, 2000). John Garrard, *Democratization in Britain: Elites, Civil Society and Reform since 1800* (Basingstoke, 2002) is a notable recent attempt to make a case for British democratisation as an essentially linear and benign evolutionary process.

At another level, the history of university representation offers an important way of connecting high politics and the evolving character and structure of higher education in this period – developments in which, of course, the state was directly involved to an ever-increasing extent. If historians note the extensions of the university franchise that accompanied reform bills, they have made virtually no effort to understand what motivated both older and new universities to seek grants of parliamentary representation during these episodes of political opportunity. Nor have historians investigated the range of arguments and activities that universities mobilised to that end, and the kinds of opposition they encountered. The universities' defence of their representative privileges against proposals to alter or abolish them has also largely been overlooked. Exploring the presence of universities within the structures of national politics in this way adds a new dimension to the history of universities, a subject that has tended to neglect direct connections with political history in favour of institutional and intellectual matters.[9]

The interaction between the developing structures of national politics and those of higher education was manifested in the shifting, if overlapping, ideological bases on which arguments for continuing and expanding university representation were made. It was first defended as a corporate vested interest, especially but not exclusively by the universities that had received the initial grants of representation. Then it became tied up with mid-Victorian debates about intellect and the nation. Later in the 19th century, a more pragmatic and partisan view took hold. Finally, and especially following the First World War, university representation was seen as a means of counterbalancing an electorate dominated by working men. Yet the growth of university representation in the 19th and early 20th centuries resulted neither from a broad political consensus that university representation was highly desirable, nor from resigned acquiescence to its enlargement. Rather, university representation was criticized and challenged throughout this period, even as, paradoxically, its enlargement was effected.

2. 'Parliament as Export' and the 'Colonial Public Sphere'

Beyond the British Isles, the idea of university representation was taken up to a greater or lesser extent around the British empire. Here the extant literature is even thinner than for the British case. With characteristic punctiliousness, Rex briefly notes some of the instances of university representation outside the British Isles in the introduction to her book, but she offers no detailed examination or comparative analysis of these instantiations.[10] A few scattered articles take up individual cases, primarily as curiosities of local interest rather than pieces of a globe-spanning patchwork of political and educational institution building. In light of the preceding discussion of the British original, accounting for the imperial spread of university representation affords a new and unprecedented perspective on the transmission and adaptation of political ideas across the colonial landscape.

[9] Recent exceptions include Keith Vernon, *Universities and the State in England, 1850–1939* (2004), and Sheldon Rothblatt, *Education's Abiding Moral Dilemma: Merit and Worth in the Cross-Atlantic Democracies, 1800–2006* (Oxford, 2007).

[10] Rex, *University Representation*, 11–13.

In the realms of both political ideas and practical policies, the empire has been understood as a great zone of export and experiment. But such transactions were rarely straightforward. Some institutions that worked well in Britain, like a hereditary aristocracy, failed to find support in the colonies. Other concepts, like federalism, which were promoted with success in imperial settings, were never considered viable ideas in Britain. It is not sufficient, therefore, to treat university representation's appearances in the empire as a simple transplanting of British political forms in colonial soil, or to reduce them to a subheading of older, unproblematised (and even self-satisfied) notions of 'parliament as an export'.[11] As Linda Colley has suggested, the study of British constitutionalism itself (and by implication its characteristic legislative formations) must necessarily be imperial in scope.[12] The debates over the function and value of university representation in 19th- and 20th-century Britain as they bore upon more general questions of representation and political developments cannot be understood to their full extent when isolated from the corresponding and contemporaneous efforts to establish versions of it in the empire.

Examined in this wider frame, the history of university representation ceases to be that of an insular British peculiarity (as it is typically treated), but rather as one of constant outward spread that went hand in hand with the adaptation of English political and educational models overseas. Following the early imperial reach to Ireland and North America, this process occurred first with Trinity College Dublin and the College of William and Mary in Virginia. Beginning in the 17th century, when they were granted the privilege of electing representatives to their respective legislatures, both institutions served politically as well as culturally as bastions of the English and anglican order. Following a host of sweeping, world-historical events including the loss of the American colonies and the beginnings of a new empire in Asia and the Pacific, parliamentary union with Scotland and then Ireland, new political ideas from the American and French revolutions and all the social and economic transformations associated with industrialisation, Britain's constitutional, imperial and educational position was substantially different by the early 19th century. At one level, then, the conception of, and debates surrounding, university representation in the colonies in the 19th and early 20th centuries continued the earlier trend of overseas expansion. At another level, however, their character was indicative of the new phase of domestic and imperial development.

India became the principal location for university representation outside the United Kingdom in this period. The universities established there under British rule initially served as the means of imposing some order on the provision of western learning required for Indians seeking employment in the channels to which the Raj gave them access and in which their labour was required to sustain the workings of imperial power. The emergence of regional universities in the United Kingdom around the same time was also directed at the need for a skilled workforce, but in India those needs were associated with imperial administration rather than industrial economy. With the creation of university seats in provincial legislative councils, and the building up of those bodies to become more functionally representative institutions, the position of these universities

---

[11] *Parliament as an Export*, ed. Alan Burns (1966).
[12] Linda Colley, *Taking Stock of Taking Liberties: A Personal View* (2008), 27–30.

must be seen as more than just another instance of the complex development of an independent, indigenous associational life, or civil society, in imperial India.[13] Notwithstanding the limitations of the provincial councils, the power to return members made universities an important means by which prominent Indians participated in the formal structures of governance. As in Britain earlier, the university seats also focused attention on questions about the role of learning in politics in India, though with substantial differences given the significant role of the western-educated elite in the effort to shake off British rule. The collective contributions of the university members to civic and political life, before and after independence, were considerable.

The history of Indian self-government under the Raj has been investigated in detail by a number of scholars. Even so, the position and indeed the presence of university representation have been characteristically neglected.[14] Yet a closer study of the factors underlying the growth of university representation opens possibilities for viewing a range of political ideas and practices in a new light. In a number of respects, the history of university representation in India can be seen as exemplifying Mrinalini Sinha's notion of a distinctive 'colonial public sphere' that 'functioned in an intermediate zone between both metropolitan and indigenous public spheres'.[15] Indeed, what Sinha writes about British clubs in India could also be said of university representation, that 'its efficacy as an imperial institution has less to do with metropolitan history – however expanded to accommodate the constitutive impact of empire – than with the practices of imperial rule in the colony'.[16]

But university representation also differs in important respects from other institutions that linked imperial and metropolitan institutions. As numerous studies have demonstrated, to borrow James Vernon's encapsulation, 'politicians, historians and lawyers used the empire as a laboratory within which they could make their constitutional experiments – if they could control "the savages" overseas, they reasoned, they would be able to manage the "Other" within'.[17] In the case of university representation, however, constitutional experimentation travelled the other way, from Britain to India. In India, university representation was not an isolated instance of institutional privilege, but rather was closely connected to the more extensive development of corporate and communal franchises within the overall representative framework. Indeed, the history of university representation in India serves to complicate understandings of the motivations, operations and outcomes of British policies grappling with questions of Indian self-governance. At the same time, it underscores some of the complexities of the position in which both the rulers and the ruled found themselves.

---

[13] See Nicholas Owen, 'British Progressives and Civil Society in India, 1905–1914', in *Civil Society in British History: Ideas, Identities, Institutions*, ed. Jose Harris (Oxford, 2003), 149–75.

[14] For example, university representation receives no mention in the major survey of the development of local government in British-ruled India: Hugh Tinker, *The Foundations of Local Self-Government in India, Pakistan, and Burma* (1954).

[15] Mrinalini Sinha, 'Britishness, Clubbability, and the Colonial Public Sphere: The Genealogy of an Imperial Institution in Colonial India', *Journal of British Studies*, xl (2001), 492.

[16] Sinha, 'Britishnes, Clubbability, and the Colonial Public Sphere', 491.

[17] James Vernon, 'Notes toward an Introduction', in *Re-reading the Constitution*, ed. Vernon, 11–12. On the empire as a 'test site' for dealing with domestic issues, see also Sinha, 'Britishness, Clubbability, and the Colonial Public Sphere', 496 and n. 31.

Without wholly neglecting Indian perspectives, the central focus in this book's discussion of India is on what the British thought they were doing when adapting this particular constitutional peculiarity – one that was already contested in Britain – to strategies of imperial governance, as well as to compare and contrast Indian and British developments. As already observed, however, university representation is a phenomenon that needs to be understood with reference to the empire more broadly. It also cropped up in a variety of ways in Canada, Australasia and the Mediterranean. In addition to filling out the history of university representation as a special aspect of the development of legislative structures, these scattered episodes help to test more general propositions about the meanings and practices of university representation as well as the conditions that tended to favour its establishment.

In this way, just as university representation can be shown to have been intertwined with a host of larger issues in domestic British politics, it also provides a window through which it is possible to view certain processes across a broad swathe of the British empire. This is not to say that university representation was a basis for intra-imperial connections, since it generally cannot be demonstrated that the arguments for and against it in each imperial setting made reference to anything other than the British precedent. Instead, the comparative history of university representation from around the empire affords a means for understanding something about the consistency and the mutability of British political ideas in their imperial transmission.

3. *The Plan of the Book*

The structure and weighting of this book correspond to its subject. Chapter 1 functions as a kind of prologue by describing university representation's origins and early development in 17th- and 18th-century England, Ireland and North America. The rest of the book concentrates on the 19th and 20th centuries, during which university representation grew to its greatest extent while also becoming ever more politically embattled. Three chapters examine the history of university representation in the United Kingdom, where the institution was most firmly established in the representative system, and where its records, including the debates over its place in political life, are the best documented. Chapter 2 provides a basic narrative of university representation's expansion, focusing on the motivations and efforts of new and unrepresented universities to become parliamentary constituencies in the context of major changes in the structure of higher education. The ways in which the conception of university representation was advanced and contested within the process of successive proposals for constitutional and electoral reform is taken up in Chapter 3. Chapter 4 then turns to the personnel of university representation by testing contemporary characterisations of university MPs against the characteristics of their backgrounds and record of contributions, and also by exploring the extent to which universities could be said to have had representation, at least in principle, in the house of lords.

The chapters that follow examine university representation's various and far-flung imperial adaptations. Chapter 5 is devoted to India, where the most extensive and one of the most durable versions of university representation outside the United Kingdom developed within the British Raj's evolving objectives and structures of governance.

Chapter 6 takes up the generally more ephemeral ways that university representation appeared in other colonies, which bring into greater relief the truly trans-imperial character of debates over British constitutional structures and their application overseas. The conclusion doubles as an epilogue by describing the afterlife of university representation following its general termination around 1950, while also drawing together the implications of university representation's global history across four centuries.

Chapter 1. University Representation in the 17th and 18th Centuries

The origins and early development of university representation in England and beyond are more than simply background for an account of the parliamentary institution's main phase after 1832. How the questions surrounding the university franchise in the United Kingdom bore on larger debates about the nature of representation during the gradual reform and democratisation of the British constitution in the 19th and 20th centuries can only be fully understood in connection with the longer history of why university seats were established in the first place as well as the characteristics of the initial university constituencies and their members in relation to the often tumultuous politics of early modern Britain. Similarly, it is impossible to develop a full account of the varied manifestations of university representation within the British empire without the context of its earliest transplantations. To date, scholarship on university representation in the 17th and 18th centuries has been spread across a number of works that cover different time periods, countries and institutions. This more synthetic account of university representation's early modern history not only covers the whole span from 1603 to the early 19th century, but also unites for the first time the early history of university seats in England, Ireland and colonial America.[1]

1. *The 17th Century*

University representation was created and rapidly instituted in 1603 (in the Julian calendar which was then in effect in England).[2] In the middle ages, Edward I had summoned members of Oxford and Cambridge to the English parliament, but as legal experts to advise the crown rather than representatives of the universities. In France, the same was true for Philip the Fair and, very occasionally afterwards, other French kings. But these instances cannot be considered as antecedents for the kind of continuous corporate right of representation that the English universities began to seek during the middle years of Elizabeth I's reign. The first documented appeal (by Cambridge) for the privilege of parliamentary representation occurred in 1566. The universities followed with several further petitions in the 1570s, 1580s and 1590s.

The universities were most probably prompted to seek representation by the breakdown of ecclesiastical supremacy and the growing influence of the house of commons

---

[1] A seven-page overview of the first two centuries of university representation is provided in T. Lloyd Humberstone, *University Representation* (1951), ch. 3. This is neither an especially detailed nor analytical account, and does not touch on contemporaneous American developments.

[2] Millicent Barton Rex, *University Representation in England, 1604–1690* (1954). Unless otherwise cited, my summary of 17th- and 18th-century developments at Oxford and Cambridge relies upon this work, which is virtually the only, and certainly the most thorough, account of the origins of university representation and its early history in England.

that took place during the Elizabethan period. With the subordination of the Church, its principal seminaries now needed to look to the crown for defence of their privileges. Under the Tudors, the universities had many other reasons to be concerned for their corporate security, including the worrying example of the dissolution of the monasteries, the multiple shifts in the state's religious policies and the government's periodic impositions on, or revisions of, the universities' statutes. For their own special reasons, therefore, the universities, like other communities during this time, appreciated the advantages of having representation in parliament. The already long history of town–gown conflict (another source of concern) made it clear that some form of representation through the borough corporations would not be satisfactory.

With the accession of James I, the universities' persistence finally paid off, though their enfranchisement seems to be due almost entirely to the agency of the attorney-general and future lord chief justice, Sir Edward Coke. It appears that James himself, though reputed to be a comparatively learned monarch with a great interest in universities, was merely the authoriser of Coke's innovation. As James VI of Scotland, the king had not contemplated introducing university representation into the Edinburgh parliament (which in any case operated along rather different lines from the corresponding bodies at Westminster and Dublin). Coke, a loyal Cantabrigian, held the universities in high regard. As the state's law officer, he had some direct acquaintance with town–gown disputes, and he had also noted the universities' inability to participate in deliberations over amending their complicated statutes. Before James called his first parliament, then, Coke had done the necessary political work to secure letters patent to Oxford and Cambridge under which the chancellor, masters and scholars of each university were empowered to elect two burgesses on a regular basis.

The stated reasons for granting parliamentary representation to Oxford and Cambridge were that, 'like other places, cities, boroughs, or vills of our Realm of England', they were subject to 'many local Statutes, constitutions, ordinances laws and institutes' and 'many Statutes and acts of Parliament'.[3] In addition to recognizing that the university 'is and for a long time has been a body politic and corporate', the letters patent for Oxford (which are more elaborate than those for Cambridge) cite two other significant justifications for granting parliamentary representation to the university (and later, by extension, to other institutions). First, it was noted that the University of Oxford was 'endowed with famous and ample rents, revenues, possessions, privileges, and other things to the honor of God'. Second, Oxford was said to abound 'in a multitude of men endowed with wisdom doctrine and integrity, for the common good of both the whole commonwealth and of the university'.[4] Thus, the grant of representation to secure the universities' corporate interests could be seen as recognizing that the universities, if not necessarily their members, possessed property, and that by virtue of their degrees the members had a stake in their university's fortunes.

At the same time, it also recognized that members of the university were holders of intellectual property who, through their burgesses, could make learned contributions to discussion of the nation's affairs. In William Blackstone's characterisation, the privilege of

---

[3] Humberstone, *University Representation*, 28–9. Taken from his translation of the letters patent to Cambridge.

[4] Humberstone, *University Representation*, 25–6. Taken from his translation of the letters patent to Oxford.

returning burgesses was granted 'to serve for those students who, though useful members of the community, were neither concerned in the landed nor the trading interest; and to protect in the legislature the rights of the republic of letters'.[5] The burgesses did not, however, need to be dons themselves (and most were not) for such contributions to be made. Indeed, from early on, even the most basic connection between the burgesses and the universities that returned them – that is, matriculation and degree holding – could be tenuous.

Several trends observable in 17th-century Oxford and Cambridge are especially relevant to the later history of university representation. First, amid much turmoil and rupture, university representation proved to be durable and continuous. This is even true for these former bastions of royalism during the Civil War and Protectorate, which saw the forms of representation modified (merged into three-member county constituencies in the Nominated Parliament; reduced to one member each under the Instrument of Government; then removed to the new upper House in 1658 during the Second Protectorate Parliament). Although occasionally threatened and sometimes vacant, the seats remained. In large measure, this durability can be attributed to a second trend: politically, university representation adapted to the currents of authority. University members tended to be strong supporters of the crown, except during the interregnum when Oxford and Cambridge meekly submitted to the lord protector's choices.

Through all the changes of regime from the Stuart accession, through the interregnum and Restoration, to the Glorious Revolution, the political tenor of university representation tended to move with the general currents, though rarely to the extremes. To a large degree, these shifts manifested the core interest of the universities as arms of the anglican church. Thus, the universities' representatives in parliament tempered their royalism with reformism in response to Charles I's personal rule, and high tory supporters of the Restoration could turn whiggish around the edges when faced with James II's catholicism. While some of the members seated during the interregnum were indeed revolutionary puritans, others were former royalists who had found their own reasons to accommodate themselves to the new regime.

The universities' general loyalty to the regime in power is due, in turn, to a third trend: that university seats had early on come to be viewed as available to the crown (or Protectorate) for its supporters, sometimes through the agency of chancellors who were members of, or closely associated with, the government. This trend was not much affected by the emergence of a de facto compromise which held to a greater or lesser extent through much of this period under which, at each university, one member would be the government's man, and the other would be the electorate's (vice-chancellors and college heads being the principal influences on the local selections). Reflecting the corporate self-interest that had animated the idea of university representation in the 16th century, the universities' choice of representatives was by and large calibrated to maintaining favour and influence with the government. In this way, university representation fulfilled its intended function, though at the price of being at least in part at the disposal of the government.

Coke had originally advised the universities to return lawyers rather than clerics, which in any case became impossible after 1642 when legislation forbade clergymen

---

[5] William Blackstone, *Commentaries on the Laws of England, Vol. I: Of the Rights of Persons* (Chicago, IL, 1979), 168.

from holding civil office. Accordingly, law was the principal occupational background for university members in the 17th century – a tradition that persisted throughout the history of university seats in both the United Kingdom and India. Coke's recommendation had been for universities to select doctors of civil law, but the legal element of university representation in 17th-century England was also increasingly sustained by common law lawyers. Not all university members in this period were lawyers, however, and the representation even reflected to some degree the new scientific currents of the age with the return of burgesses in medicine, and most especially Isaac Newton's election at Cambridge in 1688.

With respect to the nature of the burgesses' participation in parliamentary debates, the record indicates that their efforts were directed far more to matters of state than to university or religious issues. In part, this was a function of the university members' association with the government. Also, questions of state were far more prevalent during this period than those affecting universities or the Church. In practice, therefore, safeguarding the universities' corporate interests, the original idea for giving Oxford and Cambridge representation, proved to be more of an ancillary than primary function for their burgesses.

The University of Dublin was the third such institution to gain parliamentary representation in the 17th century.[6] Dublin was England's first overseas university, although its situation, both as an institution of higher learning and as a parliamentary constituency, was rather different from that of the two English universities. Originally intended as a collegiate university like Oxford and Cambridge, the University of Dublin became effectively synonymous with the one college that was ultimately established, Trinity, which was incorporated in 1592. The creation of universities was a notable feature of Britain's colonial enterprise and, as with Trinity College Dublin, the question of representation for these institutions came to be a closely associated phenomenon.

Like the original cases of Oxford and Cambridge, and also the subsequent university enfranchisements in the United Kingdom, the granting of seats to Dublin resulted from institutional self-advancement at a special moment of political opportunity. The first Irish parliament in the reign of James I was called, after much delay, in 1613 (the parliament had last met in 1585). To thwart the largely catholic opposition to the crown, the government was determined there should be a protestant majority in the lower House. Accordingly, it created 40 new borough electorates on top of the 34 boroughs that existed prior to the Stuart accession. Although reliably protestant, many of these new boroughs were places of little importance but they were selected with the idea that they could become sizeable towns in time.[7] As part of this movement, Trinity College's provost, William Temple, successfully lobbied for representation in the Irish parliament, which was granted on terms nearly the same as those for Oxford and Cambridge, the letters patent noting that the college was for all intents and purposes a university in its own right.[8] In 1613, the college had only been in existence for 21 years and was thus a relative newcomer when it sought, within the framework of a parliament that emulated

---

[6] My account of the Dublin constituency draws heavily on *History of the Irish Parliament, 1692–1800*, ed. E.M. Johnston-Liik (6 vols, Belfast, 2002), ii, 231–4.

[7] T.W. Moody, 'The Irish Parliament under Elizabeth and James I: A General Survey', *Proceedings of the Royal Irish Academy, Section C*, xlv (1939), 53–4.

[8] Denis Caulfield Heron, *The Constitutional History of the University of Dublin* (Dublin, 1847), 35 and n. 4, 213–16.

English forms, a privilege equivalent to that of the more venerable English institutions. In seeking the privilege of returning members to the parliament at so early a stage of institutional development, Trinity College exemplified another trend that would be well in evidence in the later history of university representation both in the United Kingdom and in the empire.

The right of returning members had somewhat different institutional consequences at Dublin than at the English universities due to the particular structure of the college. Primarily, it gave the provost, as head of the college and returning officer for elections, considerable political influence. The provost's position was strengthened further when the college's 1637 charter, granted by Charles I, made the position a crown appointment. Whereas Oxford and Cambridge electors could at times thwart or temper the influence of chancellors, vice-chancellors and college heads, it was much easier for provosts to control the Trinity College electorate. Like many of the other new Irish boroughs created in 1613, the number of electors at the college was very small and susceptible to influence. The few fellows essentially owed their appointments to the provost, who had the power to reward or discipline them as he saw fit. With respect to the scholars, some idea of the scale is indicated by the fact that Trinity awarded only nine BA degrees in 1613.[9] A larger number of scholars would have been in residence at that time, of course, though some of them would have been below voting age.[10]

A stronghold of the ascendancy and officially exclusively anglican, Trinity College conformed to the royalist tendencies of the English universities in the 17th century. This was not surprising since the provostship was a crown appointment. During the interregnum, although Oxford and Cambridge universities continued to be represented in some form, the Dublin University constituency was abolished under Instrument of Government, its representation being subsumed by the two-member Dublin County and City constituency in the united commonwealth parliament (in which Ireland had 30 of the total 460 members). The university's seats were revived in 1660 with the re-establishing of the Irish parliament under the Restoration. Later, however, James II's pro-catholic policies created a divide between the anglican college and the crown, especially the king's efforts to impose catholic fellows. Trinity's resistance led James to cut off financial support. Later, following James' 1689 landing in Ireland, its buildings were taken over as a military garrison and prison. Catholic priests were put in charge of the college and its library, though in fact they, and the catholic Joseph Coughlan who was then representing the university in the Irish parliament, did much to help preserve Trinity from further depredations at the hands of James' forces and supporters.[11]

2. *The 18th Century*

Although outwardly united as a species of two in the English parliament, Oxford and Cambridge universities acquired rather different characteristics as constituencies during

[9] Derived from a search of *A Catalog of Graduates Who Have Proceeded to Degrees in the University of Dublin, from the Earliest Recorded Commencements to July, 1866, with Supplement to December 16, 1868* (Dublin, 1869).

[10] According to Humberstone, the scholars were able to vote even if they had not attained the statutory age. Humberstone, *University Representation*, 34.

[11] W. Macneile Dixon, *Trinity College, Dublin* (1902), 66.

the period from 1690 to 1820.[12] Although the two universities had never behaved identically during the early decades of university representation, they were generally more alike than not. Following the Glorious Revolution, however, they diverged with respect both to political alignments and to the character of their representatives.[13]

Oxford was a seemingly impregnable bastion of toryism, a tendency that only intensified over this period. In the first half of the 18th century it was considered a jacobite stronghold. Whigs rarely put up candidates, and most of the constituency politics dealt with rivalries among the more influential colleges and the comparative rigour of candidates' toryism. The internecine tory character of Oxford elections meant that candidates would generally be agreed upon by the time of the poll in order to avoid dividing the tory vote. This minimised contests, and Oxford University seats were seen as lifetime posts for the incumbents.

The focus of Oxford politics was the Church, and the university's relationship with governments over this period was consistently guarded. Even before the beginning of the whig supremacy in 1715, tory governments had proved disappointing in their perceived failure to make a sufficient number of Oxford ecclesiastical appointments and, in the early part of the century, to produce legislation for enforcing conformity. Given its staunch toryism, Oxford's pride in its independence from the government was intensified during the long period of whig rule. While the university attracted front-ranking tory politicians at the beginning of the century, it subsequently assumed a pattern of returning midland squires for whom the principal requirement was to back the privileges of the Church to the hilt and uphold Oxford's independence from government influence.

In Cambridge, the situation was rather more fluid. Like their Oxford counterparts, the general run of Cambridge electors also consisted of tory-leaning clergymen. At both universities, heads of colleges (especially the larger and richer ones) were generally the principal actors in determining the choice of candidates. But where college heads at Oxford shared the tory sensibilities of the electors, a number of their more influential counterparts at Cambridge had whig or low church dispositions and encouraged both latitudinarian theology and Newtonian science. At Cambridge, too, unlike Oxford, politically prominent chancellors tended to exert their influence on elections. Cambridge's whig tradition may be seen to have originated with James Vernon, who was returned in 1679 to the first Exclusion Parliament, when whigs were first recognized as a distinct political group. As secretary to the university's chancellor, Vernon (later a secretary of state under William III) conformed to the patterns of influence that had developed in the 17th century. But the chancellor was the duke of Monmouth, who was then the whigs' favourite protestant candidate to succeed Charles II. Cambridge's

---

[12] The relevant volumes of *The History of Parliament* provide close studies of the university constituencies within the wider frame of political developments: *The History of Parliament: The House of Commons, 1690–1715*, ed. Eveline Cruickshanks, Stuart Handley and D.W. Hayton (4 vols, Cambridge, 2002), i, 136; ii, 49–58, 484–91; *The History of Parliament: The House of Commons, 1715–1754*, ed. Romney Sedgwick (2 vols, 1970), i, 201–2, 305–7; *The History of Parliament: The House of Commons, 1754–1790*, ed. Lewis Namier and John Brooke (3 vols, 1964), i, 35, 219–21, 359–60; *The History of Parliament: The House of Commons, 1790–1820*, ed. R.G. Thorne (5 vols, 1986), i, 62–3; ii, 32–6, 327–31, 651–4. On the virtues and shortcomings of the various sections of *The History of Parliament*, see David Cannadine, 'Parliament: Past History, Present History, Future History', in *Making History Now and Then: Discoveries, Controversies and Explorations* (Basingstoke, 2008), 59–82.

[13] Rex, *University Representation*, 327, 339, 341.

whiggish future was further foreshadowed by Newton.[14] From 1692, college heads, working with the chancellor of that period, the duke of Somerset, secured the election of at least one whig member. In the general election of 1705, the rallying cry of the 'Church in Danger' successfully fanned tory fears of the whigs' toleration of dissent and hostility toward the Established Church. At Cambridge, tory votes overcame the wishes of the college heads and thereafter the university returned tories until 1727.

The whigs regained Cambridge seats after 1727, in part owing to the crown's ability to influence the award of honorary doctorates at the university (significantly, a form of influence it lacked at Oxford). This power was evidently employed in a deliberate way to strengthen the government's hand in the university's elections. Between 1726 and 1728, nearly 400 honorary degrees were granted. Thereafter, Cambridge was seen as the whig university. Succeeding Somerset as chancellor in 1748, the duke of Newcastle – who with his younger brother, Henry Pelham, played important and influential roles in the whig ministries between 1721 and 1756 – ran the university constituency like one of his boroughs. After Newcastle's death in 1768, Cambridge politics entered a period of considerable ferment. The new chancellor, the duke of Grafton, was the whig prime minister but was less attentive than his predecessors and made less pleasing recommendations for candidates. Sharpened political divisions over the American war were reflected in Cambridge's contested and politicised elections, beginning in 1779.

In 1784, for the first time in half a century, Cambridge returned tories, William Pitt the Younger and the chancellor's son, Lord Euston. After the whigs attempted to reassert themselves in 1790, there was no further contest until Pitt's death in 1806. Thereafter, the general pattern was to have one burgess from each party. Euston himself eventually turned to the whigs and, after 1812, an electoral compromise saw tory Lord Palmerston share the university with whig John Henry Smyth, although Palmerston turned away from the tories in the mid 1820s. As Pitt, Palmerston and others (like the attorney-general, Vickery Gibbs) demonstrate, Cambridge MPs, unlike those from Oxford, continued to be prominent figures on the parliamentary stage.

In the Irish parliament during the 18th century, Trinity College remained the provost's borough. At the century's end, the electorate amounted to only 22 fellows and 70 scholars, who 'were usually put to the trouble of a poll only as the result of the ability of a candidate to divide them on both national and parochial issues'.[15] For most of the century, between 1717 and 1794, only three men occupied the provostship and all were politically active. Illustrating the power of the office, there is an account of one provost, Richard Baldwin (1717–58), a staunch whig, summoning the scholars before an election and ordering them to vote for his favoured candidate. When he subsequently changed his mind, he summoned the scholars again and ordered them to vote for the other candidate.[16] Later, the purely political appointment of the able but non-academic John Hely Hutchinson (1775–94) provoked bitter and long-lasting acrimony at the college. This resistance curtailed the provost's influence on returns, though it did not stop him from attempting to seat two of his sons (both efforts generating petitions).

---

[14] Rex, *University Representation*, 261–5, 305, 327.
[15] *HPC, 1790–1820*, i, 105.
[16] J.L. McCracken, 'Irish Parliamentary Elections, 1727–68', *Irish Historical Studies*, v (1947), 230.

With the dissolution of the Dublin parliament under the 1800 Act of Union, the Dublin University constituency survived as one of the 100 Irish seats added at Westminster. Trinity not only lost one of its two seats, but the relocation of its representation to England also meant that the college was decoupled from the considerable influence it had enjoyed across College Green as well as the patronage and support that had come from the Irish parliament and the wealthy aristocratic families.[17] Perhaps as a result, the constituency lost its autocratic cohesion. In the early 19th century, the seat was routinely contested with much internecine political manoeuvring.[18]

As with the English universities, representing Trinity College carried considerable prestige, along with a generally comfortable tenure. Members were typically well connected and respectable. More like Cambridge than Oxford, the members also tended to be people of some ability. Their politics were not always staunchly anglican and tory. Among the most divisive issues after the war was relieving catholics of their political disabilities within the United Kingdom. While Trinity College retained its protestant identity, its MP in these years, William Conybeare Plunkett (1812–27), an Ulster presbyterian, was a leading advocate of a moderate pro-catholic position.

3. *American Adaptation*

In addition to Trinity College, English higher education extended to even more remote colonial settings in the early modern period, and in one case it was also associated with a form of university representation. By the terms of its 1693 royal charter, the College of William and Mary in Virginia was granted the right to return members to the colony's house of burgesses.[19] The histories of the nine colleges established in Britain's North American colonies between 1636 and 1769 shows that they exerted sometimes decisive influence on their governments and legislatures on numerous occasions.[20] They were also among the many trade and other groups that organised themselves to lobby their legislatures for or against laws in which they had an interest.[21] But only William and Mary had formal representation after the English and Irish precedents.[22] Collegiate

---

[17] Dixon, *Trinity College, Dublin*, 150.

[18] *HPC, 1790–1829*, i, 62–3, 651–4.

[19] Rex, with her customary thoroughness, does not neglect mention of William and Mary in her foreword to *University Representation*, 12–13.

[20] See J. David Hoeveler, *Creating the American Mind: Intellect and Politics in the Colonial Colleges* (Lanham, MD, 2002), 68, 87–9, 113, 163–6, 208–12.

[21] Alison G. Olson, 'Eighteenth-Century Colonial Legislatures and Their Constituents', *Journal of American History*, lxxix (1992), 553.

[22] According to Rex, the question of whether Dartmouth College, founded in 1769, should be represented in the New Hampshire legislature was raised but never acted upon. Rex, *University Representation*, 13. Although she provides no citation, one must presume that she had this information on good authority. In the *Concise Chronological History of Dartmouth College* compiled by Hamilton Gibson (Hanover, NH, 1919), an entry for 1774 states: 'College and Hanover seek and fail to secure representation in Provincial Assembly' (p. 7). Yet, Hanover's search for representation only receives a brief mention in Frederick Chase, *A History of Dartmouth College and the Town of Hanover New Hampshire, Vol. 1* (Cambridge, MA, 1891), 423. And although it contains much about the affairs of the college, the issue of representation does not appear at all in *Provincial Papers: Documents and Records Relating to the Province of New Hampshire, Vol. VII: From 1764 to 1776*, ed. Nathaniel Buton (Nashua, NH, 1873). At the time, the leadership of town and college were closely allied, so the distinction can be a hard one to draw. For guidance on these matters, I am grateful to Barbara L. Krieger, Dartmouth College Archives, email to the author, 25 Nov. 2009.

histories and histories of colonial Virginia's legislature dutifully note that William and Mary returned members to the house of burgesses, but, in keeping with the general tendency of scholars to overlook the special characteristics and significance of university representation and its imperial dissemination, this first transplanting outside the British Isles has not been studied in detail in its own right, much less placed in its wider historical, transatlantic and imperial contexts.

William and Mary's charter granted:

> to the said President, and masters, or professors of the said College, full and absolute power, liberty, and authority, to nominate, elect, and constitute one discreet and able person of their own number, or of the number of the said visitors, or governors, or lastly, of the better sort of inhabitants of our colony of Virginia, to be present in the house of Burgesses, of the General Assembly of our colony of Virginia.[23]

This privilege was subsequently incorporated into Virginia's 1705 Election Act. One set of explanations for why William and Mary was exceptional among the American colonial colleges in this respect is that both the legislature and the new college in Virginia appear to have been especially attentive to English models.

In general, it has been argued, the American colonies developed their own forms of governance, incorporating aspects of the Westminster model only as they were deemed suitable to local circumstances.[24] Yet, as one early study of the procedure of the house of burgesses concludes, Virginia's colonial legislature was distinguished by its 'remarkable adherence to English forms and practices. From the outset they strove to model their own assembly on the great "mother of parliaments" '.[25] In the province of the Massachusetts Bay, by contrast, Harvard, the first English college established in North America, did not have representation in the assembly of the general court. There, election of representatives was based strictly on a property qualification, with no separate academic constituency.[26] (Later, the Massachusetts constitution of 1780, penned by John Adams, would explicitly bar any 'President, Professor, or Instructor of Harvard College' from sitting in the legislature.)

William and Mary's constitutional organisation, like that of Harvard, followed the English model of colleges consisting legally and practically of the resident group of academic officers. A few years after William and Mary was established, the creation of Yale College as a corporate body that would employ and oversee the resident academic officers of the school set the organisational pattern for the American colleges that followed.[27] But although both William and Mary and Harvard were organised according to the same English precedent, the Virginia college's ongoing structural connections to the English establishment were much closer than those of its elder counterpart in

[23] College of William and Mary, *The Officers, Statutes and Charter of the College of William and Mary* (Philadelphia, PA, 1817), 24.

[24] A.F. Madden, ' "Not for Export": The Westminster Model of Government and British Colonial Practice', *Journal of Imperial and Commonwealth History*, viii (1979), 13–14.

[25] S.M. Pargellis, 'The Procedure of the Virginia House of Burgesses', *William and Mary Quarterly*, 2nd ser., vii (1927), 156.

[26] Ellis Ames [Paper on the Qualification for Voting in the Massachusetts Province Charter, December 1868], *Proceedings of the Massachusetts Historical Society*, x (1867–9), 370–5.

[27] John E. Kirkpatrick, 'The Constitutional Development of the College of William and Mary', *William and Mary Quarterly*, 2nd ser., vi (1926), 96.

Massachusetts. In contrast to the independent spirit of puritan Cambridge, William and Mary's founding and long-serving president, James Blair, was head of the anglican church in Virginia and the bishop of London's colonial deputy. It was also customary for the bishop to serve as the college's chancellor.

Although the privilege of returning a burgess was granted to William and Mary in 1693 and confirmed in 1705, the representation of the college had a rocky start befitting William and Mary's early struggles to establish itself as a going concern. In the *Calendar of State Papers Colonial*, there is an entry on 10 December 1700 noting Virginia burgesses declared duly elected, including one for the college: 'The return of Thomas Cowles, Sheriff of James City County, upon the writ for election of a Burgess for the College of William and Mary was approved'. Yet, the note also indicates that there was some question over the authority by which Cowles' election to represent the infant college was effected: 'Mr James Blair, President, made answer that, there being as yet but a President and one Master, therefore they did not think it fit to elect a Burgess, that being to be done by the President and Masters of the College'.[28]

By the terms of the royal charter, the college and not its lay advisers was to elect the burgess. The faculty corporation intended by the charter to govern the college was not fully established until 1729, when the surviving members of the original, temporary corporation finally transferred the college's property to its 'President and masters, or professors'.[29] In 1710 and 1712, Blair had reminded the House that 'for want of a Sufficient number of Masters and for want of the College being Transferred by the Trustees to the President and Masters that they may Act as a body Pollitik according to the Charter We are of the Opinion that the Said Election cannot be made at this time'.[30] (As head of the Church and the bishop of London's representative, Blair was a member of the colony's council and thus the college enjoyed a kind of senatorial representation during this period.) Even so, work to seat a burgess took place well before what the college's histories refer to as 'the Transfer'.

Ironically, notwithstanding his repeated assertion that it was premature for the college to elect a representative, the next attempts came from Blair himself before the conditions for the Transfer had been met.[31] In 1715, with two masters in place (one each for the grammar school and the Indian school) and a search on to fill the professorship of natural philosophy and mathematics, Blair laid claim to the corporate right and the college returned the recently unseated Speaker of the House, Peter Beverley, as its burgess. Citing Blair's previous statements that the college did not yet meet the charter's requirements for representation, the House referred the matter to its committee on privileges and elections, which refused to let Beverley be seated.[32] In the next two assemblies, however,

---

[28] *Calendar of State Papers, Colonial Series, Vol. 18: America and the West Indies, 1700*, ed. Cecil Headlam (1910), 730.

[29] Kirkpatrick, 'Constitutional Development', 98, 100.

[30] *Journals of the House of Burgesses of Virginia, 1712–1714, 1715, 1718, 1720–1722, 1723–1726*, ed. H.R. McIlwaine (Richmond, 1912), 127.

[31] This paragraph is based on the account provided in J.E. Morpurgo, *Their Majesties' Royall Colledge: William and Mary in the Seventeenth and Eighteenth Centuries* (Williamsburg, VA, 1976), 59.

[32] *Journals of the House of Burgesses of Virginia, 1712–1714, 1715, 1718, 1720–1722, 1723–1726*, xxix, 127, 138.

even though the state of the college had still not matured to the degree required, Blair successfully arranged for the return of John Custis in 1718 and Thomas Jones in 1720.[33]

Blair's determination to see the college represented is said to have sprung from his ongoing disagreements with Virginia's lieutenant governor, Alexander Spotswood. Once Blair was finally able to arrange for Spotswood's recall in 1722, he refrained from attempting to seat a burgess until after the Transfer was effected. Accordingly, there is a gap in the college's representation for the assembly of 1723–6 and the first part of the assembly of 1727–34. Almost immediately after the Transfer, however, the House recognized that the college charter's provision for returning a burgess was now in force, and in 1730 George Nicholas, gentleman, was duly returned. He sat until his death in 1734 and, although a new writ was ordered, the assembly came to an end shortly thereafter.[34] In 1736 – in what could be seen as a successful repetition of the 1715 attempt to seat Speaker Beverley – Blair secured the election of the then current Speaker, Sir John Randolph. Thereafter, the college was represented continuously up to the calling of the revolutionary conventions in 1775 and 1776.

The burgesses for William and Mary were disproportionately influential in Virginia's affairs. Of the 630 men who sat in the House between 1720 and 1776, Jack Greene has identified 110 who dominated the proceedings of the House through their service on key committees in which the real decisions were made.[35] Seven of the 11 members returned by the college during this period are classed among that elite, and constitute a nearly unbroken succession of power in the colony: Sir John Randolph (1736–7), Edward Barradall (1738–44), Beverley Randolph (1744–50), Peyton Randolph (1752–8), George Wythe (1758–61), John Blair Jr (1766–71) and John Randolph Jr (1774–6). As this list indicates, the Randolph family was especially prominent in the representation of the college. Speaker Randolph's successor, Attorney-General Barradall, was followed by Sir John's son, Beverley, who was twice re-elected. Beverley Randolph was then succeeded by his brother Peyton, and in the last years of the college's representation, Speaker Randolph's third son, also named John, was returned after the incumbent was appointed to the colony's council.

Family connections were important in colonial Virginia politics generally, and between Peyton and John Randolph there was another familial succession in the college's representation. John Page, the future governor of the state of Virginia, elected in 1771, was the son of Mann Page II, who sat for the college in the assembly of 1761–5. Despite being descended from the powerful John Page, who had played an influential role in William and Mary's founding, the two Pages are the only college members beginning with Sir John Randolph who do not figure in Greene's listing of the house of burgesses' major actors (but the younger John Page only sat in the House for a short time before being elevated to the council). Between the Pages, the familial character of the college's representation was sustained in a different way by the return of James Blair's grand-nephew, John Blair Jr.

[33] *Journals of the House of Burgesses of Virginia, 1712–1714, 1715, 1718, 1720–1722, 1723–1726*, 181, 257.

[34] *Journals of the House of Burgesses of Virginia, 1727–1734, 1736–1740*, ed. H.R. McIlwaine (Richmond, 1910), viii n., 62, 173.

[35] Jack P. Greene, 'Foundations of Political Power in the Virginia House of Burgesses, 1720–1776', *William and Mary Quarterly*, 3rd ser., xvi (1959), 485–506.

William and Mary is famous for educating many of the American revolution's leading figures, not least George Washington and Thomas Jefferson, though its politics were mixed. In the pre-revolutionary period, the college's representatives were prominent participants in royal government and public life. In the years of revolutionary ferment before 1776, Peyton Randolph supported policies to pressure Britain into greater accommodation of colonial autonomy, but remained a loyalist. His brother, the younger John Randolph, was nicknamed 'Tory John' on account of his strong loyalist sympathies. Such loyalty to the crown among William and Mary's burgesses can thus be seen as conforming to the general politics of 17th- and 18th-century university members in England and Ireland. But not unlike the ways that the inclinations of the Oxford and Cambridge burgesses moved with the revolutionary tide in the 17th century, William and Mary also returned a number of 'independence men' in the years before 1776, including: the jurist George Wythe, who was a mentor to Jefferson and signed the Declaration of Independence; John Blair Jr, who opposed Patrick Henry's Stamp Act resolutions when representing the college, but became a committed revolutionary, even while continuing to serve as a clerk to the royal governor's council; and John Page, a close friend of Jefferson's from their student days who opposed British policies and became a key figure in the revolution in Virginia.

4. *Conclusion*

The idea and ultimate establishment of university representation originated from a very specific set of political and religious concerns that affected Oxford and Cambridge in the 16th and 17th centuries. Parliamentary representation appeared as the best means to protect the universities' corporate interests against real and potential interference from the outside. These particular circumstances notwithstanding, the justifications for permitting the two universities to return burgesses to parliament noted in their letters patent – institutional merit, the quality of electors and representatives, and the general benefit to the nation – would continue to play prominent parts in subsequent arguments for and against the extension of university representation to other institutions. Establishing university representation for the anglican strongholds in Ireland and North America also set a pattern for the later adaptation of this constitutional idea, which accompanied the spread of English educational and political models as a function of British colonialism in its next phases.

In politics, university representation in its first two centuries was distinguished overall by loyalty to the regime, so long as protestantism was secure. This was a transatlantic condition. The universities were the primary producers of anglican clergymen (as were the colleges in Ireland and Virginia) and thus the religious constitution of the nation was a core corporate concern. At the same time, university representation was more than merely the clerical representation, as later critics would claim was its function. Members were necessarily laymen and at various times the universities elected people of great ability who made significant contributions to national life in their parliamentary role.

In early modern university representation, then, it is tempting to see something of J.C.D. Clark's 'confessional state' in practice: a species of parliamentary representation closely connected to the government and bound to the Church.[36] In the extension of university representation to Ireland and America, this parcel of functions and relationships was also transported to the wider British world. For all that, however, it is also significant to observe that the character of the representation did not necessarily reflect that of the institutions. Cambridge, despite the generally tory temper of its constituents, developed a tradition of returning whigs. Trinity College Dublin could return a member sympathetic to removal of disabilities on catholics when that was an especially contentious issue. William and Mary was represented by staunch loyalists, even while the college was raising up a cohort of revolutionary leaders.

As the following chapters will show, the history of university representation in the 19th and 20th centuries exhibited plenty of continuities with its early modern phase, some of them superficial, others more substantive. Yet, although the early modern record was invoked later on (typically by critics), it is also true that the political, constitutional, imperial and educational landscape was significantly altered in the 19th century. The ways in which university representation functioned and was understood changed accordingly.

---

[36] J.C.D. Clark, *English Society, 1688–1832: Religion, Ideology, and Politics during the Ancien Régime* (2nd edn, Cambridge, 2000).

Chapter 2. The Rise and Fall of the University Franchise

It has been said that 'the spirit of English constitutional development is tender to anomalies'.[1] Even so, university representation occupies a special place in the complex history of British voting rights. The 'reformed' system after 1832 continued to include a diverse array of voter qualifications, and the university vote was one of only two franchises under which electoral participation was not directly linked in some way to owning or occupying property.[2] The university franchise was further distinguished from all other plural voting qualifications that persisted by the fact that it alone was embodied by its own members in the house of commons, and university seats remained exceptional among the vastly greater number of borough and county constituencies.

Appendix 2 offers a graphic representation of the growth of university constituencies over time and the institutions they represented. At one level, the strengthening of university representation in the period after 1832 was relative, since its growth took place while other special and historic franchises were modified or eliminated. More visibly, because universities were the only special franchise with their own seats in the Commons, the strengthening of university representation also occurred in absolute terms. As Table 2.1 shows, the number of university seats grew from five representing three universities in 1801 (0.8% of seats in the Commons) to the peak of 15 representing 21 institutions after 1918 (2.1% of seats).

In part, the expansion of university representation in the 19th and early 20th centuries was a high-political process associated with the debates and deals surrounding successive measures of reform. But it was not simply an outcome of developments at the level of party leadership and parliamentary politics. The system of higher education was growing at the same time that franchise reform and redistribution of seats became an accepted if sporadic mechanism of constitutional adaptation.[3] Universities and their friends mobilised to advance their claims when proposed legislation presented opportunities for them to gain representation. They pursued this objective through a variety of means, including petitions to both houses of parliament, delegations to leading ministers or governmental committees, and other forms of lobbying to drum up additional support from regional or affiliated MPs. To lay the essential groundwork for the more analytical chapters that

---

[1] R.B. McCallum and Alison Readman, *The British General Election of 1945* (Oxford, 1947), 215.

[2] Neal Blewett, 'The Franchise in the United Kingdom, 1885–1918', *Past & Present*, no. 32 (1965), 30–6; H.C.G. Matthew, R.I. McKibbin and J. A. Kay, 'The Franchise Factor in the Rise of the Labour Party', *English Historical Review* (*EHR*), xci (1976), 726. The other franchise not directly linked to property ownership was that for freemen (i.e., those granted freedom of the borough), a status that could be acquired not only by individual recognition, but also by birth, marriage, purchase and other means. See Rosemary Sweet, 'Freemen and Independence in English Borough Politics c.1770–1830', *Past & Present*, no. 161 (1998), 90–2.

[3] The term 'system' is used here in a general sense, and does not indicate an alternative chronology for the emergence of a recognizably co-ordinated national network for higher learning described in Keith Vernon, *Universities and the State in England, 1850–1939* (2004), ch. 5.

Table 2.1: *Growth of University Seats in the House of Commons, 1801–1950*

Constituency	Number of Seats				
	1801–31	1832–67	1868–1917	1918–21	1922–50
Oxford	2	2	2	2	2
Cambridge	2	2	2	2	2
Dublin (Trinity College)	1	2	2	2	—[a]
London			1	1	1
Edinburgh & St Andrews ⎤ Combined			1⎫		
Glasgow & Aberdeen ⎦ Scottish Us			1⎭	3	3
Combined English Us				2	2[b]
U of Wales				1	1
Queen's U, Belfast				1	1
National U of Ireland				1	—[a]
Total	5	6	9	15	12
Total Commons Seats	658	658	658	707	615
% University Seats	0.8	0.9	1.4	2.1	2.0

[a] Representation transferred to Irish Free State in 1922.
[b] University of Reading added in 1928.

follow, this chapter provides a basic chronological narrative of the factors operating in both the political and educational spheres that combined to produce this growth in the number of university seats.

1. *1832*

After the addition of a seat for the University of Dublin among the 100 Irish constituencies established at Westminster by the Act of Union, the first expansion of university representation in the United Kingdom parliament occurred with the 1832 Reform Act, under which Dublin was granted a second seat. But this was not simply a matter of restoring the two-member representation Dublin had enjoyed in the Irish parliament. The second seat had to be justified by enlarging Trinity College's small electorate of provost, fellows and junior scholars to include all holders of MA and higher degrees. This arrangement followed several proposals for expanding the Dublin electorate that had been advanced and dropped during debates over the Reform Bill. The final formulation stemmed from a private members' motion that was hastily incorporated into the bill.

With the turmoil and bitter feelings caused by catholic emancipation in 1829 still fresh, the plan for the Dublin electorate drew protests on religious grounds. Trinity College was an exclusively protestant foundation, and the original connection between university representation and anglicanism remained very much alive. Indeed, in 1831, Lord Althorp, then chancellor of the exchequer, argued that Dublin should receive a second seat specifically to protect the interests of the Established Church.[4] Because

[4] Hansard, *Parl. Debs.*, 3rd ser., iii, col. 887 (24 Mar. 1831).

catholics were not permitted to be fellows or scholars, they could not vote for Dublin's MPs before 1832. But catholics were not prohibited from receiving MAs, and those who had were thus included within the broadened franchise. Recognizing the problem too late, the whig government determined that the bill was too far along to reallocate the seat to another constituency.[5] This controversy over enlarging Dublin's franchise can be seen as a harbinger of two important characteristics of university representation's subsequent expansions. First, they rarely occurred with ease. Second, the growth of university representation was typically carried along in paradoxical ways by the larger politics and processes of reform.

The four Scottish universities' long quest to be represented in parliament like Oxford, Cambridge and Dublin involved several attempts before the object was finally achieved. The fact that an Irish university had direct representation in parliament while the Scottish universities did not may stand as one of the few instances in which Ireland was better advantaged than Scotland within the union. This owed, in the main, to Trinity College's legacy as an English colonial implant and bulwark of the anglican establishment. In addition, the Scottish universities in the early 19th century were widely seen as having declined significantly from their 18th-century prominence at the centre of the Scottish Enlightenment. A Royal Commission on the Universities and Colleges of Scotland was established in 1826 to rectify the situation, but its 1831 report, while setting important administrative, financial and academic reforms in train, came too late to gain the necessary support in parliament for proposals to grant the universities representation in 1832.[6] There was not even widespread support among the Scottish delegation to parliament and most Scottish reformers disliked the idea of extending university representation north of the Tweed.[7]

Scottish universities submitted petitions to the house of commons on at least two occasions during the debates over the Reform Bill for Scotland. In the house of commons, Sir George Murray, MP for Perthshire, advanced the claims of the Scottish universities generally and introduced a petition from Edinburgh. Several other MPs voiced support, including the former lord advocate, Sir William Rae, who also presented a similar petition from St Andrews.[8] In committee, Sir John Walsh, MP for Sudbury, announced his intention to propose a motion for extending representatives to Edinburgh, Glasgow, Aberdeen and St Andrews, but later said that, since it was clear he would find little support, he would abandon the attempt. 'He hoped, however, that a measure so just was only deferred. In better times he trusted to see such an arrangement carried into effect'.[9]

In the house of lords, the earl of Haddington, a tory peer, proposed in March 1831 to add members for the Scottish universities and was seconded by the whig earl of Rosebery (grandfather of the later 19th-century prime minister). Haddington quickly withdrew his motion in the face of questions about the nature and quality of the

---

[5] See Norman Gash, *Politics in the Age of Peel: A Study in the Technique of Parliamentary Representation, 1830–1850* (1953), 57–9.

[6] *Report Made to His Majesty by a Royal Commission of Inquiry into the State of the Universities of Scotland*, Parliamentary Papers, 1831 (310), xii, 111.

[7] Gash, *Politics in the Age of Peel*, 47.

[8] Hansard, *Parl. Debs.*, 3rd ser., iii, col. 1349 (14 Apr. 1831); vii, cols 524–7 (23 Sept. 1831).

[9] Hansard, *Parl. Debs.*, 3rd ser., vii, col. 1229 (4 Oct. 1831); xiii, col. 390 (4 June 1832).

graduates compared to those of the three universities then enjoying representation.[10] In July 1832, Haddington returned to the matter during the committee stage of the Reform Bill, citing the inequity of giving Dublin a second member while providing none for the Scottish universities. The lord chancellor, stating that he was 'not one of those who were violently enamoured of the University Representation of England and Ireland', declared himself unwilling to let the proposed amendment go forward until the 'interior Constitution for the Universities of Scotland could be considered'.[11] Haddington declined to press the matter further.

Although too late to help with their case for representation in 1831–2, the effort to reform the Scottish universities was part of a broader transformation of British higher education that began in the early 19th century. Both Oxford and Cambridge had begun to strengthen their curricular and examination regimes, beginning in the late 18th century, and this continued into the first decades of the 19th. By the 1850s, however, it was clear that neither of the old English universities, if left to their own devices, would undertake the kinds of organisational and educational reforms that the times seemed to require. Accordingly, parliament established royal commissions which mandated a broad set of changes to the two universities' administrative, bursary, examination and curricular structures, and required that henceforward degrees be open to nonconformists.

Meanwhile, new institutions were being founded in the northern provinces, though initially with minimal impact. In 1832, the dean and chapter of Durham Cathedral established a university with the goal of providing an Oxford-style education at far less cost to aspiring clergymen from the region. Two decades later, Manchester's Owens College, established in 1851, also sought to emulate the curriculum of the ancient English universities. Both institutions struggled in their early years. The Oxbridge model, prestigious and attractive in principle, was ill-suited to attract the kind of regional support that both Durham and Owens would require to become viable centres of higher education. In particular, both institutions failed to align their academic missions with the needs and interests of businesses in the region – although they would subsequently move in that direction.[12]

Arguably the most significant innovation in British higher education during the first half of the 19th century was the creation of the University of London. University College London (as it became known) was founded in 1826 as an explicitly secular and professional alternative to Oxbridge. It, and its anglican counterpart King's College (founded 1829), were brought together in 1836 under the umbrella of the University of London, an examining and degree-granting authority for its constituent colleges. Around this time, as well, a number of medical schools were founded in the provinces to prepare students for the examinations of the Society of Apothecaries and the Royal College of Surgeons. Many of the medical schools, as well as a variety of other regional colleges, spent their apprenticeship affiliated with London. In this way, London itself provided an important mechanism by which higher education in Britain (and also in the empire) could grow in an accredited manner. Further, legislation in 1858 led to the creation of

[10] Hansard, *Parl. Debs*, 3rd ser., iii, cols 177–9 (8 Mar. 1831).

[11] Hansard, *Parl. Debs*, 3rd ser., xiv, cols 180–3 (9 July 1832).

[12] Michael Sanderson, *Education, Economic Change and Society in England, 1780–1870* (Cambridge, 1995), 45–7.

the 'external student' by opening London examinations to anyone wishing to take them, even if they had not attended the institutions previously recognized.[13]

The growth and reform of higher education institutions – developments in which parliament typically played a decisive role – set the stage for a concomitant expansion of university representation. This occurred for the most part in two major bursts, 1867–8 and 1918, periods in which structural transformations in the educational and political spheres converged. The needs of an urbanising, industrialising society spurred the creation of new institutions which might eventually aspire to the franchise, while, consistent with the new values and national purposes that were increasingly attached to universities, the older institutions of Scotland reformed their institutional organisation and practices in ways that might enable them to be deemed worthy of the privilege denied them in 1832. Meanwhile, the expansion of university representation also depended on the public desire for, and political will to enact, successive measures of constitutional reform and electoral redistribution, which provided unrepresented universities and their friends in parliament with opportunities to press their case for enfranchisement.

2. 1867–8

The Reform Acts of 1867 (for England and Wales) and 1868 (for Scotland) increased the number of university seats to include one member for London and one member each for two sets of conjoined Scottish university constituencies: Edinburgh and St Andrews, and Glasgow and Aberdeen. During the preceding decade and a half in which numerous reform proposals had been advanced, these universities had been very much alert to opportunities for acquiring seats in parliament. By 1860, for example, the proponent of university reform and former MP James Heywood wrote that 'the public interest felt in a Reform Bill affords a fair opportunity of reconsidering the various restrictions which limit the elective franchise in the Universities of Oxford, Cambridge, and Dublin, and of improving the system of English University representation'.[14] Most of the abortive reform bills of the 1850s and 1860s – regardless of which party brought them in – included provisions to enfranchise London and the Scottish universities.

In the case of London, Benjamin Disraeli is said to have quipped that he enfranchised the university so that Robert Lowe, a Liberal who had opposed his own party's reform proposals in 1866, could have a safe seat.[15] But the university had pushed its case with great consistency and determination. London based its claim on Thomas Spring Rice's 1835 letter to the privy council on behalf of the government requesting the grant of a royal charter for the university. Spring Rice, then chancellor of the exchequer, had written: 'It should always be kept in mind that what is sought on the present occasion is an equality in all respects with the ancient Universities, freed from those exclusions and religious

---

[13] On the innovation of external students and degrees, see Sheldon Rothblatt, *The Modern University and Its Discontents: The Fate of Newman's Legacy in Britain and America* (Cambridge, 1997), 252–8.

[14] James Heywood, *Academic Reform and University Representation* (1860), 183.

[15] A statement reported, and repeated, retrospectively. See, e.g., *The Times*, 11 May 1899, p. 13; 9 Jan. 1900, p. 9.

distinctions which abridge the usefulness of Oxford and Cambridge'.[16] In May 1852, the prime minister, Lord Derby, assured a deputation of graduates that no other claim for a grant of university representation could come into competition with that of the University of London.[17] Shortly thereafter, Disraeli, then Conservative leader in the Commons, opined that, although London was not yet at a stage of development to warrant representation, the principles on which the claim had been urged should be respected.[18]

London's efforts continued the following year when a 'numerous and influential deputation' – including members of the university's senate, heads of colleges, principals of schools influenced by London's curriculum, representatives of the medical profession and 16 MPs – presented a lengthy memorial to Derby's successor, Lord Aberdeen.[19] Beyond simply asserting the university's claims to the long-established, uninterrupted and 'unassailed' constitutional principle of returning a member to parliament, the memorial laid particular stress on how the university had 'connected with itself, without one important exception out of the pale of the Established Church, all the theological, all the medical, and all the general collegiate institutions, not only in the Metropolis, but in the United Kingdom, and even in the colonies'. Further, to pre-empt the argument that London was not really a university proper, but simply an examining body for a congeries of diverse educational institutions, the memorial also emphasized how its functions had raised the standard of medical education throughout the country and, through mandating 'literary acquirements', had broadened the narrow theological curricula of religious colleges. Thus, London's were not merely titular degrees, but rather carried with them 'all those consequences (not ecclesiastical) which are implied by the possession of a degree elsewhere'. In response, Aberdeen assured the deputation in a 'marked and emphatic manner' that it would be agreeable to the government to organise a constituency for the university and would give the matter the most serious consideration.[20] Support for London's case was evidently as widespread as its graduates. Shortly after the university's delegation waited upon Lord Aberdeen, 'certain inhabitants of the borough of Halifax [West Yorkshire], praying for Parliamentary representation to the London University' petitioned the Commons.[21]

In 1858, the university's convocation established a high-level committee to promote the university's interests with respect to obtaining representation and to work closely with 'influential friends of the University' in its approaches to the government.[22] In

---

[16] Quoted in Univ. of London Archives, Convocation and Committees, UoL/CN 1/1/13, Proceedings of Convocation, 17 Mar. 1917: 'Statement of Sir Alfred Pearce Gould, Vice Chancellor and Returning Officer, and Sir Edward Henry Busk, Chairman of Convocation, on the Speaker's Letter to the Prime Minister Dated 27 January, 1917, Reporting the Resolutions Arrived at by the Speaker's Conference on Electoral Reform'. See also Univ. of London Archives, Convocation and Committees, UoL/CN 1/1/1: Proceedings of Convocation, 24 Nov. 1858.

[17] Heywood, *Academic Reform*, 206.

[18] Hansard, *Parl. Debs*, 3rd ser., cxii, col. 443 (10 May 1852).

[19] James Lorimer, 'University Representation', *North British Review*, xx (1854), 367.

[20] *The Medical Times and Gazette*, new ser., vi, 19 Mar. 1853, p. 294.

[21] *The Times*, 28 May 1853, p. 3.

[22] Univ. of London Archives, Convocation and Committees, UoL/CN1/1/1: Proceedings of Convocation, 24 Nov. 1858. For reports of the committee's work, see also Proceedings of Convocation, 8 May 1860, 14 May 1861; Univ. of London Archives, Convocation and Committees, UoL/CN1/1/1: Minutes of Committees, 14, 18 and 28 Mar. 1859, 14 May 1866; and Univ. of London Archives, Senate, UoL/ST 3/2/6.

March 1859, the university's senate sent a memorial to Derby (briefly back in power) 'urging upon her Majesty's government the claim of the University of London to be represented in Parliament'.[23] The memorial was followed by petitions to each house of parliament, presented by Sir James Graham in the Commons and Earl Granville (London's chancellor) in the Lords.[24] As Granville stated to a university assembly at Burlington House when the petitions were to be presented: 'The University of London was endowed with the power to confer degrees, and it was established with the distinct promise that it should be placed in all respects upon the same footing as the sister universities'.[25] Similarly, in anticipation of the 1866 Reform Bill, London's convocation convened an extraordinary general meeting which resolved 'That a petition be presented to both Houses of Parliament praying that two members may be given to the University of London'.[26]

The widespread support for enfranchising the University of London opened the door to the claims of all other universities established in the 19th century and after to be treated equitably, even without the benefit of understandings similar to those Spring Rice had urged upon the privy council when securing London's royal charter. Like London, other universities actively organised and lobbied for the franchise and their own MPs. In 1866, for instance, a group of Durham graduates formed the Durham University Society, an association dedicated to promoting the university's interests and image during the debates over a new measure of reform. Subsequently, when representation for London seemed to be assured under the 1867 Reform Bill, Durham's friends in parliament sought to avoid it having to bear 'the stigma and odium of being the only unrepresented University' through inclusion in the new constituency.[27]

Alongside the activities of the new English universities during the long build-up to the Second Reform Act, efforts also continued to obtain representation for the Scottish universities. In 1857, in response to a paper 'On the Parliamentary Representation of the Scottish Universities' read by the Glasgow MP Walter Buchanan at the Scottish Literary Institute, the lord advocate of Scotland arranged for a deputation from the society to meet with a large group of Scottish MPs in London to build support for Buchanan's propositions and those of another paper on reform of the Scottish universities.[28] Four years later, during debates over a bill to disenfranchise two small English constituencies and reapportion their seats, William Stirling, Conservative MP for Perthshire who was deeply involved in higher education issues, used the opportunity to propose transferring the additional member intended for South Lancashire to the Scottish universities. The general case he put forward for recognising the 'great unrepresented body connected with the Universities of Scotland' was not far from the one Lord Haddington had advanced 30 years earlier: Oxford, Cambridge and Dublin had a total of six seats, while the Scottish universities had none, even though they too were venerable and important

---

[23] Quoted in Heywood, *Academic Reform*, 205.

[24] *The Times*, 12 May 1859, p. 12.

[25] Quoted in Heywood, *Academic Reform*, 198.

[26] *The Times*, 22 Mar. 1866, p. 12.

[27] Hansard, *Parl. Debs*, 3rd ser., clxxxviii, col. 28 (18 June 1867).

[28] Walter Buchanan, *The Parliamentary Representation of the Scottish Universities: Being the Substance of a Paper Read at a Meeting of the Scottish Literary Institute: Held at Glasgow on the 24th April 1857* (Edinburgh, 1857). Charles Rogers, *Leaves from My Autobiography* (1876), 313–15.

institutions in their country. He further argued that, while the interests of Oxford and Cambridge were well known in parliament because so many MPs had been educated there, only a small number of the members for Scotland had been educated at the Scottish universities.[29]

In one respect, however, things had advanced from Haddington's day. As Stirling pointed out, the Universities (Scotland) Act of 1858 had reconstructed the constitutions of those institutions and opened their general councils (the proposed electorate) to non-graduates who could demonstrate that they had studied for four years. This made the councils larger bodies like Oxford's convocation and Cambridge's senate, which consisted of all holders of MAs and higher degrees. The Scottish universities' old constitutions had limited the role of graduates in their corporate affairs, so the practice of taking degrees had waned (except in medicine where degrees were needed for professional reasons). The reforms encouraged higher rates of degree taking, with the effect of reducing the councils' non-graduate element over time. Stirling claimed that these new arrangements answered the earlier objection that the university franchise in Scotland would only go to a very small number of people. In response, however, the home secretary, Sir George Cornewall Lewis, called for Stirling's motion to be rejected on the grounds that the changes brought in by the 1858 Act were too recent, and that it would be inappropriate in any case for an English seat to be transferred across the border.[30]

Things went rather more smoothly in 1868, especially in light of the London precedent. As the Edinburgh University senate proclaimed after London had been granted a seat the previous year, the 'principle of University representation is therefore fully admitted'.[31] Disraeli cited the new constitutions of 1858 as having removed the major barrier to establishing them as constituencies.[32] Although the Scottish Reform Bill originally proposed two members for the four universities, an amendment was moved to allocate them only one seat. In response, the Scottish universities argued that they in fact merited more, not fewer, representatives. Edinburgh's senate produced a statement that the Scottish universities 'might justly claim four members instead of two' and certainly more than one on the basis of numbers. The potential combined electorate for Edinburgh and St Andrews was already greater than either Oxford or Cambridge, and Glasgow and Aberdeen boasted more electors than Dublin. Further, it was argued that representation would lead to a great increase in the number of qualified voters. That London, 'which may be said to possess no property at all', was guaranteed a member caused the Scottish universities to claim appropriate representation based on educational effectiveness and 'influence on the community at large', rather than corporate wealth.[33]

---

[29] Hansard, *Parl. Debs*, 3rd ser., clxiv, cols 121–9 (1 July 1861).

[30] Hansard, *Parl. Debs*, 3rd ser., clxiv, cols 129–30 (1 July 1861).

[31] Univ. of Edinburgh Library, Special Collections Division, Miscellaneous Materials Relating to Glasgow University, Gen. 566/5: 'Statement of the Senatus Academicus of the University of Edinburgh in Support of the Proposal to Give Two Members to the Four Scottish Universities under the Scotch Reform Bill', Apr. 1868.

[32] Hansard, *Parl. Debs*, 3rd ser., clxxxvii, cols 404–5 (13 May 1867).

[33] Univ. of Edinburgh Library, Special Collections Division, Miscellaneous Materials Relating to Glasgow University, Gen. 566/5: 'Statement of the Senatus Academicus of the University of Edinburgh'; 'The Petition of the University Court of the University of Aberdeen', Apr. 1868.

Ultimately, the single-member amendment was rejected, and the bill went forward with provision for two university MPs.[34] For each constituency, a larger and more robust university was joined to a smaller one. This arrangement was informed, in the words of the lord advocate, Edward Strathearn Gordon (subsequently elected MP for Glasgow and Aberdeen in 1869), by the belief 'that some jealousy might probably exist between Edinburgh and Glasgow; and it was therefore much better that the interest of each of these Universities should be attended to by a separate Member'.[35]

Like its counterparts in the Scottish and the new English universities, the convocation of the Queen's University of Ireland – created in 1850 as a kind of Hibernian University of London for the colleges established five years earlier at Belfast, Cork and Galway – had also sought to secure representation for the university during the deliberations over the 1868 Irish Reform Bill, but to no avail.[36] Here, too, the precedents elsewhere in the United Kingdom, as well as sensitivities about institutional status within Ireland, were at the forefront. Chichester Fortescue, Liberal MP for Louth, argued that with London and the Scottish universities now to be represented, the Queen's University was at an even greater disadvantage relative to Dublin.[37]

3. *Learning and 'Fancy Franchises'*

All these activities to extend university representation, and the various proposals made in connection with the reform bills of the 1850s and 1860s, occurred during a period of considerable discussion about the role of intellectuals in national life and debates over the merits of broadening the parliamentary representation of learning and science more generally. In many respects, these positions recalled the idea advanced earlier in the century by Samuel Taylor Coleridge and others that the university-educated class should think of itself as a 'clerisy' with a duty to assume greater national responsibility for preserving culture and morals in the face of advances by the supposedly philistine middle and lower classes.[38]

With respect to parliament, such ideas took the form of proposals for 'fancy franchises' for members of learned societies, especially the Royal Society, and for distinguished professional corporations like the Royal College of Physicians, the Royal College of Surgeons and the Royal Academy of Arts. Ultimately, this approach was deemed impractical because, as Disraeli said in 1852, while such franchises were conceived of as free from 'embarrassment of political connexion, and without inconveniences of party passions', it would be too hard to draw the line between societies

---

[34] Hansard, *Parl. Debs*, 3rd ser., cxcii, cols 879–86 (25 May 1868).

[35] Hansard, *Parl. Debs*, 3rd ser., cxcii, col 883 (25 May 1868). In 1832, the earl of Haddington had proposed this arrangement, the only difference being that Edinburgh would have shared its representation with the two colleges in Aberdeen, King's and Marischal, which were joined to form the university in 1860. Hansard, *Parl. Debs*, 3rd ser., xiv, col. 181 (9 July 1832).

[36] *The Times*, 17 Oct. 1868, p. 10.

[37] Hansard, *Parl. Debs*, 3rd ser., cxcii, cols 1771–4 (18 June 1868).

[38] See Samuel Taylor Coleridge, *The Collected Works of Samuel Taylor Coleridge, Vol. X: On the Constitution of Church and State* (1830), ed. John Colmer (Princeton, NJ, 1976), esp. 46–55. See also Sheldon Rothblatt, *The Revolution of the Dons: Cambridge and Society in Victorian England* (New York, 1968), 113–15, 148 and n. 2; Ben Knights, *The Idea of the Clerisy* (Cambridge, 1979).

that merited representation and those that did not. Further, he thought that looking 'for the elements of a representation among self-elected corporations' was neither constitutional nor judicious'.[39]

The Inns of Court were another category of learned institution, and there was some discussion of whether they, too, should be represented in parliament. Historically, the Inns had been regarded as England's 'third university'.[40] In 1852, along with disposing of the idea of a parliamentary franchise for learned societies and corporations, Disraeli also rejected the idea of special representation for the Inns. Among other factors, he cited the common view that there were already too many lawyers in the House.[41] Subsequently, Lord John Russell's failed 1854 Reform Bill also proposed granting two MPs to the Inns of Court.[42] In this connection, it is interesting to note that increasing dissatisfaction with the organisation of, and education provided by, the Inns led a royal commission on legal education to recommend in 1855 that they be reconstituted as a legal university.[43] The Inns successfully resisted this extreme course and undertook to reform themselves.

Russell's proposals for university and professional franchises were not simply intended as counterweights to those segments of the artisanal and working classes that were coming into the general electorate. Rather, according to one historian of the Second Reform Act, he sought to include the whig ideal of the independent voter 'who would exercise his vote rationally and free of unworthy influence to further his own interests and so ultimately the interests of the state'.[44] John Stuart Mill had also suggested giving an extra vote to all members of the liberal professions, as well as others demonstrably endowed with a superior education.[45] In a more general way, debates over Gladstone's proposed householder franchise in 1866 turned on the extent to which intellect, in the form of bachelor scientists, academics and professionals living in lodgings, needed to be taken into account.[46]

The question of representation for the learned professions dovetailed with debates over university representation. Universities (especially those seeking to be represented in the mid 19th century) were, after all, the institutions that awarded degrees in law and medicine. Because, as Disraeli had noted, lawyers were already an established presence in parliament (including many university MPs), much of this discussion of the professions in relation to university representation focused on medicine. Beginning in the 17th century with Jonathan Goddard (Oxford, 1653), university constituencies returned a

---

[39] Hansard, *Parl. Debs*, 3rd ser., cxxi, cols 440–4 (10 May 1852).

[40] Wilfred R. Prest, *The Inns of Court under Elizabeth I and the Early Stuarts, 1590–1640* (1972), 115; J.H. Baker, *The Third University: The Inns of Court and the Common-Law Tradition* (1990).

[41] Hansard, *Parl. Debs*, 3rd ser., cxxi, cols 440–4 (10 May 1852). On the prejudices against lawyer MPs, see Joseph S. Meisel, *Public Speech and the Culture of Public Life in the Age of Gladstone* (New York, 2001), 207–19.

[42] *A Bill Further to Amend the Laws Relating to the Representation of the People in England and Wales*, 3, Parliamentary Papers, 1854 (17), v, 375.

[43] *Report of the Commissioners Appointed to Inquire into the Arrangements in the Inns of Court and Inns of Chancery, for Promoting the Study of the Law and Jurisprudence*, 55, 104, Parliamentary Papers, 1854–5 [Cmd 1998], xviii, 345.

[44] F.B. Smith, *The Making of the Second Reform Bill* (Cambridge, 1966), 37.

[45] John Stuart Mill, *Considerations on Representative Government* (1861), ch. 8.

[46] See Anna Clark, 'Gender, Class, and the Nation: Franchise Reform in England, 1832–1928', in *Re-reading the Constitution: New Narratives in the Political History of England's Long Nineteenth Century*, ed. James Vernon (Cambridge, 1996), 241–3.

number of medical practitioners.[47] Indeed, university representation became the major vehicle for medicine's parliamentary presence.[48] Yet it must also be borne in mind that having MPs with a particular professional qualification was not the same thing as giving individuals with degrees in that profession a second vote, or constituting its learned society as a separate constituency.

The potential for the university franchise to provide greater representation for medical men was most pertinent for the institutions at which medical education held the greatest importance: London and the Scottish universities. In 1854, when introducing London's deputation to Lord Aberdeen, James Heywood, then MP for North Lancashire, made the point that the university 'included among its members the major portion of the medical profession in London, and it should be remembered that at present the medical profession could not be said to be represented in the House of Commons'.[49] Twelve years later, George Jessel, QC (future master of the rolls and London's vice-chancellor from 1881 until his death in 1883) stated that, if London were to receive the franchise, 'every class of learned men would be represented, more especially the class of medical men, of whose accomplishments the University of London might justly be proud'.[50]

But not all commentators thought that extending the franchise to graduates with professional degrees was a good idea. In his 1857 paper arguing in favour of representation for the Scottish universities, Walter Buchanan made very clear that he thought the franchise should be only for holders of AM degrees, not MDs or LLDs.[51] Similarly, the natural law philosopher James Lorimer argued that the claim of the learned class to political representation was incontrovertible, but cautioned that it 'must be more than a professional class, carrying on a certain portion of the business of the community, and remunerated by the community to the full extent of its services in money'.[52] The professions (medicine, law, army, church), he asserted, were already as well represented in parliament as any other portion of the community and there was no need to confer suffrage upon them as professions. But, he thought the same could not be said for the 'learned class'.

Another set of arguments against including professional graduates in the franchise centred on the nature and limitations of their degree qualifications. Of the medical graduates from London and the Scottish universities, Lorimer wrote: 'general studies which terminate at sixteen, and subsequent duties which confine their attention to the

---

[47] Goddard, however, was a member of the Nominated Parliament. See Millicent Barton Rex, *University Representation in England, 1604–1690* (1954), 185–7.

[48] Roger Cooter, 'The Rise and Decline of the Medical Member: Doctors and Parliament in Edwardian and Interwar Britain', *Bulletin of the History of Medicine*, lxxviii (2004), 71–3.

[49] Quoted in Lorimer, 'University Representation', 368. At the time, he noted, there were only two medical men in the house of commons: Joseph Hume, a member of both London's and Edinburgh's Colleges of Surgeons, and William Mitchell, MD (p. 370).

[50] *The Times*, 22 Mar. 1866, p. 12.

[51] Buchanan, *Parliamentary Representation of the Scottish Universities*, 11. But Buchanan also advocated broadening the subjects for AM degrees beyond classics, mathematics and natural philosophy. He thought classics should be required, but that history, political economy and modern languages could substitute for the other two subjects (p. 10).

[52] Lorimer, 'University Representation', 362.

structure and changes of the human body, little qualify them for the senate'.[53] In order to be eligible for the franchise on the same footing as MAs, he thought, those taking medical degrees should *at least* have a qualification in literature like Cambridge's Previous Examination, which was required of students before they could become a bachelor of physic. The requirements for medical degrees at Oxford and Dublin, which mandated prior study of arts, were even more satisfactory in his view.

If whigs like Russell had toyed with the idea of more special franchises for the learned, and a notable radical like John Stuart Mill (anticipating concerns that would become more acute after 1918) supported plural votes for university graduates and other representatives of the educated classes 'as a counterpoise to the numerical weight of the least educated class',[54] liberals in an era of emerging mass democracy came to view special franchises as generally inconsistent with the trajectory of constitutional development. Objections to university representation had been raised in the past by a few notable figures like John Bright, but a broader hostility towards it began to emerge in the later 19th century. By 1883, one commentator would describe 'orthodox liberalism' as 'severe, even procrustean, in the simplicity of its theory of representation. An extended franchise, equal constituencies, and freely chosen candidates are all its requirements'.[55]

The next extension of the franchise and the redistribution of seats, in 1884 and 1885, respectively, did not involve any further growth of university representation. This was not for lack of trying on Durham's part. The graduates' lobbying group, the Durham University Society, sent deputations to Westminster in 1878, and another one waited on Disraeli the following year. When the question of reform and redistribution was reopened in 1884, the society set up a special sub-committee to press the university's case for representation.[56] What is most significant about the reforms of 1884–5 with respect to the university franchise is that it was preserved in the face of considerable criticism. If the liberals had become hostile to university representation, protecting it (along with the plural vote for business owners) became largely a conservative cause. One reason was that university constituencies tended to return Conservative MPs. Lord Salisbury, Oxford's chancellor as well as Conservative leader, was a particularly 'rigid' supporter of continuing the university franchise.[57] Gladstone, in order to avoid having his reform bills blocked by the Conservative-dominated Lords, was required to enter into a bipartisan compromise with Salisbury over the shape of the franchise and redistribution measures. An explicit provision of this compromise was that university seats would be left untouched.[58] Preservation of the university seats in 1884–5 set the stage for their increase 33 years later, in a much altered political and educational landscape.

[53] Lorimer, 'University Representation', 370.

[54] Mill, *Considerations on Representative Government*, 178.

[55] J. Parker Smith, 'University Representation' [pt 1], *The Law Magazine and Review*, 5th ser., ix (1883), 21.

[56] Reginald Easthope, 'Durham University Society: History of the Society', University of Durham, http://www.dur.ac.uk/dusada/history.htm. 3 Nov. 2006.

[57] Lady Gwendolen Cecil, *Life of Robert Marquis of Salisbury* (4 vols, 1921–32), iii, 123–4.

[58] See William A. Hayes, *The Background and Passage of the Third Reform Act* (New York, 1982), 121, 255, 264.

4. *1918*

In its final form, the 1918 Representation of the People Act amalgamated the two Scottish university seats into one constituency represented by three MPs; gave two members to the 'Combined English Universities', consisting of all the 'modern' universities not already enfranchised (Durham, Manchester, Birmingham, Liverpool, Leeds, Sheffield and Bristol); and created single-member constituencies for Queen's University Belfast and the federal University of Wales. Ironically but not coincidentally, the largest expansion of the special franchise for university graduates occurred at the same moment that Britain achieved full manhood suffrage and gave the vote to women aged 30 and above. Adding to the irony, the prime minister at the time, David Lloyd George, had, when firebrand chancellor of the exchequer in 1911, described university representation as 'the greatest farce in the Constitution of Great Britain'.[59] Yet, the preservation and extension of the university franchise was part of the recommendations made by the Speaker's Conference that met in late 1916 and early 1917 to work out the principles for a new measure of reform to follow the end of the Great War.[60]

Since no minutes were kept of the conference's deliberations, there is no record of how this outcome was arrived at, or the nature of the arguments for and against university representation that were marshalled. One of the 32 conference members likely to have advocated university representation was Sir Joseph Larmor, Lucasian professor and Conservative MP for Cambridge (1911–22). Yet, even if Larmor had worked to persuade his colleagues that university representation should be retained, the acquiescence to its continuation and extension was much broader. When the 1918 Representation of the People Bill was debated in parliament, there was no division on whether the institution of university representation was justifiable.

An important feature of the extension of university representation in 1918 was the presence of the new 'civic' universities that had recently come into their own. Provincial medical schools and colleges fostered under the London umbrella became key components of the new proto-university institutions that began to take shape in England after 1870 in response to the growth of new urban industrial centres (with the concomitant shifts in population away from the south) and sharpened international economic competition.[61] Provincial centres of higher education also took shape around the university extension programmes created by Oxford and Cambridge as they sought to assume a new kind of national role. While most of these institutions' early years were precarious, the perceived need for civic cultural enhancement and the requirements of growing local industries placed increased emphasis on the development of higher education in the great manufacturing towns, nurtured by local philanthropy and state support.

[59] In a speech at Bath, 24 Nov. 1911; *The Times*, 25 Nov. 1911, p. 12.

[60] *Conference on Electoral Reform: Letter from Mr Speaker to the Prime Minister*, 5, Parliamentary Papers, 1917–18 [Cmd 8463], xxv, 385.

[61] This paragraph relies upon classic studies of the late 19th- and early 20th-century development of Britain's higher education system: Michael Sanderson, *The Universities and British Industry, 1850–1970* (1972), esp. ch. 3; Roy Lowe, 'The Expansion of Higher Education in England'; and Sheldon Rothblatt, 'The Diversification of Higher Education in England', in *The Transformation of Higher Learning, 1860–1930: Expansion, Diversification, Social Opening, and Professionalizing in England, Germany, Russia, and the United States*, ed. Konrad H. Jarausch (Chicago, IL, 1983), 37–56, 131–48; as well as the more recent Keith Vernon, *Universities and the State in England, 1850–1939* (2004), ch. 3.

The chartering of the Victoria University in 1884 created a new degree-granting entity on the London model, comprising Owens College, the University College at Liverpool and the Yorkshire College of Science at Leeds. When Mason College in Birmingham (propelled by the town's former Radical mayor turned leading Unionist politician, Joseph Chamberlain) obtained its own university charter in 1900, it set off similar efforts among the other candidate institutions and their supporters at Manchester, Leeds, Sheffield, Liverpool and Bristol. By this time, a federal University of Wales had already been created in 1893, consisting of the university colleges at Aberystwyth, Bangor and Cardiff. With the exception of Reading (described below), other proto-university institutions in England such as the colleges at Nottingham, Newcastle and Southampton would attain university status only after the Second World War.

When they received their charters at the beginning of the 20th century, the new English 'civic' universities which, along with Durham, eventually formed the Combined English Universities constituency, were strongly identified with their regions through governance, funding, student composition and academic specialisation. Even before the First World War, however, many of them were becoming markedly less provincial. Interest in extending representation to the new institutions appears to have emerged first among the established university constituencies in response to legislative efforts to abolish or curtail their existing franchise.

In late 1912 and early 1913, with a bill to eliminate plural voting before parliament, London's MP, Philip Magnus, sought out the views of graduates of several universities, including unrepresented ones, in order to bolster his proposed amendment to preserve university representation.[62] In response, the convocations at Manchester and Liverpool passed resolutions advocating the extension of representation to all universities, while Birmingham's Guild of Graduates took a postal poll of members who were British subjects and resident in the United Kingdom.[63] Of the 223 replies received, 127 men and 56 women definitely approved the motion 'That in any new Redistribution or Electoral Franchise Bill, the University of Birmingham be represented in the House of Commons by one member'.[64]

Around this time, Oxford's Hebdomadal Council developed a scheme for broadening the university franchise to include all university graduates, giving representation to all English and Welsh universities, and increasing the number of university MPs. Remarkably, it also proposed to merge its representation with that of Cambridge in a single three-member constituency. The vice-chancellors of Oxford, Cambridge and London then convened a conference of university MPs, vice-chancellors and other notables to discuss these proposals, which in the event were generally agreed to.[65] Durham, meanwhile, wrote to the new universities of its willingness to co-operate in any endeavour to

---

[62] Univ. of Leeds Archive, Microfilm Reel 134.F1: secretary [to the vice-chancellor] to Dr Chapman, 18 Jan. 1913.

[63] Univ. of Birmingham Archive: Minutes of Council, 12 Feb. and 7 May 1913. Leeds' convocation, however, resolved that the letter from Magnus lie on the table. Univ. of Leeds Archive: Minutes of Standing Committee of Convocation, 17 Feb. 1913.

[64] Univ. of Birmingham Archive: Minutes of the Committee of the Guild of Graduates, 13 Dec. 1912, 16 Jan. 1913.

[65] Univ. of Leeds Archive, Microfilm Reel 134.F1: W.P. Herringham to M.E. Sadler, 18 Apr. 1913; the Hebdomadal Council's proposal is on Reel 133.F42.

secure parliamentary representation.[66] The convocations and graduates' guilds of the civic universities also communicated with one another about the idea of obtaining parliamentary representation.[67]

While these activities generated excitement in some un-enfranchised universities, especially among the organisations representing graduates (who would stand to gain the vote), governing bodies – consumed with establishing the new universities on a firmer footing with limited resources – evidently did not count the university franchise among their top priorities and resolved to let the matter drop.[68] The Great War changed the situation in two ways. First, as Leeds' vice-chancellor, Michael Sadler, wrote in 1917:

> The War has been a crucial test of the power of modern Universities to render aid to the State . . . [The] constitution of modern universities was so well designed, their activities have become so various, their association with national life so close, that, when the unexpected test came, every side of the new University life responded to it with vigorous and useful service.[69]

These universities' considerable contributions to the war effort accelerated their emergence as truly national institutions and, as with un-enfranchised workers and women, advanced the case for their enfranchisement.

A second consequence of the war was the greater degree of inter-institutional co-operation among the civic universities in relation to the government. Before the war, the universities had taken joint action to obtain a modicum of state support. Wartime experience only deepened the extent to which they pursued their interests as a collective. One result was to establish common standards for research degrees, which had previously only been obtainable on the continent and latterly in America. Equally important was the universities' joint efforts to increase substantially the funding they received from the government, ultimately leading to the creation of the University Grants Committee in 1919.[70]

Once the 1917 Speaker's Conference report recommended an extension of university representation, the officers and governing bodies of new universities became quite active in advancing the cause, and then working out the practical details. In 1913, Liverpool's vice-chancellor, Alfred Dale, had been sceptical of the Oxford–Cambridge–London proposals, as he wrote to his Manchester counterpart, Alfred Hopkinson: 'unlike you I am against any special representation for universities'.[71] By 1917, however, either Dale's outlook had changed or he at least sought to make the best out of the inevitable, as

---

[66] Univ. of Manchester Convocation Archive, CON/2/3: Minutes of Committee of Convocation, 21 Apr. 1913.

[67] Univ. of Birmingham Archive: Minutes of the Committee of the Guild of Graduates, 21 May 1913.

[68] See, e.g., Univ. of Manchester Court Archive: Minutes of Court, 28 May 1913, 19 Nov. 1913, 20 May 1914; Univ. of Manchester Council Archive: Minutes of Council, 2 May 1913, 19 Mar. 1913, 30 Apr. 1913, 26 Nov. 1913; Univ. of Leeds Archive: Minutes of Convocation, 17 Feb. 1913.

[69] H.A.L. Fisher *et al.*, *British Universities and the War: A Record and Its Meaning* (1917), 23.

[70] Vernon, *Universities and the State*, 115–18, 181–95; Renate Simpson, *How the PhD Came to Britain: A Century of Struggle for Postgraduate Education* (Guildford, 1983), ch. 5, esp. 130–4; Christine Helene Shinn, *Paying the Piper: The Development of the University Grants Committee, 1919–1946* (1986), 39–43.

[71] Archive of the Univ. of Liverpool, Vice-Chancellor, S2339, Letter Books of the Principal Later the Vice-Chancellor, xx: Dale to Hopkinson, 19 Mar. 1913.

demonstrated by his active correspondence with fellow vice-chancellors, MPs and the Board of Education on proposals and draft legislation for the new constituency.[72] The other vice-chancellors also consulted with their peers and joined with representatives of the graduates in approaching sympathetic MPs. Courts, councils, senates and convocations approved numerous resolutions describing the desired institutional composition of the constituency, and debated how to draw up registers of voters and organise the elections.[73]

As a constituency consisting of seven (later eight) geographically distributed institutions (the distance between Bristol and Durham is more than 230 miles), the Combined English Universities was well served by the experience of wartime co-operation. The universities agreed to conduct the election entirely by posted voting papers, with each vice-chancellor to act as returning officer for his university and the centrally located vice-chancellor of Birmingham to serve as the central returning officer for the whole constituency.[74] The universities also established a joint committee to select and endorse appropriate candidates. The traditional electoral practices of university constituencies also helped. In the first Combined English Universities election, the two authorised candidates, H.A.L. Fisher and Martin Conway, did not canvass for support or hold public meetings at the universities. Instead, following the custom established at Oxford and Cambridge, they campaigned by written addresses to the electors.[75] As the biographer of John Buchan, who sat for the similarly dispersed Combined Scottish Universities constituency from 1927 to 1935, wrote, 'Here was the ideal parliamentary constituency: no expenses, no preliminary campaigning, only an election address; no polling-day frenzy, for the voting was by post; voters so scattered that there could be no week-end meetings, no socials; no sales-of-work'.[76] The redoubtable Eleanor Rathbone, however, broke with tradition in 1929 and made appearances at each of the Combined English institutions.[77]

Unlike the new English universities, the University of Wales had sought to advance its case for representation before the First World War. Here, the politics of university representation outweighed the staunchly liberal and democratic sensibilities characteristic of the principality. Previously, at a meeting of the university's court of governors in 1912, Sir Herbert Isambard Owen (Bristol's vice-chancellor and earlier a major force behind

[72] Archive of the Univ. of Liverpool, Vice-Chancellor, S2344, Letter Books of the Principal Later the Vice-Chancellor, xxv: Dale to Henry Miers, 21 June and 5 July 1917; Dale to Leslie Scott, 5 and 19 July 1917; Dale to C.T. Needham, 19 July 1917; Dale to H.A.L. Fisher, 7 and 31 Dec. 1917; and Dale to N.D. Bosworth Smith, 8 May 1918.

[73] Univ. of Manchester Council Archive: Minutes of Council, 24 Oct. 1917, 13 Mar. 1918. Univ. of Manchester Court Archive: Minutes of Court, 16 May 1917. Univ. of Leeds Archive: Minutes of Standing Committee of Convocation, 20 Dec. 1917, 7 Jan. 1918; Minutes of Convocation (extraordinary meeting to discuss matters stemming from the Representation of the People Act), 20 Mar. 1918. Univ. of Sheffield Administrative Archive: Minutes of Council, 16 July 1917.

[74] On the government side, responsibility for organising the new university constituency fell to the Board of Education.

[75] *The Times*, 8 Dec. 1918, p. 10; H.A.L. Fisher, *An Unfinished Autobiography* (1940), 118.

[76] Janet Adam Smith, *John Buchan: A Biography* (1965), 299.

[77] Susan Pedersen, *Eleanor Rathbone and the Politics of Conscience* (New Haven, CT, 2004), 220. Rules about candidates holding meetings in university buildings varied somewhat across the Combined English Universities institutions. Yet, even where prohibitions were in place, candidates could still hold meetings in student unions. See Univ. of Manchester, Vice-Chancellor's Archive, VCA/7/138 (2) for the 1935 exchange of letters between Rathbone and Vice-Chancellor Stopford of Manchester, as well as Stopford's inquiries to his colleagues.

the effort to unite Wales' major colleges) had moved that steps be taken to secure representation in parliament. In response to objections that university representation was undemocratic and was likely soon to be done away with, Owen said: 'his point was that if parliament did decide to allow university representation to continue the Welsh University should see that it had a share in any plunder – legitimate plunder, of course – that might be attached', and his motion was carried by 17 votes to 12.[78] From another direction, the royal commission (1916–18) established to examine university education in Wales heard from a delegation of the university's students in 1917 arguing for parliamentary representation, although the commission's report did not take up the question.[79]

With a new franchise and redistribution bill in the works at the end of the war, there was strong sentiment in Wales that the University of Wales should have its own MP.[80] In framing the Representation of the People Act of 1918, those looking out for Welsh interests worked to get an additional seat for the principality. Giving that seat to the university was seen as the least objectionable option, since it would avoid privileging one part of Wales over another. In November 1917, David Davies, MP for Montgomeryshire and active supporter of Welsh higher education, brought in a motion to give the university representation, but the home secretary, Sir George Cave, was unwilling to complicate the passage of the bill any further by acceding to demands for additional representation. Davies' motion was supported by 12 votes.

Having failed in the Commons, advocates for giving Wales an extra seat through the university then lobbied for a favourable revision to the bill in the house of lords.[81] In January 1918, the Liberal peer Lord St Davids introduced a motion to grant the university a separate member, which was accepted by the government.[82] The following month, Ellis Jones Ellis-Griffith, Liberal MP for Anglesey, moved an amendment in the Commons to the same effect, and was supported by London's Philip Magnus. Cave then stated that he was in sympathy with the demand made on behalf of the university, while for the opposition Liberals, Herbert Samuel reiterated his party's customary objection to university representation (noting how much it was now to be enlarged), but said he did not want to see Wales placed at a disadvantage to the rest of the kingdom.[83]

In his history of the university, Gwynn Williams writes that it was 'ironical that a university which took pride in its democratic origins and constitution should at the election of 1918 have a constituency of only 1,066 and that in 1922 the member returned received less than 500 votes'.[84] At the time, A.F. Pollard, the historian and unsuccessful candidate for the London seat, observed:

> It needed a peculiar Welsh wizardry to give a seat to a Welsh University with barely a thousand voters, and leave London, which had more than nine times the number of

[78] *The Times*, 23 Nov. 1912, p. 4.

[79] J. Gwynn Williams, *A History of the University of Wales, Vol. 2: The University of Wales, 1893–1939* (Cardiff, 1997), 330.

[80] Williams, *University of Wales*, 330.

[81] See National Library of Wales, J. Herbert Lewis Papers, D79: letters between John Herbert Lewis and various correspondents.

[82] Hansard, *Parl. Debs* (Lords), 5th ser., xxvii, cols 1129–36 (23 Jan. 1918).

[83] Hansard, *Parl. Debs* (Commons), 5th ser., ci, cols 1005–2015 (1 Feb. 1918).

[84] Williams, *University of Wales*, 332.

electors, with the same amount of representation. Nor was it much fairer to give the Combined [English] Universities, with less than a quarter of London's electorate, double its representation.[85]

As Pollard's comparisons indicate, the enfranchisement of universities was driven by political imperatives which were not only outside the mainstream democratic logic of representation that emerged in 1918, but also advanced without any coherent scheme for how universities should be represented in relation to each other.

The Act also extended university representation on an individual as well as institutional basis: the new constituencies conferred the franchise on all persons of age who had obtained a degree of any kind, not just the MA previously required for the Oxford, Cambridge and Dublin vote. As part of the broader hostility towards university representation, the MA requirement had come under fire on previous occasions. In 1906, for example, Asquith had pointed out that:

> the qualification for a University vote was the possession in our ancient universities of an MA degree, and an MA degree could be acquired by anybody who had passed a not very difficult examination and was prepared to pay a sum of £20 or £25. He himself had not got a vote, because he had never been prepared to pay the £25, although a graduate of Oxford.[86]

In line with the general franchise established in 1918, the university vote was also extended to qualified women over 30. At the same time, however, the elimination of most other special franchises under the Act, and the provision that no elector could have more than two votes, reduced the overall number of plural voters, which before 1918 had amounted to more than half a million. After passage of the Act, plural voting remained the privilege of approximately 159,000 people holding the business franchise (which had also been preserved) plus a university electorate of around 68,000.[87] As one contemporary observer wrote, the university franchise, like the business premises vote, was one of the safeguards against the transition to (nearly) full democracy: 'The Conservative elements insisted upon these arrangements as a means of preventing the submerging of the more wealthy and more educated part of the electorate'.[88]

In addition to these changes, the 1918 Act sought to democratise university representation 'to accord with modern ideas'[89] by introducing, for university constituencies represented by more than one member (Oxford, Cambridge, Dublin, Combined Scottish and Combined English), proportional representation by single transferable vote. Nineteenth-century proponents of proportional representation (PR) had identified the

[85] *The Times*, 29 Nov. 1922, p. 13. The inequity of London's single member was raised again in the letters pages two years later by J. Beresford Clark, president of the University of London Union Society; *The Times*, 15 Nov. 1924, p. 6.

[86] Hansard, *Parl. Debs*, 4th ser., clxiii, col. 209 (24 Oct. 1906).

[87] Martin Pugh, 'Popular Conservatism in Britain: Continuity and Change, 1880–1987', *Journal of British Studies*, xxvii (1988), 260.

[88] Frederic A. Ogg, 'The British Representation of the People Act', *American Political Science Review*, xii (1918), 499. The business franchise allowed a man to vote in a constituency other than that in which he resided if he occupied a property for business purposes worth £10 or more per year.

[89] *The Times*, 16 Feb. 1948, p. 5.

special category of university seats as 'a most tempting subject for such an experiment'.[90] Advocates of PR were encouraged by the results. For the Scottish universities, the Liberal minority gained a seat, which had proved impossible under the old system, and while the Combined English Universities' two seats limited the ability of the minority to gain a representative, supporters of PR thought that minority now at least had a 'fighting chance'.[91] At Oxford, the university's MPs from 1832 to 1918 had been returned unopposed in 24 out of 30 elections and by-elections. Beginning with 1918, every election but one (1931) was contested.[92] With hindsight, however, the experiment produced limited results. In the 32 contests in which PR might have operated during the eight general elections from 1918 to 1945, six candidates were returned unopposed and a further seven obtained a sufficient number of first-preference votes to render any consideration of second preferences unnecessary. In 13 other contests, the successful candidate would clearly have won in a first-past-the-post election.[93]

A further development associated with university representation in 1918 had to do with British subjects residing overseas, who previously had been virtually unable to vote. Postal voting had been introduced for university constituencies in 1864 (in the short term strengthening the influence of the country clergy in Oxford and Cambridge elections). The practice was extended in subsequent university enfranchisements, but postal voting by graduates living outside the United Kingdom was practically impossible because statutes required their voting papers to be signed by a justice of the peace. In 1918, consistent with temporary provisions introduced for voters in the services stationed abroad, witnessing requirements for voting papers were broadly extended.[94] Thereafter, university electors outside the United Kingdom could vote (so long as their papers arrived before the close of the poll), and the university franchise was the only one for which British subjects resident abroad were eligible. (Absentee ballots for expatriates and those travelling at the time of an election were only introduced in 1985.) By 1930, an estimated 8% of university electors lived overseas.[95] This was used in arguments to preserve the university franchise. As a 1931 petition signed by a long and eminent list of supporters asked: 'Can it be desirable to cut off from all share in home politics the oversea members of a nation as far-wandering as ours?'[96] (The changes to the franchise and electoral procedures in 1918 also benefited some internal wanderers, such as the

[90] J. Parker Smith, 'University Representation' [pt 2], *The Law Magazine and Review*, ix (1884), 157.

[91] [Anon.], 'PR in University Elections: How the System Worked', *Representation: The Journal of the Proportional Representation Society*, xlii (1924), 30–2.

[92] *The History of the University of Oxford, Vol. 8: The Twentieth Century*, ed. Brian Harrison (Oxford, 1994), 378.

[93] D.E. Butler, *The Electoral System in Britain, 1918–1951* (Oxford, 1953), 152–3.

[94] Univ. of Leeds Archives, Administrative Records: Parliamentary Representation (in file titled 'Representation of the People Bill/Act, 1917–18'), 'University Elections Bill, 3rd Dec., 1917, ccxxii (3) 230–3'. An introductory note to the bill explains the reasoning behind the clauses, which were incorporated into the 1918 Representation of the People Act. I have referenced this bill by archival location because, even though it has a bill number, it is not listed as part of the parliamentary papers of either the Commons or the Lords, nor does it appear in the journals of either House; Mari Takayanagi, Parliamentary Archives, email correspondence with author, 13 Apr. 2007.

[95] Eleanor Rathbone, 'The Case for University Representation' (printed circular), Dec. 1930, Univ. of Manchester Vice-Chancellor's Archive, VCA/7/138 (1).

[96] *The Times*, 17 Feb. 1931, p. 8.

increasing number of university-educated wesleyan ministers whose mandatory itinerancy had previously prevented them from meeting electoral residency requirements.)[97]

With respect to the Irish universities, the political and institutional conditions at the end of the First World War had been considerably altered from those of the late 1860s. The fate of Irish university seats was inevitably bound up with the territorial and constitutional debates surrounding home rule. The 1912 Home Rule Bill – delayed by the Lords but passed in 1914, then never put into effect on account of the war and subsequent events – would have transferred Dublin's two seats to the Irish parliament without granting any additional seats to either Queen's University Belfast or the National University of Ireland (established in 1908 with the former Queen's colleges at Cork and Galway and the Jesuit University College, Dublin).

The question of university seats for both Dublin and for the newer institutions was raised again in 1917 when, during the debates over the Representation of the People Bill, it was agreed that a special conference would be established to consider the redistribution of seats in Ireland on the basis of population.[98] With the establishment of separate home rule parliaments for both the north and the south in prospect, the leadership of Queen's University Belfast was 'unwilling to trust the integrity of any Irish parliament, even a northern one'.[99] Supporters of Queen's Belfast saw representation at Westminster as a key safeguard for the institution's future. In November 1917, the university's senate convened a special meeting on the subject and appointed a committee to advance the university's claims and resist any suggestion that the Irish universities be grouped into a single constituency like their Scottish and modern English counterparts. The committee despatched a deputation to Westminster to make the university's views known and to secure the support of MPs from the Ulster province. Ultimately, the 1918 Redistribution of Seats (Ireland) Act created separate single-member constituencies for both Queen's University Belfast and the National University of Ireland. In this way, the politics of university representation both reflected and helped to reify the emerging de facto territorial division of Ireland.

In partitioning the island, the 1920 Government of Ireland Act continued the representation of both Dublin (two members) and the National University of Ireland (one member since 1918) at Westminster, while also approving four members for each institution in the southern parliament. Similarly, Queen's University Belfast continued to return one member to the house of commons, and was given four seats in the Northern Ireland parliament at Stormont. With the treaty of 1922 and the establishment of the Irish Free State, representation of the southern universities passed entirely to the Dáil Éireann, in which Dublin and the National University were each given three seats.

5. *From the Interwar Years to the Post-War Years*

Following the great expansion and extension of university representation in 1918, the interwar years saw hostility towards the institution increase still further, accompanied by

[97] Univ. of Leeds Archive, Microfilm Reel 133.F42: cutting from the *Methodist Times*, 19 Sept. 1918.

[98] Hansard, *Parl. Debs* (Commons), 5th ser., c, cols 758–96 (7 Dec. 1917).

[99] T.W. Moody and J.C. Beckett, *Queen's Belfast, 1845–1949*, (2 vols, 1959), ii, 466.

intensified efforts to abolish or weaken the university seats. Yet, it was during this period that university representation was extended for the last time, to the University of Reading, which received its royal charter in 1926 and was the only university to be so recognized between the wars. Two years later, A.A. Somerville, Conservative MP for nearby Windsor, introduced a bill to entitle Reading's graduates to vote for the Combined English Universities seats. Because Reading had been chartered after the 1918 Representation of the People Act, he made the familiar claim for equity by arguing that the university's standing among the 'young' English institutions was anomalous with respect to representation: 'There may be some objection to University representation as a principle, but as long as University representation exists, it seems unfair to deny to the graduates of Reading University the privilege which is at present enjoyed by other Universities'.[100]

The Bill was supported by the two members for the Combined English Universities and the member for Wales, as well as a Labour MP, Morgan Jones, who had been educated at Reading. Consistent with their principled opposition to university representation and plural voting generally, most Labour MPs objected to enfranchising Reading. Nevertheless, the Bill was passed (in a not very full House) by 90 votes in favour to 45 against.[101] As the account by William MacBride Childs, Reading's first vice-chancellor, makes clear, obtaining the franchise was seen as the culmination and ultimate recognition of university status: 'The effective start of the University is to be dated October, 1926; but it was not until 1928 that an act of Parliament was passed securing for graduates of the University of Reading the privileges in respect of the parliamentary franchise enjoyed by graduates of the Combined English Universities'.[102]

Although it exemplified several key aspects of the larger history of the expanding university representation, extending the franchise to Reading turns out to have been the story's coda. In early 1944, when another all-party conference chaired by the Speaker of the house of commons was convened to develop plans for revising the structures of electoral politics for the new post-war era, the extensive recommendations (for redistribution of seats, reform of the parliamentary and local franchises, and changes to the costs and methods of elections) explicitly left university representation untouched.[103] Conservatives had a decisive majority in the conference, which was constituted in rough proportion to the parliamentary membership elected in 1935. Here was another compromise that prolonged the life of university representation: leaving the university and business franchise largely unaltered was a political price Labour paid in exchange for assimilating the parliamentary and local government franchises.[104] When it came to be

---

[100] Hansard, *Parl. Debs* (Commons), 5th ser. ccxviii, col. 1364 (15 June 1928).

[101] Hansard, *Parl. Debs* (Commons), 5th ser., ccxviii, cols 1364–84 (15 June 1928).

[102] William MacBride Childs, *Making a University: An Account of the University Movement at Reading* (1933), 265.

[103] 'The existing University representation and methods of election shall be retained, Provided that every person who has received or receives a degree (or its equivalent) shall be automatically registered and that no fees shall be charged for registration expenses.' *Conference on Electoral Reform and Redistribution of Seats: Letter from Mr Speaker to the Prime Minister*, 6, Parliamentary Papers, 1943–4 [Cmd 6534], iii, 213.

[104] See the later statements by the former Conservative chief whip, Viscount Margesson, Hansard, *Parl. Debs* (Lords), 5th ser., clvii, col. 309 (5 July 1948), and by Churchill, Hansard, *Parl. Debs* (Commons), 5th ser., cdxlvii, col. 861 (16 Feb. 1948); both cited in Butler, *Electoral System*, 114–15.

debated in the Commons, the clause for retaining the institution was accepted by 152 votes to 16.[105]

The compromise was abrogated after Labour returned to power in 1945. With the party in a commanding majority for the first time, the government went against the terms agreed to by the Speaker's Conference and instead made good on the previous decade's effort at abolishing university representation. The 1948 Representation of the People Act included the elimination at the next general election of the university vote and the 12 university seats. The Conservatives charged that this was a violation not only of the Speaker's Conference agreement, but also a breach of constitutional custom by altering the structure of the Commons without the consent of all parties. In response, they pledged to restore the university seats once they returned to power – a position included in the party's 1950 and 1951 election manifestos. Indeed, the primarily Conservative or Independent university seats could possibly have altered the results of these two close elections. Nevertheless, Conservative support for university representation was not unanimous and some within the party questioned the necessity and wisdom of restoration.[106]

When the Conservatives returned to office in 1951 the expectation that university representation would be restored led some potential candidates to start positioning themselves to campaign for the seats.[107] But the government had only a slim majority, and Churchill announced that the party would not attempt to restore university representation during the life of the new parliament. In his speech on the Address, he stated that, although on a strict interpretation of the Conservatives' mandate his government should be permitted to restore university seats immediately, it would create a 'questionable precedent' for a government to add to their majority already elected to parliament. Instead, he said, any alteration to the franchise should follow the normal course of such measures, with restoration operative only at the dissolution.[108] Such ardour as the restoration of university representation may have inspired faded quickly. By 1954, it could be said that 'university representation is now regarded as an interesting phenomenon belonging already to the past',[109] and the 1955 Conservative manifesto dropped the

[105] Hansard, *Parl. Debs* (Commons), 5th ser., cdiii, cols 2019–51 (12 Oct. 1944). It is possible that nearly half the MPs in 1944 had the university vote. Based on entries in *Dod's Parliamentary Companion* for 1944, I have counted 305 MPs who were 'educated at' one of the represented universities. The number who were eligible for the franchise could be smaller than this, since most entries did not indicate whether degrees had been taken (it seems safe to assume that those MPs who did not have educational information in their entries were not university graduates). The total number of seats in the Commons was 615, three of which were vacant at the time *Dod's* was prepared.

[106] Butler, *Electoral System*, 139; Dell G. Hitchner, 'The Labour Government and the House of Commons', *Western Political Quarterly*, v (1952), 419 and n.

[107] The Manchester businessman Leonard Behrens, for example, was urged by his friends to stand for the Combined English Universities in the belief that the government would soon restore university seats. Univ. of Manchester Vice-Chancellor's Archive, VCA/7/138 (2): Behrens to J.S.B. Stopford, 27 Oct. 1951. Behrens, a Liberal who planned to run as an Independent, went so far as to begin preparing his election address. Royal Institution of Great Britain, Sir Lawrence Bragg Papers, W.L. BRAGG/56A/514: Behrens to W.L. Bragg, 28 Oct. 1951. In 1937, Bragg's father, William H. Bragg (like his son, a physicist) had declined overtures from the Manchester University Constitutional Association to stand as Unionist candidate for the Combined English Universities. Royal Institution of Great Britain, William Henry Bragg Papers, W.H. BRAGG/10A/35 and 36: A.E.G. Chorlton to W.H. Bragg, 12 and 15 Feb. 1937.

[108] Hansard, *Parl. Debs* (Commons), 5th ser., cdxciii, col. 71 (6 Nov. 1951).

[109] [Theodore Wilson Harris], 'The University Vote' [review of Rex, *University Representation*], *Times Literary Supplement*, 8 Oct. 1954, p. 634.

pledge to restore the seats. Thus, despite the stated commitment of his party, Churchill's return to power marked the true end of university representation in Britain, three and a half centuries after it was established.

6. Conclusion

In the absence of any serious debate over whether it was fundamentally appropriate or desirable for universities to be directly represented in parliament, there were few real barriers against institutions' efforts to gain the franchise after 1832. Following the 17th-century precedents, obtaining seats in parliament came to be seen by universities, old and new, as a legitimate and desirable institutional objective. Institutional aspirations can be seen particularly in the ways in which the size of the potential electorates came to be invoked. For example, the proposal to grant Dublin a second seat in 1832 as part of an overall electoral plan for Ireland had to be tied to broadening the university's extremely narrow franchise. Lord Haddington, refuting the claim made in 1832 that there was no real constituency for the Scottish universities, noted that the number of degrees taken at those institutions from 1800 to 1830 amounted to 6,879, including 2,728 MAs, of which some 1,500 were resident in Scotland.[110] When the Scottish universities fought back against an amendment to limit their representation to one seat in 1868, they could claim that their combined electorate would exceed that of either Oxford or Cambridge plus Dublin. Proponents of London's enfranchisement in 1866 could point to the growing body of graduates as part of their claim, noting that the number of eligible electors stood at 1,729 and would rise to 2,000 by the time a reform bill was passed.[111] And when the next big round of university enfranchisements was being discussed in 1917, London's vice-chancellor went further to argue that, based on the size of the university's electorate (6,072 to Oxford's 6,895 and Cambridge's 7,145), it should really be given a *second* MP.[112]

Although university constituencies would never be as numerous as those of the boroughs and counties, the growing rolls of living graduates, the expanding access to higher education, the widening of university franchises and the enfranchising of more universities gradually moved university constituencies somewhat closer to the average representation of other constituencies. In 1918, an ordinary member represented six times more electors than a university member (32,822 to 4,928); by 1945, only three times as many (52,511 to 18,114).[113]

But universities' considerations went beyond mere questions of status. Representation – both as a general practice and in the case of specific universities – was justified by its advocates on a number of grounds that reached far beyond parochial institutional concerns. For example, the arguments for London's representation, and those marshalled later on for the civic universities, could be seen as specific instances of more general

[110] Hansard, *Parl. Debs*, 3rd ser., xiv, col. 182 (9 July 1832).

[111] *The Times*, 22 Mar. 1866, p. 12.

[112] Univ. of London Archives, Convocation and Committees, UoL/CN 1/1/13: Proceedings of Convocation, 17 Mar. 1917, 11 Dec. 1917.

[113] Butler, *Electoral System*, 152.

attempts to advance the cause of political modernisation in which the universities stood for new trends that were challenging the status quo. Similarly, the civic universities' demand for parliamentary representation was an assertion not only of their strength, but also of the importance to the nation of the forms of education they provided. Beyond developments such as these, the questions surrounding university representation also connected to a set of even more fundamental constitutional issues, which are taken up in detail in the next chapter.

Chapter 3. Debating University Representation

In 1865, *The Times* described university representation as 'not a branch of the political tree, but a magnificent fungus, more defensible on its own merits than as part of the whole system'.[1] Yet it was precisely the function of university representation within the whole system that made it both significant and increasingly contentious. Over the course of the 19th and early 20th centuries, advocates for universities seeking to obtain representation advanced a wide range of arguments. The parliamentary franchise and election of members were viewed as important features of universities' corporate life, without which they would be somehow incompletely realized. Thus, institutions made claims for equity: if some universities were enfranchised, all should be; and to lack representation placed universities at a disadvantage relative to those that already had MPs. The more established Scottish universities could further argue that they, too, were old foundations and should therefore be entitled to the same privileges as Oxford, Cambridge and Dublin.

As universities advanced their claims with each new proposal for constitutional or electoral reform, the question of their parliamentary representation became ever more contentious. Critics raised two main categories of objection. The first rejected university representation on principle, although the principles changed over time. Initially, opponents focused on limiting clerical influence in parliament. Later, principled objections emphasized the undemocratic nature of fancy franchises and plural voting. This shift from religious to political criteria in critiques of university representation echoed the more general decoupling of religion from both the state and education over the course of the 19th and early 20th centuries. The second category of objection arose with the emergence of the modern party system and was centred on the political affiliation of members as well as the use of university seats strictly for party purposes. In the face of these mounting criticisms, those who favoured university representation were increasingly hard-pressed to justify and defend the institution against those who sought to restrict or abolish it altogether.

Arguments for and against the continuation and extension of university representation were deeply enmeshed with many of the larger constitutional issues that were raised (and not necessarily resolved) between the Great Reform Act of 1832 and the 1948 Representation of the People Act. Just as university seats and the place of learning in parliament more generally were bound up with evolving 19th-century theories of representation, university representation also figured in debates over the character of political modernisation in Britain, especially with respect to the constitutional position of religion, the appropriateness of plural voting, the relationship of constituent nations and regions to the United Kingdom, and political rights for women. Indeed, the debates over university representation demonstrate the degree to which all these issues were bound up with one another.

[1] *The Times*, 25 July 1865, p. 8.

1. *Religion*

For opponents of university representation, a major objection in the 19th century was the claim that university seats were de facto a form of clerical representation. The connection between universities and the Established Church featured prominently in university representation's 17th- and 18th-century history. In the 19th century, anglican clergymen constituted the majority of the MAs who were entitled to vote for Oxford and Cambridge's MPs, and nonconformists were not permitted to take degrees at those universities until the 1850s, or to become fellows until the 1870s. Dublin, despite the broadening of its franchise in 1832 to include catholic holders of higher degrees, remained staunchly anglican in character. Durham, which actively sought to obtain representation, was an outgrowth of the cathedral created to train clergymen.

The negative association of university representation with the clerical interest was still employed as a rallying cry in the 1880s, though (like the universities themselves) not always quite understood by popular audiences. At the National Liberal Federation conference held at Leeds in October 1883, for example, John Morley's rhetorical question, 'Were the clergy to retain the four seats for the two Universities of Oxford and Cambridge?' met with a mixed or confused response (reported in *The Times* as ' "No", "Yes" ').[2] In 1885, after noting that the abolition of religious tests was gradually making the Oxford and Cambridge constituencies less of the clerical strongholds they had been, Albert Grey (later the fourth Earl Grey) advocated hastening the process by admitting all graduates to the franchise, even to the inclusion of extension students.[3]

The confluence of universities' institutional concerns, religious questions and parliamentary reform in the 19th century is especially evident in the debates that surrounded two proposals to create joint university constituencies. The first occurred during the committee stage of the 1867 Reform Bill when the long-promised creation of a seat for London was briefly thrown into confusion by John Robert Mowbray, MP for the city of Durham, who moved an amendment to add the University of Durham to the new constituency. The proposed amendment was supported by other MPs from northern constituencies, and shepherded by Disraeli in his capacity as Conservative leader in the House. As Bernal Osborne, Radical MP for Nottingham, said towards the end of the debate, 'he could hardly have imagined that the question of Universities would have produced so much consternation among hon. Gentlemen'.[4]

Mowbray's amendment met with vigorous objections from Robert Lowe, John Bright, Osborne, Edward Cardwell and Gladstone. Some of them focused on London's just claims. As Bright (who reiterated that he was no supporter of university constituencies) observed, the principle of enfranchising London had already and repeatedly been proposed and accepted in successive reform bills since 1854. He saw the sudden proposal to add anglican Durham as a purely partisan move by the government, attempting to dilute London's liberal tendencies. Other objections emphasized the incompatibility of the two institutions. As Lowe put it: 'Durham is local and provincial; London is

---

[2] *The Times*, 18 Oct. 1883, p. 6.

[3] Hansard, *Parl. Debs*, 3rd ser., ccxcv, cols 350–3 (6 Mar. 1885).

[4] Hansard, *Parl. Debs*, 3rd ser., clxxxviii, col. 42 (18 June 1867).

metropolitan and cosmopolitan, extending its influence more and more every day all over the world . . . The one University is ecclesiastical, the other pre-eminently and entirely secular'.[5]

At that time, Durham's convocation included only those MA holders who were members of the church of England (although the university had recently removed religious tests for matriculation and non-theological degrees). Mowbray claimed that Durham was moving in a liberalising direction and would soon drop this restriction on the composition of its convocation. The religious dimension was even more complex because, as Disraeli wryly observed, the bill would make electors out of students at Ushaw College, a catholic seminary located in Durham which awarded London degrees, while defeat of Mowbray's amendment would exclude Durham University's anglicans from the same privilege. In addition to the religious question, other objections centred on Durham's institutional fitness for the franchise. Lowe asserted that Durham was really more a college than a university because it relied on its own teachers to examine the students. Gladstone, who also emphasized London's long-standing expectations, agreed that Durham had not achieved an appropriate level of institutional development to warrant representation. Some commentators were less charitable in their characterisations of Durham. The *London Review*, for instance, wrote: 'The examinations are placed at an inferior standard in order to encourage scholars, and to attract them to the halls of a decaying and inefficient college. There is no credit to be attained by taking a degree from it . . . It is not worth a representative; and conferring the franchise upon it, and welding it with London University, is simply an insult to the latter, for which there is no justification'.[6]

For its part, London took swift action to counter the threatened joint representation. It immediately summoned a special meeting of convocation to deal with the proposed joining of Durham to the constituency. This produced a resolution asserting that a merger with any other university would be 'entirely derogatory' to the university's position and the pledges given at its foundation that it should enjoy a status equal to that of Oxford and Cambridge. Moreover, the resolution concluded, 'a combination with Durham would be utterly heterogeneous'. MPs who were graduates of the university were mobilised to oppose the amendment, and a petition against the proposed merger signed by London's vice-chancellor and the chairman of convocation was presented to the Commons by Lowe on 18 June.[7] (Within the university, even the anglican King's College does not appear to have advanced a minority opinion in support of the idea of a merged constituency.) All these arguments and efforts notwithstanding, the vote was surprisingly close. In the end, 234 MPs voted against the proposed amendment to add the words 'and Durham' to the clause enfranchising London, producing a slim majority over the 226 who voted in favour of it.

A second disputed proposal for joining universities in a single constituency occurred the following year during consideration of the Representation of the People (Ireland) Bill. Under the previous government, Chichester Fortescue, then under-secretary of state

---

[5] Hansard, *Parl. Debs*, 3rd ser., clxxxviii, cols 20–1 (18 June 1867).

[6] *London Review*, xiv (1867), 693.

[7] Univ. of London Archives, Convocation and Committees, UoL/CN 1/1/3: Proceedings of Convocation, 15 June 1867, 23 July 1867, 12 May 1868 (Report to the Annual Meeting).

for the colonies, had proposed adding a member for the federated Queen's University of Ireland in connection with the plan then under discussion to make it an Irish cognate to London.[8] He did not renew this proposal in 1868 because there was no redistribution scheme for Ireland. Instead, he proposed that the 700 to 800 graduates of the Queen's University be included 'within the very ample representation of the University of Dublin', since Dublin had a much smaller number of electors (1,870) than either Oxford (4,190) or Cambridge (5,440) while returning the same number of MPs.[9] Fortescue argued that uniting the representation of the two universities would be less like the case of London and Durham and more like that of the Scottish universities, and he thought his scheme to join the two Irish universities into one constituency a better and less 'violent' plan than another proposal to reassign one of Dublin's members to the Queen's University.

The earl of Mayo stated his hope that the Queen's University would be granted representation under any future redistribution scheme, but objected to Fortescue's motion on the grounds that both institutions found such a scheme objectionable. He read from a letter sent to him by a member of the Queen's University convocation stating that the idea of uniting the constituencies was discussed and unanimously condemned: 'We should nominally have two representatives who would virtually represent another institution'.[10] John Thomas Ball, attorney-general for Ireland and an MP for Dublin, also raised objections on behalf of his constituency. On the other side, Fortescue's motion received vigorous support from William Gregory, Liberal-Conservative MP for County Galway, who saw the addition of Queen's electors as the first step towards breaking up the exclusively anglican character of Dublin's representation. Shortly after the clause went down to defeat, the Liberal MP Henry Fawcett picked up this fallen standard and proposed to disenfranchise the smallest Irish borough (Portlington, which had only 106 electors) and transfer the representation to the Queen's University, but this too was defeated.[11]

Against the backdrop of more general objections to university representation as representation for the clergy – especially as embodied in the older university seats – these two short-lived merger proposals, in different ways, show the spirit of modernity in conflict with tradition, both among higher education institutions and in the shaping of the reform bills of the 1860s. In each case where a constituency merger was proposed, the joining of a secular university with a broad public mandate to an institution strongly identified with anglicanism was rejected on account of the perceived fundamental incompatibility of the two. But the incompatibility was not merely institutional. Rather, the arguments in both cases (like those that accompanied the reforms imposed at Oxford and Cambridge) shed light on the shifting relationship between anglicanism and the state. The emphasis in each case was, however, quite different. In the proposed London–Durham merger, the addition of anglican Durham was closely associated with the perceived political temper of secular versus establishment institutions. In the Dublin–

[8] In 1880, the Queen's University was superseded by the Royal University of Ireland, a degree-conferring body on the London model for the former colleges of both Queen's and the Catholic University of Ireland (Magee College and University College Dublin).

[9] Hansard, *Parl. Debs*, 3rd ser., cxcii, cols 1771–4 (18 June 1868).

[10] Hansard, *Parl. Debs*, 3rd ser., cxcii, col. 1774 (18 June 1868).

[11] Hansard, *Parl. Debs*, 3rd ser., cxcii, cols 1777, 1790–1 (18 June 1868).

Queen's case, the addition of a smaller non-denominational body was seen as a healthy way to dilute Trinity College's anglican monopoly. Of course, the differences between these two episodes reflected the larger differences between England and Ireland with respect to religious concerns.

2. *1884–5*

As religious concerns in politics became less acute generally towards the end of the century (outside Ireland, at least), the focus of objections to university representation shifted to a more strictly political basis. In the 1880s, the agreement struck between Gladstone's government and the Conservative leadership under Lord Salisbury over a new measure of reform spared plural voting and university representation. As the independent-minded Conservative MP for Cambridge, Alexander James Beresford Hope (Salisbury's brother-in-law) asserted in 1885, using the language of the high culture movement, the maintenance and extension of university representation would be the intellectual counterweight to the 'philistine' thrust of the reform measures. Non-resident graduates – lawyers, doctors and other professionals – were, he claimed, the mind of the country, and even if 'among the non-residents might be found country squires, whose degree was a poll or a pass one, and whose talk was of bullocks and such things, was it not something to be able to talk of bullocks with that reasonable education which any degree indicated?'[12]

The agreement was one of several ways in which Salisbury used the 1885 redistribution bill to temper the 1884 extension of the franchise and strengthen the Conservatives' electoral advantages. Gladstone's decision to let the university seats remain has been seen as an especially important part of the compromise reached by the party leaders.[13] Indeed, the tories laid great stress on preserving university representation, possibly, it has been argued, because they did not succeed in protecting more of their interests.[14] But if the compromise limited the ability of opponents of university representation to act in the Commons, prominent Liberal ministers did not feel constrained from expressing their belief that the special franchise should be done away with. Attorney-General Sir Henry James stated that he could not defend university representation any more than he could defend plural voting. Similarly, the Radical Sir Charles Dilke, president of the Local Government Board, also aired his personal view that university representation ought to be abolished, but as a member of the government who had played a central role in negotiations with the Conservatives he was obliged to support the bill in its current form.[15]

From the Liberal backbenches, however, James Bryce, MP for Tower Hamlets, mounted the first major assault on university representation as an institution during the committee stage of the 1885 redistribution bill. A noted historian, fellow of Oriel College and regius professor of civil law at Oxford, Bryce was precisely the kind of

---

[12] Hansard, *Parl. Debs*, 3rd ser., ccxcv, col. 363 (6 Mar. 1885).

[13] Andrew Jones, *The Politics of Reform, 1884* (Cambridge, 1972), 212–13.

[14] See William A. Hayes, *The Background and Passage of the Third Reform Act* (New York, 1982), 272 n. 95.

[15] *The Times*, 18 Mar. 1885, p. 9.

member for whom some argued university representation needed to exist.[16] Bryce, however, had proved himself capable of standing and being returned for a regular constituency. From his perch of high academic qualification, he moved an amendment to eliminate university constituencies on the ground that the introduction of party politics into institutions of learning and their governing bodies distorted the impartiality with which academics should ideally approach educational questions and even, he claimed, intruded into decisions on appointments. Further, Bryce contended that the overwhelming majority of university electors would have the vote under another franchise. The motion drew further declarations of personal ambivalence from the government bench. Dilke said that Bryce had made an unanswerable case, but that the government could not accept the amendment because it would go against the bipartisan compact over the provisions of the bill. In the end, it was crushingly rejected by 260 votes to 79.[17]

In these exchanges, like those from the 1860s, the growing politicisation of university representation is clearly evident. There were no new universities to consider in connection with the bills of 1884–5 aside from Durham and the Royal University of Ireland. Although Durham as ever certainly pressed its case, both of these institutions were sufficiently marginal to be passed over in the larger struggle to equalise the franchise and electoral districts. Thus, the compromise preserved the status quo with respect to university representation, but proposed no offensive extensions. The 1884–5 episode also underscores the way that the fate of university representation was consistently dependent on the larger political forces in play.

Gladstone's subsequent governments of 1886 and 1892–4 were dominated by the effort to enact home rule for Ireland which left the Liberals weakened and divided, and strengthened the tories into the 20th century. These conditions afforded little scope for considering the future of university seats. In seeking to build a coalition to support the home rule cause in 1892, Gladstone had gestured his support for a wide range of radical positions. An erstwhile MP for Oxford, the Grand Old Man's own stance on university representation had been notably ambiguous in the past, but after the election he came out less equivocally (for him) against the institution. When, in a speech at West Calder, Gladstone noted that seven of the eight university seats had gone to the tories, a voice from the crowd expressed the hope that he would do away with university representation. 'I do not think I can pledge myself at my time of life', Gladstone said in response, 'but I cordially respond to his wish, and I may say that I hope somebody will propose it, and I will support it [cheers]'.[18]

But such tepid endorsements did not translate into policy for a ministry dedicated to seeing through home rule. Accordingly, in the last years of the 19th century and the first years of the 20th, efforts to do away with university representation occurred at the level of private members' bills. In 1892, for example, while the Liberals were in opposition, George John Shaw-Lefevre introduced a private members' bill to establish the electoral system on a one-man-one-vote basis and was backed by such notable Liberal leaders as William Harcourt, George Otto Trevelyan and Herbert Henry Asquith. On behalf of the

---

[16] See John T. Seaman, *A Citizen of the World: The Life of James Bryce* (2006), ch. 4.

[17] Hansard, *Parl. Debs*, 3rd ser., ccxcv, cols 323–38, 691–717 (6 Mar. 1885). On the second night of debate, Parnell argued that Dublin was the university of the minority, and therefore not entitled to separate representation. Hansard, *Parl. Debs*, 3rd ser., ccxcv, cols 641–9 (10 Mar. 1885).

[18] *The Times*, 8 July 1892, p. 8.

government, the chancellor of the exchequer, George Joachim Goschen, objected to the bill as undermining special franchises by an indirect process, and it was rejected on second reading.[19] Another notable private members' bill to eliminate university representation was introduced in 1894 by a group of 13 Liberal MPs, a number of whom had strong academic ties, such as Thomas Rayburn Buchanan, a fellow of All Souls College, and Sir Henry Roscoe, a noted chemist and prominent figure at Owens College (and later London's vice-chancellor).[20] Charles Dilke, now a backbencher following the divorce scandal that blighted his brilliant political prospects, worked to undo the compromise he had been obliged to uphold as a member of the government in 1884–5 by annually submitting bills to disenfranchise universities in the late 1890s and early 1900s. Government efforts to do away with university representation would have to wait until the Liberal revival in the years before the First World War.

3. *Plural Voting*

As the 'new liberalism' that emerged towards the end of the 19th century moved to embrace more progressive policies, the effort to do away with university representation came to be subsumed in a larger effort to regularise the franchise and eliminate plural voting of all kinds. Among provisions for plural votes, however, the university franchise was uniquely manifested in separate MPs, compared to other special franchises that simply permitted voting in multiple borough and county constituencies. University seats were therefore the most visible reminders of the more general inequities. Apart from the Liberals' reforming ideals, the effort to end plural voting in an era of sharpened party conflict and increasing constitutional tension was good politics. It was widely held that most of the people entitled to cast more than one ballot voted for the Conservatives, and tories continued to hold the majority of university seats.

The Plural Voting Bill was one of the Liberals' early pieces of reforming legislation after the landslide election of 1906. The Bill would have required voters to cast their ballots in only one constituency. Because it was assumed that people would be far more likely to vote in the territorial constituencies in which they lived, the measure would have the effect of reducing university electorates to such a degree that it amounted to disenfranchisement of the universities 'by instalments'.[21] Undercutting the position of the university seats, Asquith, now chancellor of the exchequer, noted that, with the exception of Oxford, Cambridge and Dublin, university representation was 'a very modern product indeed', created by Disraeli in 1867 and 1868.[22] For the opposition, Conservative leader Arthur Balfour (Salisbury's nephew and former protégé) objected to the Bill explicitly on the grounds that it would destroy university seats. During the committee stage, the Conservatives moved amendments to preserve the university vote in one form or

---

[19] Hansard, *Parl. Debs*, 4th ser., iv, cols 1181–244 (18 May 1892).

[20] *A Bill to Abolish the Representation in Parliament of the Universities of the United Kingdom*, Parliamentary Papers, 1894 (166), viii, 569.

[21] The phrase used by S.H. Butcher, MP for Cambridge University. Hansard, *Parl. Debs*, 4th ser., clviii, col. 206 (24 Oct. 1906).

[22] Hansard, *Parl. Debs*, 4th ser., clxiii, col. 209 (24 Oct. 1906).

another, but these were defeated by the Liberals.[23] The Bill was passed by a large margin but, like many such measures in these years, it was rejected in the Conservative-dominated Lords as part of Balfour's strategy of using the peers to derail measures passed by the Liberal majority in the Commons.

Six years later, after the famous 'peers versus the people' showdown resulted in the Lords' veto being replaced with the power merely to delay legislation for two years, the Liberals renewed their efforts at franchise reform. In June 1912, the government introduced a bill 'to amend the Law with respect to the Parliamentary and Local Government Franchise and the Registration of Parliamentary and Local Government Electors, and to provide for the abolition of University Constituencies'.[24] Introducing the bill, J.A. Pease, president of the Board of Education, said that the government had 'no room for fancy franchises' and that the university vote was 'inconsistent with the principle of one man one vote'. In particular, Pease pointed to the small size of the university constituencies (averaging 5,000 electors, or around one-third of the average electorate in other constituencies) as justifying their discontinuation.[25] The bill was vigorously opposed by Balfour and his successor as Conservative leader, Andrew Bonar Law, as well as by (as might be expected) the university representatives, most vocally Sir Robert Finlay (Edinburgh and St Andrews) and Sir Henry Craik (Glasgow and Aberdeen).[26]

With the Liberals dominant in the Commons and pursuing a progressive course, and with the Lords stripped of their veto, the continued existence of university representation was for the first time in serious jeopardy. In response to the Franchise and Registration Bill, the universities marshalled the resources at their disposal to preserve their special franchise. Meeting in January 1913, when the Bill was about to go into the committee stage, London's convocation approved a resolution to press for the retention of the university franchise in its present form and send a deputation to the prime minister. Proposing the resolution, the Rev. Dr A. Caldecott stated:

> Two very special qualities were required in Parliament at the present day – an extensive knowledge of the past and the capacity of dealing with general principles . . . They were not there merely to defend privileges, but they did believe that in the universities of this land they had an element capable of assisting materially in the good government of the country.[27]

With university representation under a severe threat, Caldecott's reiteration of the benefits-to-the-nation argument offered the case for its retention in the broadest terms possible.

While the Franchise Registration Bill prompted such familiar actions by individual universities, the perceived severity of the threat was also sufficient to spur a greater degree of collective action. London's senate passed a resolution requesting the vice-chancellor to invite the co-operation of other British universities to secure the retention

---

[23] Hansard, *Parl. Debs*, 4th ser., clxiii, cols 201–52 (24 Oct. 1906).

[24] Hansard, *Parl. Debs* (Commons), 5th ser., xxxix, col. 1326 (17 June 1912).

[25] Hansard, *Parl. Debs* (Commons), 5th ser., xxxix, col. 1340 (17 June 1912).

[26] Hansard, *Parl. Debs* (Commons), 5th ser., xl, cols 1733–44, 2104–13 (8 and 11 July 1912).

[27] *The Times*, 18 Jan. 1913, p. 10.

of university representation.[28] On receiving letters from the chairman of London's convocation and Oxford's vice-chancellor, the council of Cambridge's senate resolved: 'That the Council of the senate are willing to co-operate with the Hebdomadal Council of the University of Oxford and with Convocation of the University of London in pressing upon his Majesty's Government the desirability of retaining University representation in some form or other'.[29] As described in the previous chapter, this effort involved attempts to gain the support of the un-enfranchised universities. In the end, however, issues unrelated to the fate of the university franchise made this mobilisation unnecessary. The government was forced to withdraw the Bill when the Speaker (prompted by a deft question from Bonar Law) ruled that the planned incorporation of amendments granting women the vote would so alter the Bill's character that it would have to be withdrawn and reintroduced.

After the demise of the Franchise and Registration Bill, university representation was next seriously threatened by the Plural Voting Bill of 1913. Although it did not propose outright abolition of university seats, the Bill again required electors to choose between voting in their university or residential constituency. As one Conservative MP stated during debate on an amendment to exclude the universities from the operation of the bill: 'It may be said that this bill does not in so many words disenfranchise universities. That is quite true. I think that it would have been more honest if it had, but it does what is even more insidious – it strives to make the university representation ridiculous'.[30] Over a host of objections, the Bill was passed in the Commons, but then rejected by the Lords in July 1914. The suspension of regular political activity following the outbreak of the First World War in August meant that the Bill was never revived in order to override the Lords' delay. Here again, as in 1906 and 1912, university representation was spared almost accidentally by the interposition of larger political questions.

4. Nation and Region

In addition to the ways that the university franchise was bound up with questions of church and state, and of democratisation and partisanship, it was also connected to wider debates about the place of nations and regions within the United Kingdom. While some universities made their case for representation as a matter of institutional equity, others appealed to considerations of *national* equity. Advocates for granting representation to the Scottish universities, for instance, demanded that Scotland be made equal to England and Ireland in this respect.[31] Further, argued the Liberal MP Walter Buchanan, the franchise was important for building Scotland's universities as national (i.e., Scottish) institutions. Writing in 1857, he compared the long-term attachment of Oxford and Cambridge graduates to their colleges with how even the most distinguished Scottish university

---

[28] Univ. of London Archives, Convocation and Committees, UoL/CN 1/1/12: Proceedings of Convocation, 17 Jan. 1913. *The Times*, 24 Jan. 1913, p. 8.

[29] *The Times*, 22 Jan. 1913, p. 8.

[30] Hansard, *Parl. Debs*, 5th ser., lv, col. 810 (11 July 1913).

[31] The issue of university representation therefore adds a further dimension to debates over the role of nationality in Scottish higher education, neatly summarized in Stuart Wallace, 'National Identity and the Idea of the University in 19th-Century Scotland', *Higher Education Perspectives*, ii (2006), 126–7.

students tended to terminate all connection on leaving. He saw the privilege of the franchise as an important factor in sustaining graduates' connection to their universities: 'I cannot but regard this as most valuable both to the University and its members. It presents an *esprit de corps* of the best kind'. Buchanan thought that giving the franchise to the Scottish universities would help promote such sentiments and thereby strengthen those institutions. The parliamentary franchise would constitute a kind of 'life member-ship' in the university and the AM degree would become a badge of social distinction. All this, Buchanan contended, would encourage more Scottish gentlemen with ambi-tions to send their sons to Scottish universities rather than to Oxford and Cambridge.[32]

In the early 20th century, the University of Wales, like the Scottish universities decades before, argued for separate representation based on its distinctive 'national' role within the United Kingdom. As with the religious issues discussed above, the national fault lines were revealed most clearly in proposals to merge representation with other institutions. In 1912, Sir Herbert Isambard Owen, vice-chancellor at Bristol and formerly senior deputy chancellor at Wales, had rejected the notion that Wales might share a represen-tative with the younger English universities. 'It was necessary', he said, 'that the Welsh University should not be pooled with, say, Birmingham or Bristol, because the Welsh University was national and possessed distinct interests'.[33] This insistence on separate representation notwithstanding, the report of the 1917–18 Speaker's Conference pro-posed a new three-member constituency representing London, Durham, Manchester, Liverpool, Leeds, Sheffield, Birmingham, Bristol and Wales.[34]

In response to this proposal, Sir Herbert Roberts, Liberal MP for West Denbigh, in effect repeated Owen's argument by observing that the University of Wales differed from all other universities because it represented the whole principality.[35] John Herbert Lewis, Liberal MP for Flintshire and a leading advocate for granting the University of Wales a separate parliamentary seat (of which he was subsequently the first holder), argued that, if linked with seven other English universities, the University of Wales would never have a representative who could speak with authority on conditions affecting the separate Welsh education system generally. Because the main point was to find a way to give the principality an extra MP, Lewis also did not hesitate to play upon wartime emotions by pointing out to his compatriot Lloyd George that Wales had contributed a larger share of its population to the armed forces than other parts of the United Kingdom and therefore should not be 'meanly treated'.[36]

National distinctions within the United Kingdom were not the only source of resistance to the proposed new multiple-university constituency. In roundly rejecting the idea of such a merger, London's response displayed something of the clear regional separation between the metropolis and the provinces. Vice-Chancellor Gould circulated

[32] Walter Buchanan, *The Parliamentary Representation of the Scottish Universities: Being the Substance of a Paper Read at a Meeting of the Scottish Literary Institute Held at Glasgow on the 24th of April 1857* (Edinburgh, 1857), 7–8.

[33] *The Times*, 23 Nov. 1912, p. 4.

[34] *Conference on Electoral Reform: Letter from Mr Speaker to the Prime Minister*, 5, Parliamentary Papers, 1917–18 [Cmd 8463], xxv, 385.

[35] Hansard, *Parl. Debs* (Commons), 5th ser., xcix, col. 2416 (29 Nov. 1917).

[36] National Library of Wales, J. Herbert Lewis Papers, D79: J. Herbert Lewis to David Lloyd George, 21 Jan. 1918. Lewis reiterated the same points to other correspondents.

a report to members of the government, members of the Speaker's Conference and all MPs who were graduates of the university. The report rehearsed the history of London's struggle to be enfranchised, the original intention that London should hold status equal to that of Oxford and Cambridge, and the university's contributions to higher learning within Britain and around the world. The Speaker's Conference proposal was, the report stated, 'inconsistent with the position which successive governments have repeatedly acknowledged to be due to the University of London'. London's current incumbent, Philip Magnus, called a meeting of all MPs who were graduates of the university and it was agreed to send the report to every member and peer.[37]

For their part, the civic universities strongly objected to the idea of sharing a constituency with London, which had more graduates than the others combined and was viewed as a fundamentally different kind of institution on account of its external degrees – that is, its metropolitan character with respect to both nation and empire. They, too, undertook efforts to get the support of local MPs and produce statements of protest.[38] As Liverpool's vice-chancellor, Alfred Dale, sardonically summed up the situation, 'to set up a system of University representation which all the universities concerned will dislike will be a master-stroke'.[39] Magnus introduced a motion in the Commons, which was approved, to keep London out of the new English Universities constituency and for the university to retain its single seat.[40]

In Ireland, the national and (within Ireland) regional dynamics, like the religious ones, were especially involved. On being nominated as a Unionist candidate for Dublin in 1895, the historian W.E.H. Lecky advanced an interesting variation on the national case by arguing that university constituencies were *in themselves* somehow representative of the country (in this case, Ireland):

> Few things seem to me more irrational than to maintain that a constituency like the present, consisting of 4,000 highly-educated men, scattered over the whole surface of the country, belonging to many different professions, and coming in touch with quite an unusual number of the forms of Irish life, is not to be looked upon as representing the nation as truly as the voters in some decaying country town or some half-populated county district, where more than one in every five voters, according to a Parliamentary return of 1892, are unable to read the name on the ballot-paper.[41]

Here was another way of seeing the university constituency as a special case in national terms. The idea of virtual representation most famously articulated by another Irish MP,

[37] Univ. of London Archives, Convocation and Committees, UoL/CN 1/1/13: Proceedings of Convocation, 17 Mar. 1917, 11 Dec. 1917.

[38] Univ. of Manchester Senate Archive: Minutes of Senate, 24 May 1917; Univ. of Manchester Council Archive: Minutes of Council, 23 May 1917, 7 Nov. 1917, 24 Oct. 1917; Univ. of Manchester: Minutes of Court, 16 May 1917. Archive of the Univ. of Liverpool, Records of Convocation, S3681: 'Convocation Report of Standing Committee, November 8, 1917'; Archive of the Univ. of Liverpool, Vice-Chancellor, S2344, Letter Books of the Vice Chancellor, xxv: Dale to Henry Miers, 5 July 1917; Dale to Leslie Scott, MP, 5 and 19 July 1917; Dale to C.T. Needham, MP, 19 July 1917. Univ. of Sheffield Administrative Archives: Minutes of Council, 16 July 1917.

[39] Archive of the Univ. of Liverpool, Vice-Chancellor, S2344, Letter Books of the Vice Chancellor, xxv: Dale to Leslie Scott, MP, 19 July 1917.

[40] Hansard, *Parl. Debs* (Commons), 5th ser., xcviii, cols 2379–98 (8 Nov. 1917).

[41] *The Times*, 2 Dec. 1895, p. 7.

Edmund Burke, was that members represented the interests of the whole nation rather than those of the particular locality for which they were returned.[42] In Lecky's view, universities also provided a kind of virtual representation, but based on the fact that their electorates were both broadly knowledgeable and widely distributed.

National and sectarian questions associated with Irish university representation became particularly acute in the debates over the 1912 Home Rule Bill. Under the Bill, the proposed Irish house of commons would include two seats for Dublin, but none for the National University or Queen's University Belfast. These arrangements were to remain in effect for three years after the Act's passage, after which the Irish parliament would be entitled to alter constituencies and the distribution of its members. The non-denominational but largely catholic National University was naturally anxious to gain representative privileges like those of anglican Dublin. In April, its convocation resolved that 'in the event of a redistribution of seats in Irish constituencies becoming necessary, there should be equality of treatment in the matter of Parliamentary representation in the three Irish Universities'.[43]

The question of Dublin's parliamentary status under home rule generated some heat, if not much light. A *Times* correspondent speculated that, since the Irish parliament would have complete control over educational matters, maintaining Dublin's representation would set the stage for its amalgamation with the National University. According to another observer, however, 'The only explanation of the retention of those anomalies in the Irish bill is that the government hoped thereby to placate in some degree the Ulster minority, since the advantages of plural voting and university representation accrue chiefly to the protestant section of the Irish people'.[44] With the prospect of effective independence for Ireland, Dublin's historical legacy as a colonial implantation, bound in spirit to the mother country far more than to its surroundings, assumed a new prominence. Sir Joseph Larmor, the Lucasian professor of mathematics at Cambridge and Unionist MP for the university, spoke of Dublin as one of the universities of England, while one of Dublin's MPs, James Campbell, moved an amendment to exclude the university from Irish control entirely.[45] The other side of the colonial legacy came through in arguments that the mission must continue. For example, John Pentland Mahaffy, Trinity College's staunchly unionist professor of ancient history, thought it would be wrong, and possibly dangerous, to exclude the university from Irish control under home rule.[46]

In various ways, then, the questions raised by university representation lead directly to more fundamental issues about the composition of the United Kingdom itself. The institutions involved were taken to stand for — and took their stands on — the various and sometimes overlapping identities that made up the larger polity: Celtic versus

---

[42] See Burke's 'Speech at the Conclusion of the Poll', delivered on 3 Nov. 1774 following his election at Bristol, in *The Writings and Speeches of Edmund Burke, Vol. 3: Party, Parliament, and the American War, 1774–1780*, ed. W.M. Elofson and John A. Woods (Oxford, 1996), 63–70.

[43] *The Times*, 29 Apr. 1912, p. 6.

[44] Annie G. Porritt, 'The Irish Home Rule Bill', *Political Science Quarterly*, xxviii (1913), 312.

[45] Letter from Professor J.G. Swift MacNeill (Nationalist MP for Donegal South), *The Times*, 24 Oct. 1912, p. 12. Larmor, who took his undergraduate degree at Queen's Belfast, also believed that institution should be removed from Irish jurisdiction.

[46] *The Times*, 23 Oct. 1912, p. 8.

Anglo-Saxon; periphery versus centre; provincial versus cosmopolitan; and even metropolitan versus colonial. In the university franchise, these identities mapped on to ideas about representation far transcending jealousy of institutional privilege.

5. *University Representation and Women's Suffrage*

The question of votes for women was another way in which the history of university representation was tied to larger constitutional considerations. Universities' admission of women to degrees – first at London (1878), then at the Scottish universities (1892) and Wales (1893) and then by the civic universities as they acquired charters beginning in 1900 – meant that the extension of university representation also intersected with the issue of women's suffrage.[47] By 1910–11, there were no fewer than 4,600 women students in British universities, and the proportion who were attending classes with the intention of taking degrees had increased markedly.[48] The possibility of obtaining the university vote, and thereby plural voting, constitutes an additional though little noted aspect of the broader gender dynamics of franchise reform.

The first electoral registers compiled under the 1918 Representation of the People Act included nearly 8.5 million women, of whom 7,910 were also entitled to vote for universities (compared to 60,181 male university electors).[49] The provisions of the Act even explicitly allowed women to enter the electoral rolls of universities that still would not grant them degrees. Women were fully admitted to degrees at Oxford in 1920, and at Cambridge in 1948. Beginning in the late 19th century, however, both universities had permitted women to sit for most undergraduate degree examinations. Starting in 1918, women who obtained a passing mark and had kept the required terms of residence qualified for the university vote.

University representation and women's suffrage had already been linked at the end of the 19th century. Dilke's annual bills of the 1890s and 1900s had called for giving the vote to women as well as taking it away from the universities, although his linking of these two causes was inconsistent from a party political standpoint. While Liberals criticized university constituencies for returning a preponderance of Conservative MPs, a source of resistance to women's suffrage was the persistent belief that the Conservatives would be the main electoral beneficiaries.[50] University representation also figured in another backbench suffrage effort. The Women's Enfranchisement Bills of 1907 and 1908 were private members' bills which sought to extend all existing franchises – owners, occupiers, lodgers and the service and university votes – to women who held the same

---

[47] The timing of women's admission to classes and degrees is far more complex than this simplified chronology indicates. See Carol Dyhouse, *No Distinction of Sex? Women in British Universities, 1870–1939* (1995), 11–13.

[48] Dyhouse, *No Distinction of Sex?*, 24 and 248, table.

[49] *Return Showing, for Each Parliamentary Constituency in the United Kingdom, the Numbers of Parliamentary and Local Government Electors on the First Register Compiled under the Representation of the People Act, 1918*, Parliamentary Papers, 1918 (138), xix, 925.

[50] Brian Harrison, *Separate Spheres: Opposition to Women's Suffrage in Britain* (1978), 41. On the strength of Conservative efforts to include women, see Martin Pugh, 'Popular Conservatism in Britain: Continuity and Change, 1880–1987', *Journal of British Studies*, xxvii (1988), 264–8.

electoral qualifications as enfranchised men.[51] These proposals met the same fate as Dilke's annual bills and all other attempts to get votes for women through legislation. It is therefore a political irony that, as noted above, the issue of women's suffrage effectively saved university representation from being eliminated in 1913 when proposed amendments to give women the vote caused the government to withdraw its Franchise and Registration Bill.

Outside parliament, questions of women's suffrage and university representation were also linked in a 1907 suit brought by a group of women graduates from Scottish universities. Building upon the recent success in gaining full admission for women, the plaintiffs claimed that their status as graduates duly entitled them to the parliamentary franchise because the language of the relevant acts establishing the Scottish university constituencies (1868) and permitting election by voting papers (1881) did not specifically limit the electorate to men. Ultimately, the court of session ruled that women were not entitled to vote under the university franchise because the political disabilities of women took precedence over any ambiguous use of terms like 'persons' in the legislation.[52]

With the suffrage issue so prominent by the beginning of the 20th century, it made sense that universities would reflect on the position of their women graduates. In 1913, when resolving that the extension of parliamentary representation to all universities was desirable, Manchester's convocation also affirmed 'its desire that the University principle of equal privilege for all its graduates should be maintained by the inclusion of women in the exercise of this proposed privilege'.[53] Although the record gives no indication of why Manchester's council and court took no action on convocation's resolution, perhaps the vexed question of giving women the vote played some role in the decision.[54]

London and the Scottish universities had been enfranchised before they admitted women to degrees, and during a period in which sporadic movement towards manhood suffrage tended to eclipse women's aspirations for the vote. The civic universities, on the other hand, had women graduates before they were enfranchised and were granted their charters around the time that the suffrage movement was intensifying. Thus, the position of women graduates had to be considered when contemplating any extension of the franchise to new institutions. As Humberstone wrote in 1913, the test for the suffrage in university constituencies 'is purely intellectual, and it is difficult to see on what grounds or reason of expediency a sex disqualification should be introduced'. Women who had undertaken advanced training that gave them special knowledge on social and political issues, he thought, should not be denied 'the modest influence on the destinies of their country which a University vote would confer'.[55] Miss I. Thompson, warden of University Hall for Women at Leeds, went further, noting that the university franchise would have a special value to women beyond that to be gained from extension of the general franchise because many women in 'residential posts' (presumably professional women

[51] Teresa Billington-Greig, 'The Sex-Disability and Adult Suffrage', *Fortnightly Review*, lxxxiv (1908), 258–71.

[52] Elizabeth C. Wolstenholme Elmy, 'Justice between the Sexes', *Westminster Review*, clxix (1908), 29–40.

[53] Univ. of Manchester Court Archive: Minutes of Court, 28 May 1913.

[54] Univ. of Manchester Council Archive: Minutes of Council, 26 Nov. 1913; Univ. of Manchester Court Archive: Minutes of Court, 20 May 1914.

[55] T. Lloyd Humberstone, 'University Representation in Parliament', *The Arena*, iii (1913), 246.

graduates on the full-time staffs of educational, medical, charitable and other kinds of live-in institutions) would have no other voter qualification. Cambridge's vice-chancellor, S.A. Donaldson, for his part, did not see the desirability of giving women graduates the vote, but observed that his university, with no women graduates, would be unaffected. Stronger, albeit dogmatic, objections were stated by the historian Walter W. Seton, secretary of University College London, who was 'on principle opposed to granting of the franchise to women under any terms or conditions whatsoever, whether they are graduates or householders or possess any other so-called qualification'.[56]

Wartime experience muted such opposition to votes for women, and the principle was conceded in the 1916–17 Speaker's Conference.[57] For universities, the prospect of including women graduates in the electorate was an advantageous one. The newer universities would enlarge the bases of their still comparatively small constituencies. London's vice-chancellor, Sir Alfred Pearce Gould, went further. Bolstering his view that his university should be entitled to a second MP based on the number of graduates, he observed that the balance would be even more in London's favour if women graduates were enfranchised.[58] A neglected dimension of the 1918 Representation of the People Act, therefore, is that in addition to giving women aged 30 and above the vote, it also gave women graduates (with the same age qualification) the second, university vote that had been preserved by the Speaker's Conference and extended through the creation of new university constituencies. Similarly, when women gained the vote on the same terms as men a decade later, the number of women holding plural votes also increased. In this way, university representation magnified the gains made by women in both higher education and political life.

6. *The Interwar Years*

After the First World War, the Labour Party, which assumed the fragmented Liberals' place as Britain's second major party, was even more ideologically committed to democratisation and the abolition of elitist privileges in politics. Accordingly, the Labour government elected in 1929 mounted a major effort to abolish university representation. Without an absolute majority in the House, Labour was obliged to respond to pressure from the Liberals, on whose support the government depended, for a measure of electoral reform. In its insecure position and facing the pressing need to deal with the nation's deepening economic crisis, Labour's effort to undo long-standing constitutional arrangements that had become dear to the Conservatives (while not going forward with introducing proportional representation favoured by the Liberals) seems all the more remarkable.

[56] All quotations from 'Some Opinions on Questions of University Representation', *The Arena*, iii (1913), 246–7.

[57] Among other things, women's fees had been a much-needed source of universities' revenue during the war. Janet Howarth, 'Women', in *The History of the University of Oxford, Vol. 8: The Twentieth Century*, ed. Brian Harrison (Oxford, 1994), 349.

[58] Univ. of London Archives, Convocation and Committees, UoL/CN 1/1/13: 'Statement . . . on the Speaker's Letter to the Prime Minister', Proceedings of Convocation, 17 Mar. 1917.

In response to this challenge, the universities and their friends once again attempted to mobilise support for retaining their parliamentary representation.[59] At the end of 1930, the University of London Graduates' Association – of which the university's MP, Sir Ernest Graham-Little, was president – sent a circular to 21,000 graduates asking them to urge their local MPs to oppose the Electoral Reform Bill because of its threat to the university franchise.[60] Similarly, the burgesses for Oxford and Cambridge also issued a circular in early 1931.[61] One exasperated Labour MP, having received 'a considerable number of letters and post-cards from university graduates', alleged that he could not respond to most of these communications because the handwriting was so poor.[62]

Perhaps no one did more to rally opposition to the proposed abolition of the university franchise than Eleanor Rathbone, who had been returned as an Independent for the Combined English Universities in 1929. Daughter of a long-serving Liberal MP, Rathbone was one of only 14 women returned to the Commons that year and the only woman ever to occupy a university seat. The new Combined English Universities constituency was amenable to her combination of intellectual strength and independent politics stemming from long involvement with feminist and social welfare causes.[63] University seats became another one of her causes and in late 1930 and early 1931 she turned her formidable political and organisational skills to preserving them. She was correspondingly unsparing to those who should have been allies but lacked a similar resolve, like Manchester's vice-chancellor, Walter Moberley:

> As to your view that concerted action on the part of the Universities is unsuitable, because 'we are poor witnesses to the special value of our own opinions', may I just register my emphatic dissent? . . . If there is one thing that has been brought more strongly home to me in Parliament than any other, during my short experience, it is that all this kind of interest and class of question that affects universities is far less effectively organized and defended than the corresponding interests among the industrial workers. This is probably because the Universities are 'too proud to fight', like President Wilson.[64]

In contrast to such academic diffidence, Rathbone wrote and circulated a 'case' for university representation. In it, she countered charges against the franchise's undemocratic character and Conservative dominance. She also asserted the importance of university votes for counterbalancing the possibility of a 'proletarian' majority, and also for giving votes to Britons living abroad. At the beginning of January 1931, Rathbone organised a conference of university MPs, vice-chancellors, representatives of learned societies and other distinguished individuals, which resolved to organise letters of protest from university governing bodies, graduate and professional organisations and graduates

---

[59] See D.E. Butler, *The Electoral System in Britain, 1918–1951* (Oxford, 1953), 74.

[60] *The Times*, 11 Dec. 1930, p. 10.

[61] *The Times*, 27 Jan. 1931, p. 10.

[62] *The Times*, 20 Feb. 1931, p. 15.

[63] Rathbone's colleagues on the executive of the National Union of Women's Suffrage Societies had been unsuccessful in persuading Rathbone to seek election in 1918, when women were for the first time permitted to stand for parliament. Susan Pedersen, *Eleanor Rathbone and the Politics of Conscience* (New Haven, CT, 2004), 29–30, 176–7, 219–21.

[64] Univ. of Manchester Vice-Chancellor's Archive, VCA/7/138 (1): Rathbone to Moberley, 17 Jan. 1931.

residing overseas that would be sent to the prime minister, the home secretary, local MPs and the press.[65] To this end, a restatement of Rathbone's case was printed up as a form letter to which signatures could be appended.[66]

Her mobilising efforts bore fruit. As she later informed the House, 'at every convocation meeting in all the younger universities a resolution against the abolition of the university franchise has been carried by overwhelming majorities'.[67] At Birmingham, for example, members of the university's court, senate and council, along with other academic, municipal and religious worthies organised a letter of protest.[68] Several hundred notable academics and graduates signed an open letter protesting against the proposed abolition.[69] In an echo of the 19th-century discussion of university representation in relation to the representation of learning more generally, support was also forthcoming from professional bodies such as the Royal College of Physicians, which passed a resolution expressing its strong disapproval of the proposal to abolish university representation.[70]

In March 1931, the abolition clause was narrowly defeated by 246 votes to 242, primarily on account of a divided Liberal vote (19 against university representation, 16 in favour and 23 unpaired absences).[71] The Liberals' failure to provide their promised support to the government was yet one more indication of their persistent fractures and a cause of further internecine strife while also damaging the party's delicate relations with Labour.[72] With the original proposal to abolish university representation dropped, the government introduced a new provision to abolish plural voting. Under this plan, like the Liberal bills of 1906 and 1913, university constituencies would not be eliminated outright, but graduates would be required to choose between their residential and university vote. Much as they had done before, opposition critics complained that the university vote would be reduced to insignificance as a shadow without substance.[73] With the government's resignation in August, however, the bill became a dead letter.

Like Lloyd George presiding over the enlargement of university representation in 1918 after having roundly denounced it only a few years earlier, the second Labour

---

[65] Univ. of Manchester Vice-Chancellor's Archive, VCA/7/138 (1): printed copy of 'The Case for University Representation' (Dec. 1930), and letters from Rathbone to Manchester vice-chancellor, Walter Moberley, Dec. 1930 and Jan. 1931. Pedersen, *Eleanor Rathbone*, 225.

[66] Archive of the Univ. of Liverpool, Vice-Chancellor, P712/6: 'University Representation', 1930 (printed circular). This file also contains the annotated typescript of 'The Case for University Representation'.

[67] Hansard, *Parl. Debs* (Commons), 5th ser., ccxlix, col. 1803 (16 Mar. 1931). And Rathbone's work to strengthen the institution of university representation through collective action hardly stopped here. Shortly after the outbreak of war in 1939, for example, she played a key role in the formation of a university members' committee with the aim of holding regular meetings and establishing closer relations with the vice-chancellor's committee to keep abreast of universities' dealings with various government departments. Univ. of Manchester Vice-Chancellor's Archive, VCA/7/138 (2): Rathbone to J.S.B. Stopford, 26 Oct. 1939.

[68] *The Times*, 2 Feb. 1931, p. 8.

[69] *The Times*, 2 Feb. 1931, p. 8; 17 Feb. 1931, p. 8. Following publication of this letter in *The Times*, Rathbone wrote to append the names of four additional supporters now dwelling in the Elysian Fields – John Stuart Mill, Lord John Russell, Walter Bagehot and W.E.H. Lecky – and provided pertinent quotations from each. *The Times*, 16 Mar. 1931, p. 13.

[70] *The Times*, 30 Jan. 1931, p. 8.

[71] Hansard, *Parl. Debs* (Commons), 5th ser., ccxlix, cols 700–10, 1695–1806 (16 Mar. 1931).

[72] Butler, *Electoral System*, 75–6.

[73] Hansard, *Parl. Debs* (Commons), 5th ser., cclii, e.g., cols 2006 [John Buchan], 2023–4 [Gerald Hurst] (21 May 1931).

government's attempt to end university representation had its own ironic aftermath. In 1931, William Jowitt, attorney-general under Labour and slated to continue in that role in the new National Government, stood for the Combined English Universities. This caused Harold Nicolson, rival candidate from the New Party, to remind electors that, only ten months before, Jowitt had been 'anxious to suppress the constituency for which he is now standing'.[74] More famously, a few months after his rejection at Seaham in the general election of 1935, Ramsay MacDonald – expelled from Labour for agreeing to lead the National Government – re-entered parliament as a member for the Scottish Universities.[75] In response, Labour MP Samuel Viant introduced a motion to abolish the university franchise. After a debate added nothing new to these matters, university representation was spared by an even larger majority than in 1931 when Viant's motion was defeated by 227 votes to 130.[76]

7. *Conclusion*

As David Butler noted a few years after the final, ultimately successful, assault on university representation in 1948, the 1946 replacement of the late Independent, Rathbone, who had been 'so often cited as the strongest argument for university representation, by Mr. H.G. Strauss, one of the most avowedly partisan of Conservatives, can hardly have encouraged enthusiasm for the university franchise'.[77] But just as university representation had been extended by something like benign neglect, and then accidentally preserved by larger historical developments, its end was not necessarily based on principled objections to an inequitable anachronism. In the end, abolition of university constituencies as a category of plural voting may have had less to do with one-man-one-vote than with the hard political calculus of offsetting the effect of the new electoral map which eliminated a number of traditional Labour constituencies, especially in London.[78]

In genteel protest against the abolition, Oxford's vice-chancellor, W.T.S. Stallybrass, wrote to *The Times* on behalf of the Hebdomadal Council 'to express its concern and regret at the decision which the Government has taken, and hope that even now the Government may be willing to reconsider its proposals on this point'.[79] His Cambridge

---

[74] Univ. of Bristol Library, Special Collections, Papers of the National Liberal Club, DM.668: Election Addresses 1931, p. 39.

[75] MacDonald had also lent his support to earlier efforts that involved abolishing the university franchise, such as Arthur Henderson's Representation of the People Bill of March 1912. *Bill to Extend the Parliamentary Franchise to Men and Women and to Amend the Registration and Electoral System (Electors and Representation of the People: Absent and Infirm Voters)*, Parliamentary Papers, 1912–13 (109), v, 85.

[76] Butler, *Electoral System*, 86.

[77] Butler, *Electoral System*, 120.

[78] *The Times*, 16 Feb. 1948, p. 5. In 1945, 62 contests in the London area returned 48 Labour MPs. In 1950, 31 Labour MPs were elected in 43 contests. Wartime and post-war demographic trends also favoured the Conservatives in the capital. Thomas P. Jenkin, 'The British General Election of 1950', *The Western Political Quarterly*, iii (1950), 184.

[79] *The Times*, 6 Feb. 1948, p. 5. In a subsequent letter, A.J.P. Taylor and G.D.N. Worswick regretted Stallybrass' defence of university constituencies and the Hebdomadal Council's assumption of authority to speak for university opinion on political matters. Many resident graduates, and they themselves, would prefer abolition to the retention of the current system. *The Times*, 10 Feb. 1948, p. 5.

counterpart, C.E. Raven, also 'made representations to the Government' for the continuance of the university franchise.[80] This time, however, armed with a huge majority and backed by a heightened popular democratic sentiment, the position of the government was impregnable.

The ways in which university representation was debated in the 19th and 20th centuries show clearly that the arguments on either side extended much further than the merits of this institutional distinction and the advantages afforded by giving graduates a plural vote. At the same time, it is not clear that representation provided much in the way of direct benefits to the universities' affairs.[81] The presence of MPs for Oxford and Cambridge in parliament did not, for example, significantly alter the government's determination to reform the two universities in the 1850s and 1870s, while the Inns of Court, with no seats, successfully resisted government intervention. It is possible that, in the face of waning influence on the state, the universities' interests – especially those of Oxford and Cambridge – were looked after in a wholly different way by the increasing number of their graduates occupying decision-making positions throughout the state's expanding bureaucracy and serving as members or secretaries of the increasingly frequent official boards and commissions concerned with matters directly or indirectly affecting higher education.[82] If so, this would help explain why the debates over university representation centred on whether its contribution to national affairs justified its continued existence, rather than accusations of universities using their MPs for narrowly self-interested ends.

In a period of constitutional development, these arguments and parliamentary considerations were rooted in central constitutional issues about religion, nation, gender and much else. Given all the energy expended over the years by advocates for extending and preserving university representation on the one hand, and those dedicated to extinguishing that quasi-invented tradition on the other, it is ironic that the termination of the university seats occurred as it did, and that it went out with a whimper rather than a bang.

---

[80] *The Times*, 9 Feb. 1948, p. 5.

[81] See, e.g., W.R. Ward, *Victorian Oxford* (1965).

[82] See, e.g., the statistics on higher civil servants' university education in W.D. Rubinstein, 'Education and the Social Origins of British Élites, 1880–1970', *Past & Present*, no. 112 (1986), 190.

Chapter 4. University Representatives

The arguments for and against university representation described so far mainly revolved around institutional and political concerns, but a substantial portion of this persistent debate also focused on the representatives themselves, both their performance in parliament and the extent to which it measured up to the ideals ascribed to university representation. The ways, both favourable and unfavourable, in which university members were regarded provide further evidence of the ways in which university representation was strongly connected with larger political issues. At the same time, especially because they were embedded within larger political developments and concerns, contemporary claims (and allegations) cannot be taken at face value but must be tested against detailed analysis of the background, characteristics and accomplishments of the MPs. In addition, it is important to see the parliamentary representation of universities and its personnel more broadly, beyond the formal institution of members in the Commons, by also looking at the extent to which the interests of higher education were present in the house of lords.

1. *Seats of Learning?*

Advocates for university representation insisted that learned electors would naturally choose to be represented by people of superior quality and integrity who otherwise might not become involved in public life. As *The Times*' parliamentary correspondent wrote in 1948: 'One of the strongest arguments for the university constituencies has been that, in addition to bringing the interests of education to the forefront in national affairs, they have enabled many distinguished men who have not been mainly politicians to make their contribution to the work of the Legislature'.[1] Such justifications differed little from early 19th-century arguments upholding close boroughs as a means for bringing 'the aristocracy of talent' into the house of commons:

> In this manner the greater part of our distinguished statesmen have entered Parliament; and some of them perhaps, would never have found admittance by any other way. The use of such members to the house itself, and to the country, is incalculable. Their knowledge and talents give a weight to the deliberations, and inspire a respect for Parliamentary discussion, which in these times it is difficult for any assembly to obtain.[2]

---

[1] *The Times*, 16 Feb. 1848, p. 5.

[2] Lord John Russell, *An Essay on the History of the English Government and Constitution from the Reign of Henry VII to the Present Time*, (2nd edn, 1823), 344–5. Ideas about the positive qualities of university representatives in the modern period exhibit clear continuities with those which obtained under the unreformed electoral system; cf. Frank O'Gorman, *Voters, Patrons, and Parties: The Unreformed Electoral System of Hanoverian England, 1734–1832* (Oxford, 1989), 122–5.

Ironically, this specimen from the early 1820s was written by none other than Lord John Russell, later one of the authors of the reform bill that eliminated the most egregious of these constituencies. Yet, there are also clear continuities with Russell's later championing of mechanisms to give learning in various forms greater parliamentary representation.

In the years leading up to the Second Reform Act, advocates for granting representation to the Scottish universities and those who made the case for London argued that they would be high-minded constituencies that would return equally high-minded MPs. In 1857, for example, the Scottish politician Walter Buchanan claimed that 'those who have been accustomed to study and reflection, and who can bring to their senatorial labours that familiarity with principles which is most usefully found among men trained to intellectual exercises' were less likely to succeed in regular constituencies, where election depended on factors such as flattery, familiarity with current topics or personal celebrity. He could conceive of 'no better means for securing the return of educated men to the House of Commons than by enfranchising the Scottish Universities'.[3] Similarly, when moving in 1866 that London's convocation send a petition to parliament in favour of granting representation to the university, the barrister (and London graduate) George Jessel presented a similarly idealised view:

> there could not be a better constituency than a number of learned and accomplished men, for it was impossible that such a body of men would consent to be represented by a man who was inferior to the bulk of them in knowledge and education. Such a constituency, moreover, would be above all bribery and corruption, and beyond all suspicion of it.[4]

This argument for university representation runs throughout much of its history. In this sense, the university seats provided an institutionalised basis for the perpetuation of Coleridge's notion of the 'clerisy'. Speaking to his Edinburgh and St Andrews constituents in 1884, Lyon Playfair said that the anomaly of giving graduates 'a second vote for a University could only be justified on the ground that it was necessary to promote those higher interests of learning upon which the culture and even the material interests of a nation so much depended'.[5] In the 20th century, the Combined English Universities agreed among themselves to return only members of suitable intellectual accomplishment.

Critics of university representation liked to point out that in practice the universities had not for the most part selected notably superior representatives, though this charge was typically made at a high level of generality. In 1831, for example, the Radical Henry Warburton claimed (without offering specifics) that, far from representing literature, science or art, university MPs had mainly 'distinguished themselves for violence in politics, or for extreme political opinion'.[6] Thirty years later,

---

[3] Walter Buchanan, *The Parliamentary Representation of the Scottish Universities: Being the Substance of a Paper Read at a Meeting of the Scottish Literary Institute Held at Glascow on the 24th of April 1857* (Edinburgh, 1857), 5.

[4] *The Times*, 22 Mar. 1866, p. 12.

[5] *The Times*, 21 Nov. 1884, p. 10.

[6] *The Times*, 24 Sept. 1831, p. 4; stated much more mildly in Hansard, *Parl. Debs*, 3rd ser., vii, col. 526 (23 Sept. 1831).

Edinburgh's town council voted 19 to 7 to petition parliament *not* to grant a member to the Scottish universities in connection with the reforms then being discussed. In response to a motion to petition parliament in favour of enfranchisement, Duncan McLaren (later to become one of Scotland's most influential MPs) argued that the universities did not in general return useful representatives: 'The University men were always the moles that could never see light'. He also raised the objection, to be repeated by others later, that even when universities did select talented representatives, they ended up rejecting them precisely for demonstrations of their statesmanship. Oxford, he noted, had proved an inhospitable seat for Peel and Gladstone once their policies ran counter to the electors' narrow and intolerant views. But McLaren's opposition flew in the face of the broader desire to see the Scottish universities take their place in parliament alongside the other older foundations of England and Ireland. In carrying this amendment, the Edinburgh town council became, as *The Times* observed, 'almost the only public body north of the Tweed that has actively opposed the movement for Scotch University representation'.[7]

During the debates leading up to the Second Reform Act, John Bright also evinced a dim view of university representatives:

> The representation of the ancient Universities of Oxford and Cambridge was created in times about the worst in our history. The Members they have sent to this House, learned as some of them have been, and amiable as many of them have been, have not been representatives such as it would be wise – I speak of their political views – for the House of Commons to follow.[8]

Such criticisms continued into the 20th century, while also acquiring a somewhat greater degree of personal specificity. In November 1911, when the government was announcing its intentions to introduce a franchise reform bill that would abolish university constituencies, Lloyd George mocked the idea that 'by this means you get a specimen of the cultured, impartial, calm, judicial, fair-minded sort of person – a kind of superman: somebody who is above the rancour and the excitement of party'. The reality, he said, was very different: 'No constituency in the land turns out narrower, more bigoted, or more fierce partisans'. His examples were Oxford's Lord Hugh Cecil, 'a sort of male suffragist who howls down the Prime Minister . . . in a fit of hysteria because he does not approve of his policy', and Dublin's Edward Carson, 'a man who advocates rebellion unless he gets his way'.[9]

The election of a particular individual could draw praise even from the critics. When the historian W.E.H. Lecky was returned for Dublin in 1895 (a rare exception to the university's general pattern of electing lawyers, described below), *The Speaker*, a radical organ, parroted one of the arguments that supporters of university representation had long been propounding:

> No choice they could make would convert wicked Radicals like us to a belief in University Representation, but we confess that if all the Universities were represented

---

[7] *The Times*, 22 Mar. 1861, p. 9.

[8] Hansard, *Parl. Debs*, 3rd ser., clxxxviii, col. 25 (18 June 1867).

[9] In a speech at Bath, 24 Nov. 1911; *The Times*, 25 Nov. 1911, p. 12.

by men like Mr Lecky – men too much hampered by the pursuit of learning to get to the House of Commons by the road where the noisy advocate or the much respected local man excels – we should be inclined to put off the disenfranchisement of the Universities until we had carried a great many measures that are still in the clouds.[10]

But this was very much an exception to the general rule.

Complaints about the character and contributions of university MPs came to be strongly connected with members' party affiliation. Indeed, supporters of university representation could assert that narrow partisan concerns constituted the real objection underlying 'the argument *ad hominem*, which might be used with equal effect to condemn nearly every institution in the country'.[11] In response to James Bryce's attack on university representation during the 1885 redistribution debates, *The Times* noted that the 'readiness to extinguish the [university] seats, so far as it exists, springs rather from impatience with the manner in which they have sometimes been filled than from any sense of anomaly, or from any such desire as Mr Bryce expressed to screen the Universities from the blighting interests of party politics'. In the future, it was hoped, university seats would be 'less associated with the territorial aristocracy and the range of political ideas which have their home in the Carlton Club [and] will be apt to insist that their representatives shall be men of political eminence and personal distinction, and not merely displaced or undistinguished politicians for whom the party leaders are anxious to find a safe and inexpensive seat'.[12]

There is some evidence that this message and its corollary threat were not wholly lost on the ancient universities, notwithstanding their reputations as bastions of toryism. In 1891, the master of Corpus Christi (a rigid Conservative) wrote to the eminent classicist Richard Claverhouse Jebb about the possibility of his standing for the Cambridge seat that had previously been occupied by the late Henry Raikes:

> Now I have long felt that it may be very desirable to have as representatives of the University men whose claims are not political but academical – not men who already represent (or might represent) constituencies of another kind, who are unacquainted with the life of the University, and whose election by us might be read as an argument for disenfranchising the Universities.[13]

On the prospect of balancing his duties as regius professor of Greek with those of an MP, Jebb quipped: 'Happy thought: "When is a Chair not a Chair?" Answer: "When it is incompatible with a Seat" '.[14]

---

[10] *The Speaker*, 2 Nov. 1895, p. 461.

[11] T. Lloyd Humberstone, 'University Representation in Parliament', *The Arena*, iii (1913), 243.

[12] *The Times*, 11 Mar. 1885, p. 9.

[13] Edward Henry Perowne to R.C. Jebb, 5 Sept. 1891. Jebb's correspondence is mostly in private hands but is currently being edited for publication by Dr C.A. Stray, Swansea University. I am grateful to Dr Stray for bringing this letter, and the following one, to my attention.

[14] R.C. Jebb to Arthur Jebb, 12 Oct. 1891.

2. The Characteristics of University MPs

Arguments for or against university representation based on the qualities of the MPs were, as one would expect, understandably focused at the extremes: great statesmen versus party hacks; valued contributors versus somnolent backbenchers. To get beyond the limitations of such allegedly exemplary characterisations, it is necessary to study the group as a whole. Between 1832 and 1950, 101 people were returned for university seats.[15] A number of these MPs had varied careers and it is not easy to place each one into a single occupational group. For the purposes of general analysis, however, they may be categorised as shown in Table 4.1.

That the largest group consists of lawyers of one kind or another may at first glance seem to bear out in some measure Coke's original advice to Oxford and Cambridge when the first university seats were established. In fact, however, the reasons for the size of the legal contingent in the 1832–1950 period are highly localised. More than half of those categorised here as lawyers represented Dublin, and 19 of the 21 MPs who sat for Dublin in these years may be said to have had primarily legal careers. The character of Dublin MPs was well known. As the Irish nationalist MP J.G. Swift MacNeill wrote in 1896, of all the members returned for Dublin since 1801, 'all save one have been placemen and Irish barristers, and fifteen have been Law Officers of the Crown. The Bar of Ireland . . . has long considered the representation of Trinity College to be a perquisite of their profession'.[16] Yet, even leaving aside the Dublin factor, legal careers were prominent among university representatives, and it should also be borne in mind that, in common with the backgrounds of MPs generally, a number of those best classified under other occupations had training in the law but did not pursue legal careers.[17]

After the lawyers, the next largest category consists of people who pursued essentially professional political careers. These include one prime minister to be (Gladstone) and one ex-premier (MacDonald), three who served as chancellor of the exchequer (Goulburn,

Table 4.1: *University MPs by Career Category, 1832–1950*

Lawyers	35
Politicians	23
Scholars & Scientists	16
Medical Professionals	11
Other	16
Total	101

[15] The following analyses draw in the main from the biographical index of university members compiled by Ian Grimble and included in T. Lloyd Humberstone, *University Representation* (1951), 73–123. I have augmented this information where necessary (for example, by including Eoin MacNeil, the Sinn Fein candidate for the National University of Ireland, who was elected in 1918 but never took his seat), and regularised the career categories noted.

[16] Hibernicus [J.G. Swift MacNeill], 'Hibernia Irredenta: I – Mr Lecky and Irish Affairs', *Fortnightly Review*, lix (1896), 18.

[17] On lawyer-MPs, see Joseph S. Meisel, *Public Speech and the Culture of Public Life in the Age of Gladstone* (New York, 2001), 207–19.

Table 4.2: *Tenure of University MPs, 1832–1950*

≤4 years	33
5–9 years	22
10–14 years	14
15–19 years	19
20–29 years	11
≥30 years	2
Total	101

Gladstone again and Lowe) and two who served as home secretary (Gathorne-Hardy and Walpole). Numerous others in this set held a variety of minor offices. In the third largest group, many of the scholars and scientists held or came to occupy distinguished chairs, including a regius professor of Greek at Cambridge, a regius professor of zoology at Glasgow, two Lucasian professors and a Slade professor of art. Some of those classified here as lawyers also held university chairs. The last large grouping is made up of physicians and surgeons, including an obstetrician, a laryngologist and an oculist; several of these also held professorships. Other occupations of university MPs include four educationists, four writers, three social reformers, three civil servants, one banker and one businessman.

The principle that sitting members should not be opposed had been established from the early days of university representation, and the contesting of university seats before 1918 was rare in comparison to the increasing frequency of contested elections over the course of the 19th century.[18] Length of service averaged 10.5 years for the whole group: 11.8 years for those first returned before 1918 and 8.4 years for those returned beginning in that year when the introduction of proportional representation in multi-member university constituencies encouraged more electoral challenges. Table 4.2 shows the distribution of MPs' tenure in university seats.

On average, MPs were 53.5 years old on first being returned for their university seats. The youngest new university MP was David Plunkett, returned for Dublin at the age of 32. The oldest was Alfred Hopkinson, who began sitting for the Combined English Universities at the age of 75. Around one-quarter (27) of university MPs died while occupying their seat or within a year of vacating it.

With respect to career groupings, the professional politicians occupied their seats for the longest amount of time on average (13.0 years). The average tenures for university MPs in the scholars and scientists category and those who were lawyers were close (9.7 and 9.2 years, respectively), and that for medical professionals somewhat less (8.4 years).[19] Institutionally, in part because both of the university members who sat for more than 30 years represented Oxford – Sir Robert Mowbray (1866–99), a former barrister, and the backbench politician John Gilbert Talbot (1878–1910) – that constituency had the

---

[18] See W.R. Ward, *Victorian Oxford* (1965), 21. Ward describes in detail the increasing difficulties Gladstone experienced during his years as burgess for Oxford (1847–65), and views his difficulties as symptomatic: 'A university which preferred Inglis to Peel, and Gathorne Hardy to Gladstone, courted political insignificance' (xv).

[19] Two MPs, Sir Henry Craik and Sir William Cheyne, sat for the Glasgow and Aberdeen and the Edinburgh and St Andrews constituencies, respectively, before being returned for the new Combined Scottish Universities seats in 1868. For the purposes of this analysis, I have counted the total of their service.

longest average tenure, 18.8 years. Tenure in other universities' seats averaged 13.5 years at London, 11.5 years at Cambridge, 8.6 years at Dublin (which might be greater but for the fact that all the Dublin lawyers, many of whom held government legal offices, kept being elevated to the bench) and 8.3 years for all Scottish constituencies. The constituencies established in 1918 were too short-lived for proper comparison of their representatives' stability.

3. *Political Affiliations*

With respect to party, the record of university representation after 1832 amply bears out the claims of Conservative preponderance.[20] The oldest constituencies of Oxford, Cambridge and Dublin, which together held six seats, were unimpeachably Conservative in orientation. Conservatives won both Oxford seats in every election from 1832 to 1931, except for losing one seat to the Liberals in 1859. Thereafter, internecine divisions among the tories allowed some Independents to prevail.[21] Notwithstanding its earlier whig identification, Cambridge, too, was represented almost entirely by Conservatives, with the exception of Independents elected to the second seat in 1940 and 1945. (Political developments over the course of the 19th and early 20th centuries drove many whig families to assimilate with the Conservative party.) And even independent status hardly equated to non-partisanship. As one analysis observed, 'the addresses of Independent candidates [for university seats] usually made clear to which end of the political spectrum they were nearest'.[22] The politics of the Oxford and Cambridge Independents were hardly anathema to dominant Conservative sensibilities.

Dublin was staunchly, and extremely, tory, with the mild exceptions of one Liberal Unionist (Lecky) and one Independent Unionist (Sir Robert Henry Woods). Sympathetic historians of Trinity College have written that 'the peculiar circumstances of Ireland forced into Toryism many who would in England have been Whigs or even Liberals'.[23] But contemporary views were less charitable. In 1893, during a debate over whether the seats for Trinity College ought to be preserved in the new legislative assembly being proposed for Ireland under the Home Rule Bill, John Morley, then chief secretary for Ireland, observed that 'To continue the representation of the University of Dublin is simply to secure two seats for one particular shade of the Irish minority. Those seats have not been given to learning and eloquence, but to Tory Law Officers to secure Tory votes'.[24]

In a 1923 diatribe in the *Fortnightly Review*, Swift MacNeill (who came from a tory anglican background himself) pointed out that the extension of the Dublin franchise

---

[20] Although plural voting in general was thought to benefit the Conservatives, this effect was most pronounced in the case of the university franchise. Neal Blewett, 'The Franchise in the United Kingdom, 1885–1918', *Past & Present*, no. 32 (1965), 48–51.

[21] *The History of the University of Oxford, Vol. 8: The Twentieth Century*, ed. Brian Harrison (Oxford, 1994), 381.

[22] R.B. McCallum and Alison Readman, *The British General Election of 1945* (Oxford, 1947), 221.

[23] R.B. McDowell and D.A. Webb, *Trinity College Dublin, 1592–1952: An Academic History* (Cambridge, 1982), 155.

[24] Hansard, *Parl. Debs*, 4th ser., xiv, cols 1364–5 (11 July 1893).

in 1832 to include MAs had led to the hard tory character of the constituency. For most of its existence as a one-member constituency at Westminster between 1801 and 1831, MacNeill contended, Dublin was represented by men of a more liberal temperament. During that period, the scholars of Trinity College (the largest group within the small electorate) were inclined to take their voting cues from popular fellows or tutors. After the more numerous group of MAs were added in 1832, the constituency came to be managed by 'a self-constituted clique of wire pullers and pretentious sense carriers who imposed their will on an electorate largely composed of clergy, who placidly acquiesced in their recommendations of candidates'.[25] This, he thought, explained why Dublin could function as essentially a government nomination borough for the tories.

The record of London and the Scottish universities, with a total of three seats from 1868 to 1918 and four thereafter, is more varied, but also substantially weighted towards the Conservative side. In keeping with the university's progressive origins, London's first three MPs were elected as Liberals, but the third, Sir Michael Foster, became a Liberal Unionist. These were followed by two Unionists, the educationist Philip Magnus and the physician Sydney Russell-Wells, and finally by the 'Independent (Conservative)' Ernest Graham-Little, also a physician. All of London's members were academics, medical men or otherwise connected to the world of learning.

The Scottish constituencies were also mixed but more consistently weighted towards the Conservatives. As Edward A. Freeman, a Gladstonian and soon to be the regius professor of modern history, wrote in 1883, 'The Liberalism of the Universities of Scotland lags a long way behind the Liberalism of the Scottish people in general'. Observing that the record of members' party affiliations was then roughly balanced, Freeman noted that 'Even in the most Liberal part of the kingdom, the university constituencies are the least liberal part of the electoral body'.[26] The overall record was more strongly tory. The Scottish universities elected 16 Conservatives and five Liberals, supplemented by one Independent elected in 1945 and the anomaly of the National Labour leader Ramsay MacDonald, elected in 1936, on whose behalf Stanley Baldwin had campaigned.

For the last group of university constituencies, enfranchised in 1918 and holding a total of five seats to 1922 and four thereafter, the record is even more mixed but still with a marked Conservative tilt. Of the seven MPs who sat for the two-member Combined English Universities constituency, three were Conservatives (art professor Martin Conway, and lawyers Alfred Hopkinson and Henry George Strauss), one was a National Liberal (the historian H.A.L. Fisher) and three were Independents (social reformers Eleanor Rathbone and Thomas Harvey, and the Indian civil servant Reginald Craddock).[27] Between 1918 and 1926, the constituency returned one Liberal and one Conservative. Thereafter, the general pattern shifted to the election of one Conservative and one Independent.

---

[25] J.G. Swift MacNeill, 'A Lusus Parliamenti: Dublin University Representation, 1801–1922', *Fortnightly Review*, cxiv (1923), 494.

[26] Edward A. Freeman, 'University Elections', *Contemporary Review*, xliii (1883), 21.

[27] See Susan Pedersen, *Eleanor Rathbone and the Politics of Conscience* (New Haven, CT, 2004), 226–8, regarding Rathbone's influence on the trend towards Independent university MPs.

The University of Wales (one member) returned four Liberals and one 'Christian Pacifist' (George Davis). But being a Liberal bastion after 1918 could be interpreted in this context as a kind of relative conservatism. There was, for example, no Labour candidate in 1945.[28] The by-election of 1943, however, is regarded by some as a minor landmark in the history of regional nationalism because, of the two leading candidates, one was the ex-president and the other an erstwhile vice-president of the Welsh nationalist party, Plaid Cymru, although the latter, ultimately successful candidate, Professor W.J. Gruffydd, had switched affiliation to the Liberals before the election.[29]

The two Irish university seats created in 1918 delivered diametrically opposed results. The three MPs elected (unopposed) for the single Queen's Belfast seat were, as one would expect, all Unionists. The sole MP briefly elected to the Westminster parliament for the National University of Ireland before its representation shifted to the Irish Free State parliament was a member of Sinn Fein and therefore, according to that party's general policy, never took his seat.

By 1913, the 'present monopoly of University Seats by the Conservative and Unionist Parties' was both an established and increasingly controversial fact.[30] But Conservative dominance did not spring from a single source. Some factors were institutional, while others reflected broader political trends. Historically tied to the Established Church, Oxford, Cambridge and Dublin obviously had a long tradition of lining up with the Church's tory defenders. Later, by virtue of its political geography, Queen's University Belfast was a bastion of the protestant and unionist cause. The regional and confessional bases of partisanship that operated for Belfast were mirrored by Wales, which reflected the principality's contribution to the Liberal Party's nonconformist electoral base and, in particular, support for church disestablishment.

A second group, comprising London, the Scottish universities and the Combined English Universities, sought in the main to nominate and elect individuals who reflected the intellectual qualities and professional qualifications of their constituents. For the Combined English Universities, this was an explicit goal from the outset. When working out the complicated business of how the widely dispersed constituency would organise the nomination and voting processes, there was general agreement among convocations and vice-chancellors that representatives should be chosen, not on the usual party lines, but rather on the basis of educational pre-eminence. The activities of political associations like the new 'Combined University Conservative and Unionist Association' to nominate candidates were deprecated.[31] At the suggestion of Leeds' acting vice-chancellor, Charles

---

[28] Millicent Barton Rex, 'The University Constituencies in the Recent British Election', *The Journal of Politics*, viii (1946), 205.

[29] National Library of Wales, 'University of Wales By-Election 1943'. http://www.llgc.org.uk/ymgyrchu/Pleidleisio/Is/1943/index-e.htm 3 Nov. 2006.

[30] As indicated by the requests sent by *The Arena* magazine to several individuals to comment on university representation. The other major issues noted were the possibility of including new universities and giving women graduates the vote. Univ. of Manchester Vice-Chancellor's Archive, VCA/6/24: M. Tatham to Alfred Hopkinson, 2 June 1913.

[31] Univ. of Leeds Archive: Minutes of Convocation (extraordinary meeting), 20 Mar. 1918; Minutes of Standing Committee of Convocation, 10 Apr. 1918; Minutes of Inter-Convocation Conference Held at the Univ. of Manchester, 13 July 1918. Archive of the Univ. of Liverpool, Records of Convocation, S3681: 'Convocation Report of Standing Committee, 1917–18'. Univ. of Birmingham Archive: Minutes of the Guild of Graduates, 14 June 1918.

Melville Gillespie, the convocations organised a joint standing committee to identify desirable candidates who could then be approached with the promise of substantial support.[32]

That many of the MPs for London and the English and Scottish universities were Conservatives or Conservative affiliates may have more to do with the generally 'small-c' conservative nature of universities, where curricula and degree requirements are carefully structured, research must conform to peer-evaluated disciplinary standards, and governance requires a high degree of consensus. Graduates of these universities also overwhelmingly entered the professions in a period during which the Conservative Party had made substantial gains in middle-class allegiance. Related to this, it is important to recall that university representation reached its apogee after 1918, when the Liberals' fragmentation and collapse, Labour's class basis and newcomer status, and a succession of national crises left the Conservatives as the sole established major political party. When not in power outright, the Conservatives were the dominant partner in a succession of centre-right coalitions.

Manhood suffrage and the rise of the Labour Party after 1918 formed the background against which earlier political and cultural ideas of counterbalancing democratisation evolved into the notion that the university franchise was the best means to ensure the continued presence of 'learning' and high culture in parliament. During the debates over the failed 1931 Franchise Bill, Rathbone advanced the Millite argument that the university franchise offered some safeguard against the danger of permanent working-class dominance of the electorate.[33] Yet her position was not based on exclusive notions of class, but rather the representation of 'interests' – and, as she asserted, the interests of learning were no longer the exclusive preserve of the upper classes. Earlier, Rathbone had noted that the addition of the 'newer and more democratic' universities to the franchise was enlarging the meritocratic and non-elite element in university representation while also moderating Conservative predominance, as her own Independent status exemplified.[34]

Knowledgeable observers thought the tendency of candidates beginning in the second quarter of the 20th century to list themselves as Independents reflected the changing tastes of newer and younger electors who 'appear increasingly favourable to candidates who will be bound by no narrow party orthodoxy and obey no Party Whip'.[35] The principle of independence was not new. In the earlier days of university representation, Oxford in particular had jealously guarded its independence from government influence in its choice of burgesses. This tradition continued into the 19th century, as Sir William Heathcote (Oxford, 1854–68) averred before his election: 'He will not place his vote at the disposal of the present Ministry as one of their adherents; neither will he give it

---

[32] Bodleian Library, Oxford (Bodl.), H.A.L. Fisher Papers, MS Fisher 63, f. 200: Charles Melville Gillespie to H.A.L. Fisher, 20 Oct. 1918. The joint standing committee endured after university representation ceased in 1950, eventually becoming the present-day Congress of University Convocations and Graduate Associations. Adrian R. Allen, *University Bodies: A Survey of Intra- and Supra-university Bodies and Their Records* (Liverpool, 1990), 81–3.

[33] Hansard, *Parl. Debs* (Commons), 5th ser., cclii, cols. 2012–18 (21 May 1931).

[34] Archive of the Univ. of Liverpool, Vice-Chancellor P712/6: Rathbone, 'Case for University Representation'.

[35] McCallum and Readman, *British General Election of 1945*, 218–19.

merely for the purpose of displacing them. A Conservative in principle, he will deal with measures which may be proposed according to their intrinsic merits'.[36]

In the 20th century, party candidates in other university constituencies also thought it important to emphasize their independence. When Manchester's vice-chancellor, Alfred Hopkinson, stood as the Unionist candidate for the Combined English Universities in 1926, he looked forward, if elected, to joining 'as a University representative should, in an independent spirit in resisting ill-considered changes and in promoting sure and orderly progress toward better conditions for the people of our country in the future'.[37] John Buchan, too, although elected as a Unionist, felt he could operate with a great deal of political latitude and made this clear during campaigns.[38] By contrast, although Ernest Graham-Little stressed the idea that university representatives should be as free as possible from party domination when standing as an 'Independent (Conservative)' for London in 1924, 1929 and 1931, he also made it clear that he had been a lifelong 'convinced Conservative'. In 1929, he even went so far as to quote the Conservative Party Whip's satisfaction with his record.[39]

Oxford's tradition of independence stemmed from the priority given to upholding the privileges of the Established Church amid a succession of dramatic changes in the constitutional order during the 17th and 18th centuries. In the 20th century, the idea of members' independence came to be married to the 'aristocracy of talent' argument for university representation. In 1935, Oxford's first Independent MP, A.P. Herbert, a humorist for many years on the staff of *Punch*, wrote: 'I regard the principle and prestige of University Representation as, in the long run, a very much more important matter than the addition of one dumb vote to the official list of any Whip'.[40] According to Millicent Rex, writing a decade later: 'To stand as an Independent has the advantage of advertising the much vaunted "objectivity" of the university mind which is now the chief argument in favor of university representation'.[41] In the face of abolition, Oxford's vice-chancellor, W.T.S. Stallybrass, wrote: 'The university franchise has enabled men and women to enter Parliament who would not be likely to stand for an ordinary constituency, and by reason of the independence of their views and refusal to toe the party line would find no organization to support them'.[42]

Certainly, formal independence enabled Herbert and Rathbone to undertake sustained campaigns for particular causes – divorce reform and family allowances, respectively – that lay outside the main parties' legislative priorities and required cross-party support to succeed. Nevertheless, as Rex observed, 'during the last quarter century the universities

---

[36] *John Bull*, 28 Jan. 1854, p. 57.

[37] *The Times*, 17 Feb. 1926, p. 10.

[38] Janet Adam Smith, *John Buchan: A Biography* (1965), 321.

[39] Univ. of Bristol Library, Special Collections, Papers of the National Liberal Club, DM.668: Election Addresses 1929, ii, 207; Election Addresses 1931, 91. In 1929, the University Unionist Association nominated a candidate to stand against Graham-Little, which accounts for his need to emphasize his Conservative bona fides.

[40] *The Times*, 12 Nov. 1935, p. 15. A split within Oxford's Conservative ranks between traditionalists and evangelicals in the 1930s was instrumental in enabling Independent candidates to capture one seat in 1935 and both in 1937 and 1945. *Twentieth Century*, ed. Harrison, 381.

[41] Rex, 'University Constituencies', 207.

[42] *The Times*, 6 Feb. 1948, p. 5.

have remained essentially Conservative in their politics, just as they have always been'.[43] As the *Evening Standard* columnist Charles Wintour perceived, independence and conservatism were not unnaturally linked. In 1949, after praising the superior quality and performance of university MPs, he observed that 'Of course the Socialists are glad to see university representation abolished because most of the university members, being individualists, vote against them'.[44]

4. *Contributions to Debates*

When evaluating the record of university MPs, it is also important to take stock of their contributions to parliamentary deliberations. During the debates over the 1906 Plural Voting Bill, Asquith opined that, although the ancient institutions had been represented by some very distinguished people,

> some hon. Members might have thought from time to time as they had seen those great scholars and mathematicians sitting silent on these Benches hour after hour, and trudging through the Division Lobbies, that perhaps their time and energies might have been better occupied if they had remained in the sequestered seclusion of the great seats of learning from which they were unhappily sent to mix in the uncongenial turmoil of political parties in this House.[45]

Claims that academics were professionally and even temperamentally incompatible with life in the Commons were hardly limited to those making partisan arguments for reform. For example, while paying due respect to Lecky as a 'learned historian', the cartoonist and parliamentary observer Harry Furniss went on to describe how Dublin's MP 'delighted the House with his lady-like manner, and gave further illustration that Professors in Parliament are either out of place, or not a success'.[46]

Yet, such views also suggest that the cases made for and against university MPs are best tested, not against the performance of the lawyers (many of whom held office and were thus required to speak) and the professional politicians, but rather against the record of members whose primary occupational backgrounds were closest to the universities' cultivation of knowledge and spirit of learning: scholars, scientists, medical professionals, educators and writers. Together, these groups – which for convenience can be called the 'academic' university MPs – comprised slightly more than one-third (35%) of university members returned between 1832 and 1950.

The first point to make about this group is that after 1918 they were both more numerous and formed a larger proportion of all university MPs than before. For much

---

[43] Rex, 'University Constituencies', 205. The questionable status of Independents has a longer history, even when party structures are thought to have been less rigid; see Derek Beales, 'Parliamentary Parties and the "Independent" Member, 1810–1860', in *Ideas and Institutions of the Victorians: Essays in Honour of George Kitson Clark*, ed. Robert Robson (1967).

[44] The National Archives, Kew (TNA), Beaverbrook Papers, BBK/H/253: Charles Wintour to Lord Beaverbrook, 24 Nov. 1949. In defending the virtues of university representation, Wintour claimed to be 'advocating a viewpoint with which I know you [Beaverbrook] disagree'.

[45] Hansard, *Parl. Debs*, 4th ser., clxiii, col. 209 (24 Oct. 1906).

[46] Harry Furniss, *Pen and Pencil in Parliament* (1897), 185–6.

Table 4.3: *'Academic' University MPs' Contributions to Debate, 1832–1950*

Average/Session	Elected before 1918	Elected from 1918
Fewer than 10	7	9
11–20	1	6
21–40	2[a]	2
41–60	1	3[c]
Greater than 90	0[b]	3
Total	11	23

[a] Excludes the years in which Lyon Playfair served as chairman of the Ways and Means Committee and Deputy Speaker. Including these years, when he was required to speak often and on many subjects before the House, means that Playfair's average contributions per session rise from 28 to 107.
[b] Excludes the author and agriculturalist Rowland Prothero, who sat for Oxford from 1916 to 1919 (when he received a peerage), and served as president of the Board of Agriculture during nearly his entire tenure. Prothero averaged 190.5 contributions per session.
[c] Excludes H.A.L. Fisher's years as president of the Board of Education. Including these years, his average contributions per session rise from 37 to 158.7.

of the 19th century, only the chemist Lyon Playfair (Edinburgh and St Andrews, 1868–86) properly falls into this meta-category, and only 11 others with such backgrounds took their seats before 1918. Together, these 12 constituted 20% of all pre-1918 university MPs. From 1918 to the end of university representation, however, this proportion was nearly trebled. There are 23 individuals who may be classified as primarily scholars, scientists, educators or writers, and these made up 58% of the 40 university MPs who were returned in this period.

There is also a significant difference in the extent of the post-1918 'academic' MPs' participation in debates from that of their predecessors. As shown in Table 4.3, more members (the majority) of the post-1918 group made a greater number of contributions on average than those returned before 1918. Of course, parliamentary sessions vary greatly in length, but it is hardly necessary to incorporate sophisticated statistical weightings in order to illustrate the basic point about the more active participation of 'academic' university MPs elected from 1918 onwards.

Only two 'academic' members turned in abysmally minimal performances: George Gabriel Stokes, Lucasian professor of mathematics (Cambridge, 1887–91), who spoke on only three occasions; and the surgeon Thomas Sinclair (Queen's University Belfast, 1924–40), who spoke only nine times. The biggest producers of the post-1918 group were Kenneth Lindsay, former secretary to the Board of Education (Combined English Universities, 1945–50), who averaged 152 contributions; the author and journalist Henry Wilson Harris (Cambridge, 1945–50), who averaged 125 contributions; and the historian Kenneth Pickthorn (Cambridge, 1935–50), who averaged 94 contributions per session.

Further differences between the two groups emerge when examining the subjects on which members spoke. Overall, 20 of the 35 'academic' university MPs may be seen as having confined their parliamentary interventions to narrowly circumscribed briefs. For example, the educationist George Morrison (Combined Scottish Universities, 1934–45) averaged around eight contributions per session, but they were almost entirely limited to educational questions, especially those affecting Scotland. Similarly, Ernest Graham-Little, MD (London, 1924–50) averaged roughly 64 contributions per session, but they were almost all on medical, public health or educational matters. The pre-1918 group included only three MPs who spoke on a broad range of topics: Playfair, Magnus and the classical scholar Samuel Henry Butcher (Cambridge, 1906–10). By contrast, the 23 post-1918 'academic' university MPs included 12 who could be considered wide-ranging speakers, three of them especially broad in the reach of subjects addressed: the historian Charles Oman (Oxford, 1919–35), H.A.L. Fisher and Wilson Harris.

What these analyses reveal is not only that the 'academic' university MPs were far more active as members than Asquith and others alleged, but also that, overall, the frequency and range of their contributions were considerably enlarged in university representation's last phase beginning in 1918. This, combined with the greater prevalence of this type of representative among university MPs and the increasing tendency towards at least nominal political independence, leads to the rather ironic conclusion that, in general, university MPs after 1918 were (consistent with Rathbone's case for university representation) increasingly resembling the positive characterisations that had long been made on their behalf.

5. *Lords Educational?*

University representation is understood primarily with respect to the house of commons, as the return of a member for a special constituency following the original 17th-century creations. But it is also the case that universities had forms of representation in the house of lords that should not be wholly overlooked. To begin with, 21 of the 101 university MPs who sat between 1832 and 1950 were elevated to the peerage. Almost all of these were judges or politicians, although five came from the group of fields identified above as closest in spirit to university life: the writer John Buchan (created Baron Tweedsmuir, 1935); Martin Conway, Slade professor of art (Baron Conway of Allington, 1931); the agricultural scientist John Boyd Orr (Baron Boyd-Orr, 1949); the chemist Lyon Playfair (Baron Playfair, 1892); and the author and agricultural expert Rowland Prothero (Baron Ernle of Chelsea, 1919).

There was also another way in which universities were, in principle, represented in the Lords, as the author of an 1893 treatise observed:

> Nearly all the Universities have for their Chancellors members of the House of Lords . . . The Chancellors of the Universities of Oxford, Cambridge, London, St Andrew's, Glasgow, and Aberdeen, are the marquis of Salisbury, the duke of Devonshire, the Earl of Derby, the Duke of Argyll, the Earl of Stair, the Duke of Richmond and Gordon. The Earl of Rosse, an Irish Representative Peer, is the Chancellor of Dublin; and Lord Dufferin is Chancellor of the Royal University of Ireland.[47]

Indeed, through the Second World War (and beyond), the overwhelming majority of university chancellors were titled members of the aristocracy, supplemented in later years

[47] William Charteris Macpherson, *The Baronetage and the Senate: The House of Lords in the Past, the Present, and the Future* (1893), 312.

by notable commoners who had been raised to the peerage.[48] (At the Scottish universities, it was also not uncommon for lord rectors, elected by the students, to be peers.)

Between 1832 and 1950, the universities that came to be represented in the Commons during that period had a total of 107 chancellors, 88 (82%) of whom sat in the Lords. Some, like Arthur Balfour (Edinburgh and Cambridge) and Stanley Baldwin (Cambridge), began their chancellorships as commoners but were subsequently raised to the peerage. A further seven chancellors (mostly at the University of Wales) were members of the royal family. Of the two ecclesiastical chancellors, one, the archbishop of Armagh (Dublin, 1851–62) appeared in the Lords under the rotating scheme for church of Ireland bishops. Only ten chancellors in this period never sat in the house of lords, including such notable commoners as J.M. Barrie (Edinburgh), Joseph Chamberlain (Birmingham), Austen Chamberlain (Birmingham), Winston Churchill (Bristol) and Jan Smuts (Cambridge).

Historically, chancellors in the Lords involved themselves in a variety of matters related to university representation. In the 17th and 18th centuries, they served as a direct link to the centres of power and were also very influential in the selection of candidates for the university seats. Beginning in the 19th century, aristocratic chancellors also worked to assist their universities' efforts to obtain representation in the Commons. Chancellor-peers, like university MPs, varied in the degree to which they exerted themselves in matters relevant to higher education in parliament. Some were very attentive to university-related legislation, while others spoke about educational matters seldom or not at all. Outside the Lords chamber, a number of chancellor-peers proved effective in securing treasury funds for their universities, and they also served the interests of their institutions (and of universities generally) as members of government inquiries into higher education.[49]

Anticipating the focus of the next two chapters, there was also a colonial dimension to the idea of university representation in the Lords. The author of the 1893 treatise on Lords reform suggested that, in addition to ennobling all chancellors who were not already peers and granting life peerages to all vice-chancellors and rectors, the chancellors of the major universities in the colonies also ought to receive life peerages. At the same time, however, representation of Indian universities posed a problem. Although 'the presence in the House of Lords of one or two distinguished Orientalists might be of advantage both to politics and Asiatic studies', the writer claimed that Indian universities, unlike their counterparts in the settler colonies, were 'an alien importation, not rooted in the soil, but planted and maintained by ourselves, and it is held by high authority that they have done much harm in giving the wrong direction to a certain class of natives'. Excluding Indians would be offensive, he thought, yet the idea of sharing imperial enfranchisement with non-white colonial subjects would surely lead proponents of imperial federation to abandon the cause. Thus, he concluded, it would be better to avoid India (and Africa, the West Indies and East Asia) altogether.[50]

At one level, the concept of imperial university representation in the Lords was not unlike the argument that the university franchise provided the only opportunity for

[48] See David Cannadine, *The Decline and Fall of the British Aristocracy* (New Haven, CT, 1990), appendix F.
[49] Cannadine, *Decline and Fall*, 577–8.
[50] Macpherson, *Baronetage and the Senate*, 314–15.

graduates on service overseas to vote. Indeed, the chancellors and former chancellors of some universities in the empire did have seats in the Lords. The first instance of this was the College of William and Mary, where chancellors before 1776 were traditionally the bishop of London, who sat as one of the Lords Spiritual. In India, there was a similar *ex officio* arrangement for chancellors. The viceroy, almost invariably a peer, served as chancellor of the University of Calcutta. The governors of Bombay and Madras and the lieutenant-governors elsewhere served as chancellors of the universities in their respective territories. Although they were less frequently peers than the viceroy, they were generally ennobled later. A number of viceroys and provincial governors displayed particular interest in the condition of Indian higher education. First among these was Lord Curzon (viceroy, 1899–1905), 'a university man to the core of my being', as he proclaimed in his first convocation address as Calcutta's chancellor.[51] In the settler colonies, university chancellors were largely drawn from the ranks of important local politicians and judges rather than the proconsular aristocrats in the governor-general's house. John Buchan, Lord Tweedsmuir after 1935, is the only person to have served as a university MP (Combined Scottish Universities 1927–35), a governor-general (of Canada, 1935–40) and a university chancellor (Edinburgh, 1938–40).

In addition to the direct role chancellors could play in parliament on behalf of their universities, the convergence of growing controversy over university representation and considerations of reforming the Lords raised the more general question of whether members representing universities – or learning, or education more broadly – would be more properly located in the upper House. Unlike the Commons, in which university seats were anomalous among constituencies that were otherwise determined by geography and population, the Lords already included two special, institutionally based categories: the bishops and the law lords. In the 19th century, abortive proposals to enrich the Lords with life peerages specified the world of learning and letters as one of the categories that would gain a stronger presence in the upper House through such a scheme. Earl Russell's 1869 Life Peerages Bill sought to include, alongside other categories of meritorious contributors to national life, men 'distinguished for their attainments in science, literature, or art'.[52] In 1884, Lord Rosebery unsuccessfully moved the creation of a select committee to promote the 'efficiency' of the Lords, during which he listed medicine, science, literature and the arts as areas lacking in representation or insufficiently represented.[53] He revived the same proposals four years later, but they met with the same end.[54]

The general interest in Lords reform increased as the conflict between the two houses of parliament became a significant issue at the end of the 19th century, especially following the unceremonious defeat of the 1893 Home Rule Bill by the large majority of tory and Unionist peers (causing the aged Gladstone to consider launching a popular crusade against the Lords), and only came to be resolved in 1911 after a major constitutional crisis. During the First World War, in parallel with the deliberations of the

---

[51] Quoted in Suresh Chandra Ghosh, 'The Genesis of Curzon's University Reform, 1899–1905', *Minerva* (1988), xxvi, 490.

[52] Hansard, *Parl. Debs*, 3rd ser., cxcv, col. 459 (9 Apr. 1869).

[53] Hansard, *Parl. Debs*, 3rd ser., cclxxxix, col. 946 (20 June 1884).

[54] Hansard, *Parl. Debs*, 3rd ser., cccxxiii, cols 1548–606 (19 Mar. 1888).

Speaker's Conference over creating a fully democratic franchise, there was a major official effort to devise the basis for a restructured second chamber. The committee's recommendations listed education among the numerous elements of national life that ought to find a place in the new upper House.[55] That the committee's recommendations did not make distinctions between the different parts of the education sector, or single out universities, is perhaps not surprising. The proposals for the Commons being developed at the same time included a great expansion of university representation, and the committee's chairman, James Bryce, now Viscount Bryce, had distinguished himself when an MP by attacking the continuation of university seats under the 1885 Reform Bill.

Although all these failed proposals considered the representation of learning and education in broad terms, the idea that the representation of universities specifically would be most appropriately situated in the Lords was also raised at various points. A university, one writer opined, 'is an aristocratic, not a democratic, constituency, and should be represented in the aristocratic Chamber'.[56] The wider currency of this idea can be seen in the debate held in the mock parliament of the Newnham College Political Society the following year, when the Liberal 'government' in power proposed replacing the hereditary chamber with a new 'Upper House' composed of one representative from each county of the United Kingdom and one from each university.[57] In 1931, an essay in the *Saturday Review* asserted that, if the justification for university representation is that quality as well as quantity should be represented in parliament, then 'surely it is in the Upper, rather than in the Lower, House that quality should be represented, and if the burgesses of the universities are to represent the aristocracy of intellect in the counsels of the nation, in our opinion they should sit in the House of Lords, and keep company with other forms of aristocracy'.[58]

In 1937, university representation was in fact transferred to the upper chamber in the Republic of Ireland, but Britain's persistent inability to carry out Lords reform before the abolition of university seats in the Commons precluded any similar consideration. Yet, even with abolition in prospect, the case for university representation in the Lords continued to be aired. In 1948, the historian A.J.P. Taylor, writing to *The Times*, claimed that, while many graduates favoured abolition of plural voting, and hence of the university franchise to which they were entitled, some 'would like to see alternative possibilities considered, such as university representation in a reformed House of Lords'.[59] In the same year, a new conference on Lords reform was convened, but it broke down without producing a unified plan for moving forward. The participants did agree, among other things, that the new upper House would consist of life peers (styled 'lords of

---

[55] *Conference on the Reform of the Second Chamber: Letter from Viscount Bryce to the Prime Minister*, 4, Parliamentary Papers, 1918 [Cmd 9038], x, 569.

[56] Macpherson, *Baronetage and the Senate*, 313.

[57] Newnham College Archives, Newnham College Political Society Minute Book, 1894–5, 12 Feb. 1894. Given the preponderance of tories among university MPs at this time, it is interesting that the Newnham Liberals should think it advisable to bolster the Conservative element in their reformed upper House. It might be ascribed to the enthusiasm and idealism of an intellectual elite that (as women) had only recently gained conditional access to the most prestigious universities and were still barred from sitting in either house of parliament.

[58] *Saturday Review*, 10 Jan. 1931, p. 40.

[59] *The Times*, 10 Feb. 1948, p. 5.

parliament') who would be 'appointed on the grounds of personal distinction or public service'.[60] The conference made no specification that the field of education should be included, much less a suggestion that the specific representation of universities, on track to be eliminated from the Commons, should, following the Irish precedent, be recreated in some way in the reformed Lords.

6. *Conclusion*

The qualities and the quality of university members were central issues in arguments over whether university representation should stay or go. Characterisations of the members were not based on the kinds of analyses undertaken here, but rather emerged from prevailing assumptions within the wider political culture. Although their emphases shifted over time, these assumptions fell into two opposing camps. On the one hand, there was the view that it was desirable for parliament to include talented people with a high calibre of intellect, broader perspective and independent judgment, but who might not be willing or able to put up with the customary rigours and humiliations of electioneering. On the other was the view that this was a bogus ideal with scant reflection in the reality of who university members were and what they did.

Examination of the record reveals that neither set of assumptions was wholly right or entirely wrong. A significant portion of the university members between 1832 and 1950, and perhaps even the majority, can be said to have been people of learning and culture in various forms. It is also the case that their record of activity, while uneven, was also not insubstantial. The Conservative dominance of university seats was a fact, but one that calls for more nuanced understanding of the differences among institutions in response to their political geography and the eras in which they were enfranchised. The demonstrable move to some form of cross-bench independence after 1918 was insufficiently developed, while the greater presence of more members whose backgrounds reflected the university world and the stronger record of their parliamentary contributions were inadequately recognized to temper critics' opinions or slow the momentum behind efforts to eliminate university seats within a continued programme of constitutional modernisation.

Transfer of university representation to 'another place', where the interests of higher education were already present to some degree, might have afforded some kind of compromise position that all parties could have lived with, but the possibilities were precluded by the chronic failure after 1911 to pursue Lords reform in any substantive way. While it may have improved in many respects, after such a long history in which the characteristics and performance of the members had been so prominent in the more general debates over university representation, the role university MPs played within the parliamentary system proved unable to adapt with sufficient rapidity or thoroughness to the political requirements of full democracy.

[60] *Parliament Bill, 1947: Agreed Statement on Conclusion of Conference of Party Leaders, February–April 1948*, 3, Parliamentary Papers, 1947–8 [Cmd 7380], xxii, 1001.

Chapter 5. University Representation in India

Outside the British Isles, the most extensive and one of the longest-lasting instantiations of university representation occurred in India between 1892 and 1950. Like the extension of university representation in the United Kingdom in the 19th and early 20th centuries, India's version also resulted from the intersection of educational and political developments. The creation of new universities under British auspices was initially intended to facilitate recruitment of Indians into government service. The creation and extension of legislative structures at the provincial level was intended to provide for some measure of 'native' representation, of which the university constituencies that came to be established formed a part. The bases and indeed the utility of university seats were repeatedly debated in the course of successive efforts to reform the political structures in India, exemplifying the tensions inherent in maintaining imperial control while grappling with the implications of widening the inclusion of Indians in their own governance.

In comparison with the contemporaneous expansion of university representation in Britain, the history of university representation under the Raj provides an opportunity to study the translation of political ideas across the divide between the metropolitan power and the imperial territory while also offering some new perspectives on the distinctive articulations of imperial political development in India. In these ways, the Indian case both broadens and complicates how university representation needs to be understood as a political institution on several levels: generically, as a trans-imperial phenomenon, and as part of India's own political history.

1. *Indian Universities*

Educational reformers in the early 19th century argued for improvements in schooling and the extension of higher education in India.[1] They gained a significant victory in 1813 when the East India Company, by custom reluctant to meddle in Indian society but looking to a renewal of its charter by parliament, bowed to reformist and evangelical pressure and agreed to assume an active role in Indian education. Around the same time, Indian reformers, most notably Rammohan Roy, also sought to introduce western-style higher education, beginning in 1817 with the founding of Hindu College (later renamed Presidency College). British utilitarians and Indian reformers agreed that traditional literary education in Sanskrit and Arabic was an inadequate basis for the general advancement of Indian civic and economic life. For the British, the paramount concern of education was to be the requirements of imperial rule, as famously formulated in 1835

---

[1] When not otherwise cited, this and the following paragraph draw upon older but useful overviews of the subject: P.J. Hartog, 'The Indian Universities', *Annals of the American Academy of Political and Social Science*, cxlv (1929), 138–50; and Bruce Tiebout McCully, *English Education and the Origins of Indian Nationalism* (New York, 1940), ch. 3. Hartog wrote on good authority as former vice-chancellor of the University of Dacca from 1920 to 1925, a member of the viceroy's commission on the University of Calcutta (1917–19) and the secretary of the educational section of the Simon commission.

by Thomas Babington Macaulay, the whig statesman, historian and a founding father of the progressive University College London: 'We must at present do our best to form a class who may be interpreters between us and the millions whom we govern; a class of persons, Indian in blood and colour, but English in taste, in opinions, in morals, and in intellect'.[2] Macaulay thus articulated the critical link between education, cultural co-optation and the manpower needs of empire on a continental scale. Accordingly, in the wake of his minute on Indian education, English was made the official language of British India, and state spending on 'Oriental' education was discontinued.

Advancing Macaulay's goal of creating a class of intermediary rulers, the 1854 Educational Despatch issued under the authority of Sir Charles Wood, president of the Board of Control (the ministerial position responsible for overseeing the affairs of the East India Company), proposed establishing government-supported universities at Bombay, Calcutta and Madras, and later wherever else there might be a sufficient number of eligible students. The function of these institutions would be to rationalise the recruitment of the most able Indians into government service, while also nurturing a westernised intelligentsia that would transmit European values and promote British economic interests to the broader populace.[3] The three universities duly chartered in 1857 were organised on the University of London model as examining and degree-granting bodies for affiliated collegiate institutions. Following the rebellion of 1857–8 and the inauguration of crown rule, the approach to higher education outlined in Wood's despatch was upheld and continued. The University of the Punjab was founded in 1882 at Lahore, and the University of Allahabad five years later. Unlike their three predecessors, however, these two universities were empowered to teach as well as to affiliate, although they did not use their teaching powers immediately.

With the general strengthening of secondary schooling and the establishment of numerous new colleges, the number of students eligible to present themselves for degrees had increased substantially in the period between 1857 and 1885. Secondary and collegiate curricula were now all determined by the requirements of the universities' entrance examinations, which emphasized English language and European knowledge.[4] In the first half of the 19th century, English education, such as that provided by schools like Bombay's Elphinstone College, had enabled Indians to obtain clerical employment in government departments or government-supported educational institutions. These jobs could even lead to more prominent careers in law, education and commerce.[5] But the system of recruitment into government service based on lists of able graduates provided by the colleges had been inchoate. The universities' common degree examinations established not only a set of organising principles for school and college curricula, but also a more regular and systematic method of bringing Indians with

---

[2] Thomas Babington Macaulay, 'Minute on Education in India', reproduced in *Politics and Empire in Victorian Britain: A Reader*, ed. Antoinette M. Burton (New York, 2001), 18–20, quotation from p. 20.

[3] See Gauri Viswanathan, *'Masks of Conquest': Literary Study and British Rule in India* (New York, 1989), 146–51.

[4] Success in the entrance examination admitted students to any of the colleges affiliated with the university. After two years' attendance (one year for the University of Bombay), students could present themselves for a first examination in the arts curriculum. The BA examination occurred two years after the 'First Arts' qualification (except in Bombay, which required an intermediate examination). McCully, *English Education*, 168.

[5] Mridula Ramanna, 'Profiles of English Educated Indians: Early Nineteenth-Century Bombay City', *Economic & Political Weekly*, xxvii (1992), 716–21, 723–4.

recognized accomplishments to the government's notice.[6] At the same time, the greater coherence in educational advancement encouraged increasing numbers of Indians to seek out the professional and personal advantages to be gained under this system.

By the turn of the century, however, British authorities viewed the state of Indian higher education as increasingly problematic, especially with respect to the continued multiplication of university-affiliated colleges, the growth of student numbers and the seemingly uncontrolled appointment of fellows to the universities' senates. These conditions led Lord Curzon (viceroy, 1899–1905) to establish a commission for reforming and improving Indian universities.[7] In his speech launching the effort, Curzon directed the commission's attention to the weaknesses of the system developed over the previous 70 years for 'imparting an English education to an Asiatic people'. For the universities in particular, these weaknesses included: their organisation as examining and qualifying agents for a loose and dispersed federation of colleges rather than enjoying a proper corporate identity (including powers over appointments, finance and facilities); the inadequacy of residential arrangements; the absence of systematic principles for the constitution, size and powers of governing bodies; and academic standards.[8]

The recommendations of Curzon's commission led to the Universities Act of 1904. The Act required that all universities should be teaching institutions, colleges should meet more rigorous standards for affiliation, faculty should have a say in governance, and senates should not be too unwieldy. In addition, the Government of India was empowered to provide grants-in-aid to help the universities effect these changes. The Act proved highly controversial. Nationalists saw these measures as an attempt to extend the influence of British officials in the running of universities in which Indians had hitherto enjoyed a measure of autonomy. Implementation of the Act's provisions was resisted in a variety of ways. Indeed, even though Curzon's decision to partition Bengal was the main cause, the Universities Act also played a role in triggering the Swadeshi movement of 1905, which involved not only the boycott of foreign goods but also calls for national education.

If British officials viewed the changes imposed by the Act as leading to improved standards, Indian universities were nevertheless clearly some distance from operating as fully independent corporations like their occidental counterparts. They had been established in the first instance to impose government regulation and control over the colleges and schools within a given area, and the strong connection with government was maintained. The universities' chancellors were the viceroy (Calcutta), the governors of Bombay and Madras or the provincial lieutenant governors. Further, chancellors continued to nominate the majority of the members of governing bodies. The election of some members to university senates approved under the 1904 Act still had to be approved by the chancellor. Vice-chancellors continued to be appointed by the government and the hiring of professors and lecturers also remained subject to government approval.[9]

---

[6] Viswanathan, *'Masks of Conquest'*, 148.

[7] See Suresh Chandra Ghosh, 'The Genesis of Curzon's University Reform: 1899–1905', *Minerva*, xxvi (1988), 463–92.

[8] Curzon's opening address to the Educational Conference at Simla convened in 1901, reproduced in George Nathaniel Curzon, *Lord Curzon in India: Being a Selection from His Speeches as Viceroy & Governor-General of India, 1898–1905* (1906), esp. 315–26.

[9] Calcutta University Commission, 1917–19, *Report*, iii, pt I: *Analysis of Present Conditions* (Calcutta, 1919), 223.

Further growth in student numbers and continued concerns about standards led to another viceroy's commission in 1917–19 ostensibly focused on the largest university, Calcutta, but also including detailed reviews of the other Indian universities. As a member of the Calcutta commission later wrote: 'There can be no doubt that the Government, in setting up the Commission during the war, had clearly in view the democratic reforms which came into force afterwards and the desirability of raising the standard of western education in India, to meet the needs of western political ideals'.[10] The commission's report recommended the creation of a new university at Dacca, and subsequently a number of other institutions (Aligarh, Rangoon, Lucknow, Nagpur, Andhra and Agra) were also created in line with the report's recommendations.

In India as in Britain, the creation of new universities coincided with reforms that widened the scope of political participation. One outcome of these overlapping processes was the creation and growth of university representation. But to understand the specific reasons for the emergence of university representation in India and the particular shape it took there, it is first necessary to account for the emergence and growth of the provincial legislative bodies that came to include university seats.

2. *Provincial Councils and the Origins of University Representation*

Responding to complaints of overwork and demands for increased establishments from the British imperial administration, Lord Ripon (viceroy, 1880–4) identified the pressing need to incorporate (as he would state in 1884) 'the growing body of Natives educated by ourselves in Western learning and Western ideas' into the structures of imperial rule.[11] In his 1882 Resolution on Local Self-Government, Ripon stated that it was 'imperatively necessary to look around for some means of relief', by which he meant the Indians themselves: 'as education advances, there is rapidly growing up all over the country an intelligent class of public spirited men whom it is not only bad policy, but sheer waste of power to fail to utilize'.[12]

Local self-government in the form of the provincial legislative councils developed in stages over the late 19th and early 20th centuries. The first provincial councils were established in Madras, Bengal and Bombay in 1861 and 1862 to function concurrently with the viceroy's central council. Although these councils did include a number of nominated non-official members, some of them Indians, their powers were limited and their reputation was low. The inadequacy of the provincial councils led to demands for their expansion, especially from the Indian intelligentsia. Ripon's successor, Lord Dufferin (viceroy, 1884–8), was more concerned with strengthening imperial control, but to that end saw the further development of legislative councils as a means of

---

[10] Hartog, 'Indian Universities', 140.

[11] Quoted in Briton Martin Jr, 'Lord Dufferin and the Indian National Congress, 1885–1888', *Journal of British Studies*, vii (1967), 68.

[12] *Report of the Indian Statutory Commission, Vol. 1: Survey*, 229–300, Parliamentary Papers, 1929–30 [Cmd 3568], xi, 1.

securing greater co-operation from the educated section of Indian society. Even so, it took some time for his ideas to be accepted in London.[13]

In 1892, councils were enlarged through the addition of more non-official members. The councils' functions were also expanded to include participation in financial policy and the ability to ask questions on matters of public interest. The same act also introduced the elective principle, which Dufferin had advocated, although election was indirect and, formally, governors still nominated those who had been so elected. The councils and their functions were further enlarged in 1909, although official and nominated unofficial members together still outnumbered the elected members. Following the 1919 Government of India Act, the majority of provincial council seats were chosen by direct voting under a limited franchise. The Act also introduced the diarchy system under which certain areas of activity (such as local government, education, industry, agriculture and public works) were reserved for the provinces and placed in the hands of Indian ministers chosen from among the legislators. The 1935 Government of India Act, which took effect in 1937, made several councils bicameral, and also increased the councils' scope by limiting the governors' reserve powers.

The idea for including university seats in the provincial councils appears to have originated with Dufferin's 1887 recommendations for incorporating the representation of organised civic interest groups more generally.[14] At one level, Dufferin's recommendations can be seen as a version of the more widespread problem colonial administrators faced with respect to identifying suitable raw material for populating new colonial legislatures.[15] At the same time, however, there was considerable resistance to increasing the participation and authority of even the best educated Indians. Immediately before Dufferin assumed the office, the passions that could be ignited by official efforts to broaden the inclusion of Indians in the public sphere had been clearly demonstrated by the controversy over a bill that would have allowed Indian magistrates to preside over cases involving British subjects. Indeed, the animosities aroused by the bill were not only against the handful of native civil servants who would have gained this authority, but extended to the entire western-educated Indian middle class.[16]

Dufferin's impulse can be seen as fully consistent with the British whig and liberal thinkers of the 1850s and 1860s who advocated the incorporation of 'learning' into the qualifications for political participation. In the imperial context, his approach exemplified the classic whig strategy of enacting moderate reforms aimed at the more prosperous and educated segments of society in order to diminish the popular appeal of more extreme forces, in this case the Indian National Congress.[17] Although Congress in its early years was far from the radical mass independence movement it would become in the early 20th century, as a body of elite, western-educated reformists looking to increase the

[13] See Madhvi Yasin, 'Lord Dufferin and the Liberalisation of the Provincial Councils', *Journal of Historical Research*, xix (1977), 78–81.

[14] Yasin, 'Lord Dufferin and the Liberalisation of the Provincial Councils', 81.

[15] See, e.g., Ged Martin, *Bunyip Aristocracy: The New South Wales Constitution Debate of 1853 and Hereditary Institutions in the British Colonies* (Sydney, 1986).

[16] Mrinalini Sinha, *Colonial Masculinity: The 'Manly Englishman' and the 'Effeminate Bengali' in the Late Nineteenth Century* (Manchester, 1995), 40–1.

[17] R.J. Moore, 'The Twilight of the Whigs and the Reform of the Indian Councils, 1886–1892', *Historical Journal*, x (1967), 400–14.

participation of people like themselves in the governance of India it was still viewed with concern by the British administration.

Given the background of its members, it is not surprising that Congress endorsed the principle of university seats. This was of a piece with a broader set of such appeals which had been emanating from the educated class, the press and other bodies in the late 1880s.[18] In 1885, the third resolution of the first Congress called for an expansion of legislative councils through additional elected members, and the extension of councils into provinces in which none existed.[19] K.T. Telang of the Bombay legislative council (later a judge of the Bombay high court and the university's vice-chancellor) suggested that constituencies be formed from universities, along with other corporate groups (municipal corporations, chambers of commerce, universities, well-established political associations and the rural and municipal boards).[20] (In an obituary tribute, Telang, who was educated at Elphinstone College and held MA and LLB degrees from Bombay, was described as 'the best product of the new English system of education', though he was also a noted Sanskritist.)[21] Thus, at the same time that the idea of university representation appealed to Dufferin as one means of deepening British rule, it was also seen from the Indian perspective as a special kind of opportunity for further extending 'native' agency through the evolving frameworks of representative political structures being conceded by the British.

Dufferin's recommendations, in a more moderate form, came to be embodied in the Indian Councils Act of 1892, under which the senates of four universities – Calcutta, Bombay, Madras and Allahabad (a new legislative council had been established for the United Provinces in 1886) – became one of several kinds of corporate bodies entitled to recommend non-official members.[22] When the elective principle was introduced to the provincial councils in 1892, the general connection with the educated segment of the population was viewed with scepticism in more conservative quarters. *The Pioneer*, for example, wrote that, however it might be carried out, 'electoral systems in India can only mean the representation of the partially anglicized Indian university students congregated for the most part in Bengal'.[23] The *Times of India* took a more expansive view, arguing that 'It would be unjust to the people of India to make their interests the sport of the one percent [i.e., "Congress wire-pullers"] as it would to deny the anglicized element in the Indian population its full share of political influence, if it had indeed attained a magnitude which justified us in regarding it as a constituency of the Indian people'.[24]

As more provincial councils were established, more university seats were created. The Punjab gained a provincial council in 1897, though the University of the Punjab only

---

[18] Yasin, 'Lord Dufferin and the Liberalisation of the Provincial Legislative Councils', 79–80.

[19] The resolutions of the 1885 Congress are reproduced in *Politics and Empire in Victorian Britain*, ed. Burton, 189–90.

[20] Cecil Merne Putnam Cross, *The Development of Self-Government in India, 1885–1914* (Chicago, IL, 1922), 137, 150.

[21] R.P. Karkaria, *The Late K.T. Telang and the Present Political Movement in India, Reprinted from the 'Calcutta Review'* (Bombay, 1895), 5.

[22] Cross, *Development of Self-Government in India*, 163 n.

[23] Quoted in the *Times of India*, 4 May 1892, p. 5.

[24] *Times of India*, 4 May 1892, p. 5.

acquired its own representative with the council's enlargement beginning in 1909.[25] The state of Bihar came into existence in 1911, and the University of Patna duly acquired a seat on the council when it was inaugurated in 1917. Indeed, to a far greater degree than in Britain, once the principle of university representation was established in India, it expanded almost automatically as new provincial legislatures and new universities were added.

In addition to enlarging the councils of the major provinces to give them non-official majorities, the Indian Councils Act of 1909 – part of the reforms set in motion by John Morley (secretary of state for India, 1905–10) and Lord Minto (viceroy, 1905–10) – also created separate electorates for Muslims. Here university association and communal representation intersected, since being fellows of universities also qualified Muslims to vote for the seats established to represent the 'Mohammedan community'.[26] More broadly, however, the creation of communal constituencies, like enfranchising large landholders, was a strategy to offset the influence of the now more radicalised western-educated middle-class elites through forming electorates from groups thought by the British to have a more traditional and conservative outlook.[27]

Striking an acceptable balance between reform and control in a dynamic political context was a complex business, and the idea of university representation throws those processes into some relief. For instance, not long after he had taken up his post, Lord Minto considered adding a university seat to the viceroy's legislative council as a means of including a 'native' member. The notion was given salience by Minto's personal regard for the mathematician and high court judge, Asutosh Mookerjee, who had served two terms as the representative of Calcutta University in the Bengal legislative council between 1899 and 1903, and in 1906 had been appointed the university's vice-chancellor. At that time, Calcutta's governing bodies were still controlled by government-nominated European members, and they were under heavy criticism from nationalists for providing an education suitable only for colonial subservience. The Dawn Society in particular had called for higher education suited for nation building, especially the inclusion of scientific and technological fields in contrast to what was seen as the excessively literary focus of Calcutta's curriculum.

Mookerjee, who had also served on Curzon's university commission, was a reformist who addressed many of the nationalist critiques by strengthening the university's academic foundations through modernising the curriculum, expanding the range of departments and raising examination standards. Minto was impressed by Mookerjee's ability to deal effectively with the new, more radical political influences while seeing through a programme of sensible reforms. As the viceroy wrote to Morley in July 1906:

> Dr Mukerji, the Vice-Chancellor of the Calcutta University, who has been attending a Committee here in connection with University regulations, came to see me before he left a few days ago, and, in reply to a reference of mine as to the possibility of University representation on the Viceroy's Legislative Council and my apprehension

[25] William W. Reinhardt, *The Legislative Council of the Punjab, 1897–1912* (Durham, NC, 1972), 71.

[26] Cross, *Development of Self-Government in India*, 221–2 n.

[27] J.H. Blomfield, 'The Vote and the Transfer of Power: A Study of the Bengal General Election, 1912–1913', *Journal of Asian Studies*, xxi (1962), 172.

that such representation might bring with it too much of a Congress element, he said that as far as his University was concerned that would not be so.[28]

The idea of adding a native member to the viceroy's council came as a shock to Minto's aides, who thought it would be impossible to entrust an Indian with state secrets. Minto responded that 'though I fully admit your arguments, may it not be possible that you and I are ourselves unjustly prejudiced and that, if we put our own race prejudices aside, there may be a native gentleman in whom one might repose implicit trust?'[29] Eventually, the ideas of university representation and native representation on the viceroy's council were decoupled. University representation faded (as had the idea of bringing in an Indian as the council's law member, without creating an explicit 'native' seat), but, in Mookerjee, Minto had seen precisely that brand of Indian in whom he felt he could have implicit trust. As he wrote at the beginning of 1907:

> So far, I have avoided mentioning any Indian gentleman as a possible Member of my Council, but if we decided to have one, the man I should name is Dr Mukerji . . . His evident force of character has always impressed me. He has kept quite clear of Congress associations, and I believe if we accepted him as a Native Member his appointment would be generally approved throughout India. Moreover, his advice would be of the greatest assistance to us in the consideration of possible reforms.[30]

If the idea of establishing university representation at the level of the viceroy's council was stillborn, there were further developments in the provincial councils following the 1917 declaration by Edwin Montagu (secretary of state for India, 1917–22) that British policy aimed to introduce responsible self-government to India. In general, the 1918 report that bore the names of Montagu and Lord Chelmsford (viceroy, 1916–21) advocated limiting special electorates as much as possible, but nevertheless suggested that they would probably be necessary for the universities, along with the mining and planting interests, and the chambers of commerce.[31] Accordingly, the 1919 Government of India Act retained these special constituencies along with continuing the separate Muslim electorate throughout India and extending further the separate representation established for various other groups in most provinces. In this context, the function of university representation became less about extending political participation to what had been deemed to be a reliable segment of society, and more a part of an emphasis on directing electoral and legislative politics into communal and class channels.[32]

As part of the effort behind the Government of India Bill, the committee that had been established to consider the franchise question, chaired by the former civil servant Lord Southborough, not only proposed retaining the existing representation of universities, but also recommended admitting certain planned new universities – Dacca (est.

---

[28] British Library, London (BL), Morley Collection, IOR MSS Eur D573/9, f. 1: Minto to Morley, 18 July 1906.

[29] BL, Morley Collection, IOR MSS Eur D573/9, f. 1: Minto to Morley, 18 July 1906.

[30] BL, Morley Collection, IOR MSS Eur D573/11, f. 17: Minto to Morley, 23 Jan. 1907.

[31] *Report on Indian Constitutional Reforms*, 189, Parliamentary Papers, 1918 [Cmd 9109], viii, 113.

[32] James Chiriyankandath, ' "Democracy" under the Raj: Elections and Separate Representation in British India', *Journal of Commonwealth and Comparative Politics*, xxx (1992), 44.

1920) and Nagpur (est. 1923) – to the same privilege, for a total of eight university seats. In the Montagu-Chelmsford spirit, the committee's general intention was to get rid of special electorates as far as possible, except where it was deemed advisable to guarantee the protection of minority interests. In addition, however, the proposals for continuing representation for the universities were animated, it was said, by the wish 'to follow the English analogy, that the university representative should be a person of position elected by a large constituency' (a somewhat strange assertion given the comparatively small size of British university constituencies).[33]

The stated impulse to adhere to the British precedent notwithstanding, the proposals represented a major deviation from the British pattern, in which constitutional reforms recognized established institutions – as when Burma was incorporated into the Raj and Rangoon University became a constituency when British constitutional reforms took effect in 1923.[34] In the cases of Dacca and Nagpur, Southborough's committee endorsed expanding university representation *prospectively*. This was, however, more consistent with a wider colonial pattern in seeking representation for universities that had not yet been created, as in the cases of Toronto and Queensland (see Chapter 6). More immediately, this departure from the practice in Britain may indicate the extent to which those charged with thinking about Indian constitutional reform felt the pressure of events and the need to press forward with establishing further outposts of Indian representation within the evolving framework.

3. The University Franchise

As the Southborough committee recommendations indicate, the British government viewed the continuation of university representation as an asset for political development within the gradually devolving relationship of imperial power. Yet this was not the view taken by the Government of India, which asserted that the university seats were not necessary for minority interests and that representatives returned by universities would be no different from those elected by the professional classes generally. The Government of India also claimed that the seats would 'carry politics into academic circles'.[35] On one level, this is similar to objections that had been raised in Britain claiming that university representation would inappropriately politicise university life. In India, however, the stakes were considerably greater than the preponderance of one of the established parties among the university seats. The political influences about which the Government of India was concerned were increasingly vigorous in their challenge to British rule.

Other commentators applied to the Indian case the same arguments regularly used to support university representation in Britain. The *Times Educational Supplement*, for

---

[33] *East India (Constitutional Reforms: Lord Southborough's Committee), Vol. I: Report of the Committee Appointed by the Secretary of State for India to Enquire into Questions Connected with the Franchise and other Matters Relating to Constitutional Reforms*, 170, Parliamentary Papers, 1919 [Cmd 141], xvi, 449.

[34] *Draft Rules under the Government of India Act Required to Give Effect to the Notification Issued under Section 52A(1) of the Act of 27th October 1921, by the Governor-General of India in Council, with the Sanction of His Majesty, Constituting Burma as a Governors Province Under the Act*, 27, Parliamentary Papers, 1922 [Cmd 1672], xvi, 521.

[35] Hansard, *Parl. Debs.*, 3rd ser., ccxcv, cols 323–38 (6 Mar. 1885). *East India (Constitutional Reforms: Lord Southborough's Committee), Vol. III: Views of the Government of India upon the Reports of Lord Southborough's Committees*, 7, Parliamentary Papers, 1919 [Cmd 176], xvi, 865.

instance, cited the eminence of several university representatives and agreed with the view expressed by the *Times of India* that the contributions of such men were very important for the new legislative councils, but that it would be unfitting for them to be involved in the turmoil of a regular electoral contest. An important variation for India, however, was the need cited for such figures to be involved as the country moved towards the stated goal of a self-governing future: 'The universities have a great part to play in the transitional era upon which India has embarked; and it would be unfortunate if they now were deprived of a share of direct influence upon traditional legislation'.[36]

In contrast to the Government of India's interest in containing the influence of the educated elite, the Southborough committee's approach was entirely consistent with the Conservative emphasis (shared earlier by the whigs) on university representation as affording some measure of stability in the face of the unknowns of greater democratisation. In this sense, the domestic politics of university representation in Britain extended to the imperial sphere. But what was understood as a conservative measure in Britain was not necessarily seen the same way in India, and the question of university representation exemplifies the very different perspectives that London and New Delhi could bring to bear on constitutional matters. When questioned in 1919 by the parliamentary joint select committee on the Government of India Bill, Southborough said he thought the Government of India's position on doing away with special representation to be 'very radical'. His committee, he said, had proposed maintaining university representation along with other special voting groups, 'thinking it the conservative line to take', but the 'Government of India are not attracted by that conservative and stabilising line at all'. In addition to recommending university seats, the committee had also recommended giving the vote only to fellows, and not graduates – the representative scheme, Southborough noted, that was favoured by the Indian universities' dons.[37] Here again, the conceptualisation and configuration of university representation in India underscores the degree of sensitivity in negotiating the balance between reform and control.

Southborough claimed that his committee was put under 'extreme pressure' to maintain university representation and was given to understand that 'the abolition of this existing privilege, which is supported by British precedent, would be greatly resented' by 'the class of people interested in it'. He did not state from which quarters the committee had been put under such pressure, but he had clearly been impressed by the forces in favour of maintaining the graduates' enfranchisement. While the graduates themselves would certainly be against losing their voting privileges, which enhanced the status of their university qualifications, it is also possible that other advocates for retaining their participation feared the greater potential for revolutionary leadership of a disgruntled educated elite once this significant benefit under the British system had been insultingly discontinued.

As summarized by Southborough, retaining university representation in India was understood principally as a means for counterbalancing the extension of political rights to social groups at a further remove from British education and culture.

You see, we tried to view the whole situation. We have the Ryots [i.e., cultivators] and the small people coming in for the first time. We did honestly look round to see

---

[36] *Times Educational Supplement*, 28 Aug. 1919, p. 436.

[37] *Report from the Joint Select Committee on the Government of India Bill*, 55, Parliamentary Papers, 1919 (203), iv, 1.

where we could find steadying influences. We thought – my Indian friends quite agree with me – that where we could find good men and introduce them into these new Legislative Councils – men of knowledge of government and experience of history, and so on – it was quite the right thing to do at the beginning, and for that reason we did it.[38]

This 'conservative and stabilising' logic is little altered from that of Dufferin, not to mention that of Macaulay. But Southborough's explanation is also fully consistent with views of university representation in Britain from John Stuart Mill, to Lord Salisbury, to Eleanor Rathbone that a chief aim of fancy franchises for the educated should be to ensure the representation of learning and high culture within a contemplated mass electorate. At the same time, the logic runs counter to the Government of India's interest in extending the electorate to groups that would effectively serve as a counterweight to the western-educated middle classes.

Although arguments in favour of maintaining university seats within an expanded electorate were quite consistent between the British and Indian cases, the question of who should receive the university vote was rather more vexed in India. After 1918, the franchise for all British universities, old and new, extended to all male graduates and, consistent with the general electorate, women graduates (and their Oxbridge equivalents) aged 30 or older. In India, however, the university franchise had been much more circumscribed, and the issue of giving graduates the vote was a source of considerable tension between official British policy recommendations and the Indian administration.

Southborough's claim that university representation was supported by British precedent was disputed by the former secretary of the Scottish Education Department and MP for the Combined Scottish Universities, Sir Henry Craik. On the question of voting privileges, Craik asserted that 'the University representation in India has no remote resemblance to University representation in this country as we understand it' because the constituencies were restricted to the universities' governing bodies and excluded the body of registered graduates which 'alone would be the expedient for putting it upon a footing of University representation in this country'. Craik returned to the differences later when questioning the Indian civil servant Sir Frank Sly, who acknowledged that 'there is no real parallel between the proposals put forward in the Franchise Report for University representation in India with the corresponding University representation in Great Britain'. Later, he said the proposal for restricting the electorate to fellows only was 'a perfect farce'.[39]

The same year, Lord Selborne, chairman of the joint select committee on the Government of India Bill, stated his ambivalence towards continuing university representation at all, but suggested that if it were to continue it should be broadened to include the graduates.[40] The recommendations that were finally approved kept the eight university seats, but proposed extending the franchise to all graduates of at least seven

---

[38] *Report from the Joint Select Committee on the Government of India Bill*, 56, Parliamentary Papers, 1919 (203), iv, 1.

[39] *Report from the Joint Select Committee on the Government of India Bill*, 56, 139, 380, Parliamentary Papers, 1919 (203), iv, 1.

[40] *Report from the Joint Select Committee on the Government of India Bill*, 161, Parliamentary Papers, 1919 (203), iv, 1.

years' standing – a probationary period that stands in marked contrast to the way that graduates of British universities were eligible for the franchise almost immediately after obtaining their degrees. It is possible to infer that the recommendation was rooted in the notion that university graduates of seven years' standing would be more likely to be established householders, landowners and members of the professions, and thus be less liable to be swayed by the claims of radical politics. Ultimately, this broadening of the university electorates was adopted in most, but not all, cases. When a constituency was established at Rangoon in 1923, for example, the electorate consisted of fellows, honorary fellows and graduates of not less than three years' standing resident in Burma.[41]

The limited nature of the graduates' franchise drew some protests. In 1920, for example, the Madras League of Youth passed a resolution, duly submitted to the joint committee of the houses of parliament on Indian affairs, objecting to the seven-year requirement for graduates. Noting that the general age qualification was 21, the League argued that the measure discriminated against those best suited by virtue of education to hold the franchise. Further, since young men are less able to occupy a separate house or own land, and would not necessarily have a vote under other franchises, they should have the right to exercise the university vote. The resolution also cited the fact that the 1918 Representation of the People Act had given the vote to all graduates, as well as the rules in effect at the University of the Punjab under which all holders of MA degrees could vote.[42]

The question of university representation in India was raised again in the late 1920s when the Indian statutory commission under the chairmanship of Sir John Simon was established at the end of 1927 in accordance with the pledge made in 1919 to evaluate the constitutional reforms after ten years. The commission's 1930 report advocated replacing the diarchy system erected in 1919 with strengthened representative governments in the provinces. As part of these arrangements, the Simon commission recommended, 'though with considerable hesitation, that university seats should be preserved' but not increased.[43] In response, the Indian central committee and nearly all the provincial governments agreed that university representation should be retained. Even so, there were renewed efforts to restrict the franchise. In the main, the numbers were not large. Holders of the university franchise around 1930 amounted to 37,809, or 0.6% of the total Indian provincial electorate.[44] And while the 12,683 university electors in Madras were on the same numerical plane as some British university constituencies, the other Indian university electorates were considerably smaller: 7,886 electors for Calcutta;

[41] *Draft Rules under the Government of India Act Required to Give Effect to the Notification Issued under Section 52A(1) of the Act of 27th October 1921, by the Governor-General of India in Council, with the Sanction of His Majesty, Constituting Burma as a Governor's Province Under the Act*, 27, Parliamentary Papers, 1922 [Cmd 1672], xvi, 521.

[42] BL, IOR/L/PJ/9/14, ff. 359–60: Submission from the League of Youth, Madras, to Joint Committee of the Houses of Parliament on Indian Affairs, 4 Apr. 1920. A minute of 4 June 1920 responds to the League's proposals, all in the negative: BL, IOR/L/PJ/9/14, f. 356.

[43] *Report of the Indian Statutory Commission, Vol. 2: Recommendations*, 73, Parliamentary Papers, 1929–30 [Cmd 3569], xi, 443.

[44] Calculated from constituency data in *East India (Constitutional Reforms – Elections), Return Showing the Results of Elections in India in 1929 and 1930*, Parliamentary Papers, 1930–1 [Cmd 3922], xxiv, 363. The total electorate for the legislative councils was approximately 6.8 million. The figures exclude Burma, where the University of Rangoon constituency consisted of 171 electors out of a total legislative council electorate of more than 1.9 million.

7,400 for Bombay; 4,335 for Allahabad; 3,097 for Punjab; 1,577 for Dacca; 534 for Nagpur; and 297 for Patna.[45]

From the universities' perspective, the case for restricting the franchise was summarized by Patna's new vice-chancellor, Stuart Macpherson, in his 1930 convocation address:

> As at present the electoral body consists of the registered graduates and registered College and School teachers of the University and contains elements possessing divergent and sometimes conflicting views, the member whom it elects does not, as experience proves, necessarily represent the views of the Senate which is the real administrative authority of the University. Accordingly the Syndicate has re-commended to Government that in any future scheme of Reforms, the University Member be the elected representative of the Senate.[46]

In the official sphere, the central committee supported by the governments of Madras and Bengal suggested 'that, in order to secure a more adequate representation of learning and the return of representatives possessing special academic qualifications, the franchise in these special constituencies should not extend to graduates generally, but should be confined to members of the Senate or the governing body'. The 'general body of graduates', claimed the Government of India, would not be disenfranchised by such a change, since they would retain their vote in general constituencies.[47]

The question of the franchise was taken up by yet another committee, appointed at the end of 1931 and chaired by Lord Lothian. Supported by the provincial governments and committees, the Lothian committee endorsed maintaining university representation, but was not unanimous about the composition of the electorate. The majority, however, favoured 'election by the registered graduates and not by the senate or the court alone, one important argument in favour of this view being that in many cases the senate is largely formed by [government] nomination'.[48] Again, questions of university representation shed light on the different perspectives and interests of the British government and the Government of India where the former could consider issues with reference to constitutional principles and the latter had to bear in mind the practical realities of governance and control.

The 1935 Government of India Act incorporated these recommendations, but left open questions about which universities should form the basis of the constituencies, and about the qualifications for electors and candidates for university seats. On the first question, the situation in Bombay, the Punjab, Bihar and the Central Provinces was simple. In each of these provinces there was only one university which already served as the basis for the existing constituencies. In Bengal, which was unique in having two university seats on its council, the question was also easily answered since these seats were

[45] *East India (Constitutional Reforms – Elections), Return Showing the Results of Elections in India in 1929 and 1930*, Parliamentary Papers, 1930–1 [Cmd 3922], xxiv, 363.

[46] Stuart Macpherson, 'Patna University Convocation: New Vice-Chancellor's Address', *The Ravenshavian*, xv (1930), 19.

[47] *Government of India's Despatch on Proposals for Constitutional Reform, Dated 20th September, 1930*, 32, Parliamentary Papers, 1930–1 [Cmd 3700], xxiii, 679.

[48] *Report of the Indian Franchise Committee, Vol. I*, 137–8, Parliamentary Papers, 1931–2 [Cmd 4086], viii, 489.

assigned to the province's two universities, Calcutta and Dacca. In Madras and the United Provinces, the situation was more complicated. The committee appointed to address these matters agreed with the recommendation of the Simon commission and the government of Madras that henceforth the Madras University constituency should also incorporate the two new 'universities of standing': Andhra and Annamalai (following the British precedents of the joint Scottish university constituencies and the Combined English Universities). Similarly, in the United Provinces, the committee recommended amalgamating the universities of Lucknow and Agra with the established constituency, Allahabad.[49] (Burma had been granted effective home rule in 1935, so Rangoon University was not part of these considerations.)

With respect to the electorate for these seats, the committee had to sort out not only the variation among existing arrangements, but also the different recommendations from the provinces. In Madras, Calcutta, Bombay, United Provinces and Punjab, the electorate consisted of members of the university senate (or equivalent body), fellows or honorary fellows and graduates of seven years' standing. In the case of the universities of Dacca and Patna, the electorate consisted of members of the court and registered graduates with no restrictions on standing, and in the case of Nagpur of registered graduates without restriction. The government of Madras wanted to restrict the university's electorate to members of the senate; Bombay wanted to retain the present qualification; Bengal, Bihar and the United Provinces wanted to restrict the electorate to registered graduates; Punjab favoured the admission of graduates; and the Central Provinces wanted to restrict the Nagpur electorate to members of the court.[50] The committee thought the university franchise should be uniform throughout India. It acknowledged the advantages of a strictly limited electorate distinct from graduates for producing a representative of the university. Nevertheless, it was impressed by the strong exception to reducing the franchise evident in most provinces. Further, the report noted, it was 'brought prominently to our notice [that] the practice of the ancient English universities' was to include graduates. The committee concluded that it would be a mistake to restrict the electorate to members of a university's senate or court and recommended that all registered graduates of seven years' standing be granted the vote.[51]

Although representation had not been limited, as some had hoped, to the universities' senates, new limitations placed on the university electorate by the 1935 Government of India Act reduced the overall university electorate from what it had been in 1929–30. In 1937, when the first elections were held under the Act, the electorate for provincial legislative assemblies totalled 30.1 million, approximately 20% of the adult population.[52] The university electorate totaled 16,122, or roughly 0.05% of the total provincial electorate: 8,065 electors for Madras, Ahndra and Anamali; 4,395 for Bombay; 404 for Calcutta; 1,075 for Dacca; 919 for the joint constituency of Allahabad, Lucknow and Agra; 757 for

[49] *Government of India Act, 1935: Report of the Committee Appointed in Connection with the Delimitation of Constituencies and Connected Matters, Vol. I*, 139–40, Parliamentary Papers, 1935–6 [Cmd 5099], ix, 1.

[50] *Government of India Act, 1935: Report of the Committee Appointed in Connection with the Delimitation of Constituencies and Connected Matters, Vol. I*, 140–1, Parliamentary Papers, 1935–6 [Cmd. 5099], ix, 1.

[51] *Government of India Act, 1935: Report of the Committee Appointed in Connection with the Delimitation of Constituencies and Connected Matters, Vol. I*, 141, Parliamentary Papers, 1935–6 [Cmd 5099], ix, 1.

[52] *East India (Constitutional Reforms – Elections), Return Showing the Results of Elections in India, 1937*, Parliamentary Papers, 1937–8 [Cmd 5589], xxi, 205; Chiriyankandath, ' "Democracy" under the Raj', 51.

Punjab; 140 for Patna; and 358 for Nagpur.[53] For all university constituencies, the electorate consisted of members of the governing body and graduates of no less than seven years' standing. Excluded from the electorate were fellows and honorary fellows who previously qualified. These changes affected the Calcutta electorate dramatically. In addition, five of the eight constituencies (Bombay, Calcutta, Dacca, Allahabad/Lucknow/Agra and Punjab) required that eligible electors be resident in the relevant province.[54]

By this time university electorates also included some women graduates, their small numbers reflecting the huge disparity between the levels of education for men and women. Beginning in the early 19th century, schools established by missionaries and social reformers were the major providers of education for girls, but this was a comparatively small-scale enterprise and directed primarily at improving women's capabilities for fulfilling their traditional roles as wives and mothers. Gradually, however, the educational system originally intended to train men for government service began to include women. At the university level, Calcutta permitted women to present themselves for the entrance examinations in 1877, and for the BA examinations the following year. Calcutta graduated its first two women in 1883, the same year that Bombay began admitting women. Other Indian universities also started admitting women in the 1880s and, in 1916, a women's university was founded at Poona.

The number of women receiving higher education, while growing in this period, remained very small. In 1881–2, six women were enrolled at colleges and universities. Twenty years later, that number had grown to only 256, and by 1921–2 a mere 905 women were enrolled. The liberationist ethos of the freedom struggle, along with the example of prominent women in the movement, substantially advanced women's participation in higher education. By the time of independence, more than 23,000 women were enrolled at colleges and universities, although this was obviously a small fraction of the population and only 0.5% of total female participation in the education system.[55]

Suffrage campaigners had failed to persuade Southborough's franchise commission to give women the vote throughout India. Instead, the 1919 Government of India Act empowered provincial legislatures to decide for themselves whether and when to remove the sex disqualification. More localised campaigning, especially when harnessed to nationalist politics, saw some women incorporated into provincial electorates in the 1920s: Bombay and Madras in 1921; the United Provinces in 1923; Punjab and Bengal in 1926; and Assam, the Central Provinces and the especially obstinate Bihar and Orissa in 1930.[56] Thus, by 1923 – five years after women in the United Kingdom gained the

---

[53] *East India (Constitutional Reforms – Elections), Return Showing the Results of Elections in India, 1937*, Parliamentary Papers, 1937–8 [Cmd 5589], xxi, 205. The figure for Madras does not appear in this report, but has been calculated by the author based on the report's data for the number of votes cast (5,968) and voters as a percentage of electors (74.0%).

[54] *Government of India Act 1935: Report of the Committee Appointed in Connection with the Delimitation of Constituencies and Connected Matters, Volume II: Proposals for the Delimitation of Constituencies*, Parliamentary Papers, 1935–6 [Cmd 5100], ix, 331.

[55] Government of India, Department of Social Welfare, Ministry of Education and Social Welfare, *Toward Equality: Report of the Committee on the Status of Women in India* (New Delhi, 1974), 234–9.

[56] On women's gaining provincial votes generally, see Geraldine Forbes, *Women in Modern India* (Cambridge, 1996), 101–3. For Bengal, see Barbara Southard, 'Colonial Politics and Women's Rights: Woman Suffrage Campaigns in Bengal, British India in the 1920s', *Modern Asian Studies*, xxvii (1993), 397–439. For Bihar and Orissa, see Umeshwari Charan, *Responsible Government: A Case Study of Bihar, 1919–1937* (New Delhi, 1985), 72–3.

Table 5.1: *Indian University Electorates with Women Electors, 1923*

	Men	Women
Allahabad	3,272	4
Bombay	4,646	31
Madras	7,804	36

Source: *East India (Constitutional Reforms – Elections), Return Showing the Results of Elections in India, 1923*, Parliamentary Papers, 1924 [Cmd 2145], xxviii, 497.

university franchise – women were allowed to vote in three provinces with university electorates: Bombay, Madras and the United Provinces. The official election returns of that year provide figures for both men and women electors, which are shown for the relevant university constituencies in Table 5.1.

The proportion of women in the provincial electorates generally was quite small, but the limited nature of women's education caused their presence in university constituencies to be even smaller. And not all of these women exercised their franchise. Only 31 of the total 71 women university electors actually voted in 1923 (20 in Bombay, eight in Madras and three in Punjab). It is unknown, of course, whether or not these women, or the 40 who did not cast their votes as university electors, voted under other qualifications in addition to, or instead of, their university franchises. Unfortunately, the reported returns for subsequent election years do not break down the electorates or votes by sex, so useful comparisons with the status of women electors and their voting in the 1930s and 1940s are precluded. At least one woman sought election to a university seat. In 1930, Shoila Bala Das, a prominent women's rights advocate and fellow of the university, stood for Patna, but was defeated by S.M. Hafeez.[57]

Between the outbreak of the Second World War in 1939 and the independence period, seven of the 11 provincial councils were suspended following the resignation of Congress Party ministers in protest over the lack of a firm promise of post-war independence from Britain. Of the seven provinces where governors took over direct administration, five had university constituencies: Bihar (Patna University), Bombay, Central Provinces (Nagpur University), Madras (Madras, Andhra and Annamalai Universities) and United Provinces (the united university constituency of Agra, Allahabad and Lucknow). University seats continued in two of the four provinces where legislatures had not been suspended: Bengal (Calcutta and Dacca Universities) and the Punjab. Elections, which had been postponed for all constituencies for the duration, resumed in 1946 (the 1935 franchise by then extended to include all those who had served in the war). Yet university seats were to have no place in the new independent Indian democracy.

In July 1947, not long before the Attlee government's 1948 Representation of the People Act would abolish the university seats at Westminster, members of the Indian

[57] Macpherson, 'Patna University Convocation', 19. Das, the adopted daughter of the Orissa lawyer and social reformer Madhusudan Das, was an important advocate for women's rights, especially in the area of educational opportunity. Among other accomplishments, she was instrumental in obtaining the right for women to practise in the law courts. A fellow of the university and member of the syndicate, she became the first woman in India to hold the position of honorary magistrate. Following independence, she represented Orissa in the Rajya Sabha in 1952–3. *Literature and Social Reform in Colonial Orissa: The Legacy of Sailabala Das (1875–1968)*, ed. Sachidananda Mohanty (New Delhi, 2006), 42–3.

Constituent Assembly charged with establishing the guidelines for provincial constitutions resolved that 'There is to be no special representation in the Legislative Assembly either for universities, or for labour, or for women'.[58] In an odd coincidence, just as the abolition of university seats in Great Britain took effect with the general election in 1950, so in India the provincial university seats were expunged when the new constitution took effect the same year. Two universities, Punjab and Dacca, were located in territories that became part of Pakistan, where it took until 1956 to produce a national constitution. During the extended period of constitutional limbo, the province of Western Punjab's legislative council continued to have a university seat until 1955, when four provinces were reorganised into a unitary West Pakistan.[59] In the Pakistani province of East Bengal, the university seat, albeit without a member, remained part of the legislative assembly until it was abolished with other special constituencies in 1954.[60] It is also worth noting that the constituent assembly, which also served as Pakistan's legislature during this period, included several distinguished academics.[61]

4. *University Members*

For those who occupied university seats in India, the issues to be considered are somewhat different than for their UK counterparts. In Britain, arguments for both abolishing and preserving the university franchise often centred on claims about the overall character of university members. In India, university seats existed within a set of representative institutions that were evolving, and they were less anomalous within each provincial legislature's patchwork of corporate and communal electorates (see Appendix 6). Accordingly, understanding the characteristics of Indian university representatives is important, but it must be framed in relation to other questions. In particular, university members must be seen in light of the wider criticism – from both the British and Indian nationalist sides – that provincial legislative councils mattered little. Examination of the university members, however, reveals the overall seriousness and quality of their contributions, as well as their significance for the future Indian state.[62]

The inclusion of Indian members on the provincial and then central legislative councils was certainly part of the emergence of a cross-race public sphere. In a small but

[58] *Constituent Assembly Debates* [India] (12 vols, Faridabad, 1946–50), iv, 596, 661.

[59] Historical lists of members are available on the Punjab Assembly's website: http://www.pap.gov.pk/html/1193897152_e.shtml 10 May 2010. No university member is listed for the first post-independence assembly (1947–9). In the second assembly (1951–5), however, the university seat was held by the Speaker, Dr Khalifa Shuja-ud-Din, a barrister.

[60] Najima Chowdhury, *The Legislative Process in Bangladesh: Politics and Functioning of the East Bengal Legislature, 1947–58* (Dacca, 1980), 17–20.

[61] G.W. Choudhury, 'The First Constituent Assembly of Pakistan, 1947–1954', Columbia University PhD, 1956, p. 35.

[62] Assembling the list of university members and obtaining information on their backgrounds involved consulting a wide variety of source materials. Online research using both South Asian websites and digitised books and periodicals was critical to this enterprise. Some of the university members were very well-known and well-documented figures. For some others, little more information was available than their name. In all cases, I have sought to obtain the most authoritative information possible, though in some more obscure cases I was obliged to make use of whatever information was available, regardless of the source. Because of their multiplicity and, in some cases, their ephemerality, not all sources used for this biographical research are listed in the bibliography.

important way, Indian representation also spanned the divide between the Indian sub-continent and the British imperial metropole. In 1892, the year in which the Indian Councils Act was passed with the intention of giving Indians greater participation in the reformed provincial councils (part of which involved the establishment of university seats), Britain's first Asian MP, Dadabhai Naoroji, was returned in the Liberal interest for Finsbury Central.

Significantly, in light of ideas about the representation of learning that were used to justify university representation, the pioneering Naoroji, a charter member and twice president of the Indian National Congress, had been professor of mathematics and natural philosophy at Elphinstone College (the first Indian to hold a professorship), and later professor of Gujarati at University College London. He had also served as the Indian representative on the Bombay legislative council from 1885 to 1886.[63] Thus, had Naoroji returned to (or remained in) India, he might have been considered an ideal candidate for a university seat when they came into being after 1892.

Britain's second Asian MP, Mancherjee Bhowanaggree, was returned as a Conservative for Bethnal Green North East in 1895.[64] As a prominent and prosperous lawyer with fine academic credentials, Bhowanaggree would not have been out of place among the university members on Indian legislative councils. More directly relevant to this study, however, the same election saw Calcutta University's first provincial council represen-tative, Womesh Chandra Bonnerjee, contest Barrow as a Liberal candidate, albeit unsuc-cessfully. Shortly before his death, Bonnerjee also contested Walthamstow in what would turn out to be the Liberal landslide election of 1906, but ill health forced him to withdraw.[65]

Before he ventured into British electoral politics, Bonnerjee had been among the first of what would become a substantial group of Indian university representatives. From 1893 to 1950, a total of 68 men represented eight university constituencies in seven provincial legislatures.[66] When compared to the UK, this seems like a somewhat high turnover for a 57-year period, especially since only four of the seats existed for the whole time period. The turnover might have been even higher but for a number of cases where members retained their seats for more than one electoral cycle and several instances in which elections were delayed.

At the outset, elections for provincial councils were on two-year cycles. The statutory period was extended to three years by the 1919 Government of India Act. The elections that would have been held in 1934–5 were postponed in light of the constitutional

---

[63] David Lewis Jones, 'Naoroji, Dadabhai (1825–1917)', *Oxford Dictionary of National Biography*, ed. Colin Matthew and Brian Harrison (Oxford, 2004), online edn, http://www.oxforddnb.com/view/article/37802 2 Mar. 2007.

[64] A third Indian, Shapurji Saklatavala (Labour then Communist), was returned for Battersea North in 1922. Sixty-five years later, in 1987, the next British Asian MP, Keith Vaz (Labour), was returned for Leicester East. On the late 19th-century elections, see Sumita Mukherjee, ' "Narrow-Majority" and "Bow-and-Agree": Public Attitudes towards the Elections of the First Asian MPs in Britain, Dadabhai Naoroji and Mancherjee Merwanjee Bhownaggree, 1885–1906', *Journal of the Oxford University Historical Society*, ii (2004), 1–20. On the racial and symbolic politics leading up to Naoroji's election, see Antoinette Burton, 'Tongues Untied: Lord Salisbury's "Black Man" and the Boundaries of Imperial Democracy', *Comparative Studies in Society and History*, xlii (2000), 632–61.

[65] Roger T. Stearn, 'Bonnerjee, Woomes Chunder (1844–1906)', *Oxford Dictionary of National Biography* (Oxford, 2004), online edn. http://www.oxforddnb.com/view/article/76337 2 Mar. 2007.

[66] For the purposes of this discussion, I have excluded the representation of the University of Rangoon.

changes being proposed for what would become the 1935 Government of India Act. Accordingly, members at this time sat continuously between 1930 and 1937. With the outbreak of the war, electoral activity was again delayed until 1946. For the provinces in which constitutions were suspended at the end of 1939, members of the legislature nevertheless continued to be officially listed as such.

Overall, the members returned to represent Indian universities were an accomplished group, with careers marked by high levels of academic, professional and political distinction. The vast majority of university members were lawyers: no fewer than 43 (63%) had legal training. Lawyers were also the largest career category for university MPs at Westminster after 1832, but that was owed in large measure to the almost exclusively legal character of the members from Dublin. Although scholars in recent years have made much of the colonial linkages and analogues between Ireland and India, the prominence of the law in university representation should probably not be understood in those terms. It is true that the law was a major vehicle for upward mobility generally in colonial settings (as it was for the British middle classes), but Trinity College in this period was a bastion of the anglican establishment and a bulwark of the Union, and its MPs behaved accordingly. In stark contrast, most Indian university members supported the cause of independence, and lawyers were especially prominent in efforts to bring an end to British rule.

This preponderance of members supporting independence ran completely counter to what British administrators had hoped for in creating the universities in the first place, and later the university constituencies. Yet it is fully consistent with the record of India's western-educated elite which, as has long been recognized, played a central role throughout the independence movement's various phases (most famously encapsulated in 1931 by Churchill's description of Gandhi as a 'seditious Middle Temple lawyer'). Concerns about the socio-political consequences of universities producing more educated Indians than the needs of government service could absorb were long-standing. As one historian has written, 'It was natural for the educated unemployed as well as for those professionals who were not patronized by the British establishments to become increasingly alienated from the British Raj'.[67] Although more recent scholarship has sought to bring to light the neglected contributions of non-elites in India's freedom struggle, a discussion of university representatives necessarily maintains focus on a more privileged group.

Although it began as an organisation advocating a greater role for educated Indians within the structures of British rule, the Indian National Congress soon evolved into a mass movement and the leading political force for independence, the official goal of the party starting in 1928. Most university members were associated with one or another faction within Congress. Five university members served as Congress presidents, including Bonnerjee, who was elected president of the first Congress in 1885 and again in 1892; A.M. Bose (Calcutta) in 1898; N.G. Chandavarkar (Bombay) in 1900; Bhupendranath Bose (Calcutta) in 1914; and S. Srinivasa Iyengar (Madras) in 1924. Other university members played important roles in Congress at both the national and provincial levels.

In politics, university members ran the full gamut from moderate reformers like M.R. Jayakar (Bombay) and T.V. Sheshagiri Iyer (Madras), to Hindu nationalists like

---

[67] Ghosh, 'Genesis of Curzon's University Reform', 491–2.

Shyamaprasad Mookerjee (Calcutta). While some Muslim members were affiliated with Congress, like Rafi Ahmed Kidwai (Allahabad), other members such as Mian Fazl-i-Husain (Punjab), Zia-ud-din Ahmed (Allahabad) and Fazlur Rahman (Dacca) were prominent in the Muslim League. A few seemed more inclined to co-operate with the Raj. Bhupendranath Bose (Calcutta) moved closer to the government as the nationalist movement became more extreme; Mian Fazl-i-Husain (Punjab), though a founding figure in the Muslim League, later formed the loyalist Unionist Party; and R.P. Paranjpye (Bombay) was widely thought to be pro-British.

A number of university representatives who were active in the independence movement attained that supreme qualification of political dissidents: arrest and imprisonment. For example, K.M. Munshi (Bombay) resigned his seat in 1929 during the Bardoli Satyagraha, was sentenced to six months' imprisonment in 1930 for participating in the Salt Satyagraha and was imprisoned again for two years in 1932 for political activities. Another notable university member, Sarat Chandra Bose (Calcutta), was imprisoned in 1932 and again in 1941 on account of his contacts with the Japanese, who would encourage the creation of the Indian National Army led by his brother, Subhas. The case of Bose is especially interesting in exemplifying that nationalist politics were hardly epiphenomenal with respect to the university constituencies. Indeed, in his campaign letter for the Calcutta University seat in 1926, Bose made a direct link between the goals of the institution and the nationalist cause:

> My Alma Mater has as its motto – 'The Advancement of Learning'. I feel this is not the motto of the University alone, but a national motto, the battle-cry of our struggling militant nationalism seeking ever to express itself and to fulfil itself against the forces of injustice, oppression, squalor, poverty and ignorance. 'Freedom and Advancement' – that is the problem for you and me . . . This is the national problem and to its solution, the University, the lecture hall, the press, the platform and the Council Chamber must all co-ordinate their resources.[68]

Bose was one of the large contingent of lawyers among university representatives. With respect to the professional background of members, it should come as no surprise that lawyers were so prominent in Indian university constituencies. Lawyers were envisioned as best suited to fill university seats when they were first established in 17th-century England. More proximately, in late 19th- and early 20th-century India, law was the elite profession for Indians and, despite much prejudice and resistance from the British, a profession that had rapidly become Indianised.[69] It is also the case that lawyers were a substantial presence in local government generally, not least because of their local influence and clientele, as well as their access to funds.[70] Lawyers, or people with legal training in their backgrounds, were an important component of the Indian intelligentsia.

---

[68] Subhas Chandra Bose, *Correspondence, 1924–1932* (Calcutta, 1967), 246–7.

[69] Looking at the Bombay high court as an example, in 1871 it had 62 advocates and solicitors of which 17 were Indian; by 1911, Indians made up 364 of the 400 solicitors and advocates. J.S. Gandhi, 'Past and Present: A Sociological Portrait of the Indian Legal Profession', in *Lawyers in Society: The Common Law World*, ed. Richard L. Abel and Philip S.C. Lewis (Berkeley, CA, 1988), 373.

[70] See Hugh Tinker, *The Foundations of Local Self-Government in India, Pakistan, and Burma* (1954), 50, 51 n1, 58 n3, 153–4; and Chiriyankandath, ' "Democracy" under the Raj', 48, 55.

The universities were themselves centres of legal education, and many of these lawyers retained ties to the universities at which they were trained and on whose senates, syndicates and councils they often sat.

The law also provided useful structures for electioneering among the widely dispersed university constituencies. As Subhas Chandra Bose (writing from prison in Mandalay) advised his brother, Sarat, after he decided to contest the Calcutta seat in 1926:

> Regarding your constituency it is most important to have the support of the [Bar] libraries and Associations throughout the province. Each Bar Library is a place where you can get so many solid votes, if only the members could be approached. Every district and sub-divisional bar library will have to be requested to support your candidature and at least one person should be made responsible for the votes of each Bar Library. All things being equal, pleaders are bound to support a lawyer and any one who gets the solid support of the pleaders of the province is bound to be returned as the University representative.[71]

If they were of the first importance for university candidates, the Bar organisations were not, of course, the whole story. In the same letter, Subhas Bose also stressed to his brother that the next most important group to court were the teachers. Like lawyers, they, too, had professional organisations – the two unions organised for teachers at government schools and private schools – that provided useful structures for soliciting votes.[72]

While some legally trained university members became primarily involved in political activities and journalism, others remained practising lawyers and achieved high professional standing. Seven (16%) of the 43 lawyers became high court judges, including Shadi Lal (Punjab), the first Indian to become a permanent justice of any high court.[73] Lal's legal distinction was further recognized in the early 1930s when he served in Britain as a member of the judicial committee of the privy council. Bonerjee and C.P. Ramaswami Iyer (Madras) declined offers of judgeships in order to continue their lucrative law practices. Another nine members (20% of the lawyers) were high court advocates and pleaders.[74] Several university members in the law also served as advocates-general for provincial governments.[75]

For university members in general, the combination of high professional standing and provincial council experience could often lead to other kinds of public service. No fewer than 11 university members (16%) also sat on the viceroy's council, the central legislative council or the central legislative assembly, and several others also sat on the provincial governors' executive councils. A considerable number of members also came to hold important leadership posts. Chakravarti Rajagopalachari, who would later form the free-market Swatantra Party, served successively as chief minister for Madras, governor of

---

[71] Bose, *Correspondence*, 234.

[72] Bose, *Correspondence*, 234–5.

[73] The other high court judges were K. Bhashyam (Madras), N.G. Chandarvarkar (Bombay), C.P. Chatterjee (Punjab), V. Krishnaswami Iyer (Madras), T.V. Shesagiri Iyer (Madras) and Asutosh Mookerjee (Calcutta).

[74] C.H. Setalvad (Bombay); Deva Prasad Sarvadhikari (Calcutta); Jogendra Chunder Ghose (Calcutta); Munshi Gajadhar Prasad (Allahabad); Sasanka Kumar Ghosh (Dacca); Fazlur Rahman (Dacca); B.K. Bose (Nagpur); M.K. Gowalkar (Nagpur); D.T. Mangalmurti (Nagpur).

[75] Including P.S. Sivaswami Iyer (Madras), C.P. Ramaswami Iyer (Madras) and Beldeva Sahay (Patna).

West Bengal, the last governor-general of India (succeeding Mountbatten before the post was abolished in 1950), home minister of India and chief minister of Madras State. K.M. Munshi (Bombay) was home minister in the first Congress government of the Bombay legislative assembly, and would later become governor of Uttar Pradesh. B.G. Kher (Bombay) was twice chief minister of Bombay and subsequently high commissioner for India in London. B.C. Roy (Calcutta) became chief minister of West Bengal. C.P. Ramaswami Iyer (Madras) was a long-serving diwan of Travancore who sought a separate independence for his state before ultimately agreeing to accede to India. N.G. Chandarvarkar (Bombay), who had been the first non-official president of the Bombay legislative council, served for a time as prime minister of Indore. T.S. Ramaswami Iyer (Madras) served as mayor of the corporation of Madras, and S. Satyamurti (Madras) as mayor of Chennai.

University members also held important ministries or other notable public posts: Rafi Ahmed Kidwai (United Provinces Universities) became home minister in the United Provinces, and subsequently served independent India as minister for communications and then minister for food and agriculture. Fazlur Rahman (Dacca) served as minister for education, industries and commerce in Pakistan. K. Bhashyam (Madras) was a minister in Madras State. S.M. Hasan (Nagpur) became health minister in the post-independence government of the Central Provinces and Berar. R.P. Paranjpye (Bombay) was Bombay's first minister of education and later India's high commissioner to Australia. Shyamaprasad Mookerjee served as finance minister of Bengal Province in 1941–2, and after independence joined Nehru's government as minister for industry and supply. Sarat Chandra Bose was a member of the interim government as minister for works, mines and powers. D.P. Sarvadhikary (Calcutta) was, among other things, a member of the League of Nations Assembly.

Indian universities seem to have prized academic distinction in their representatives to a greater extent than their British counterparts. Jogendra Chunder Ghose, Tagore professor of law at Calcutta, is most widely known as the editor of Ramohan Roy's works. Ahmad Fazlur Rahman (Dacca) was a noted historian. C.R. Reddy (Madras) was a great scholar of Telugu literature and also taught economics and history. Several members made their mark in mathematics and science. Raghunath Purushottam Paranjpye (Bombay) was professor of mathematics and principal of Fergusson College.[76] Ganesh Prasad (Allahabad), regarded as the father of Indian mathematical research, held chairs at Calcutta and Benares Hindu universities. Zia-ud-din Ahmad (Allahabad) was also a mathematician. Although Asutosh Mookerjee was a lawyer by profession, he also made notable contributions in mathematics in the 1880s and founded the Calcutta Mathematical Society. Seyd Husain Zaheer (United Provinces Universities) became the first director of India's council for scientific and industrial research. Ram Dhar Misra (United Provinces Universities) was head of the mathematics department at Lucknow. Ruchi Ram Sahni (Punjab) became professor of chemistry at Government College, Lahore, and a popular lecturer on scientific subjects.

In addition to the scientists and mathematicians, four representatives were medical doctors. Sir Balchandra Krishna (Bombay) was an expert on leprosy. The medical

---

[76] *Dictionary of National Biography*, ed. S.P. Sen (4 vols, Calcutta, 1972), iii, 212–14; *The Times*, 9 May 1966, p. 14.

educator and one-time member of the Provincial Health Service, Bidhan Chandra Roy (Calcutta), later, as noted above, became the chief minister for West Bengal. Seyd Minhajul Hasan (Nagpur) would become the first post-independence health minister in Central Provinces and Berar, where he succeeded in establishing a medical college in Nagpur.[77] Birenda Nath Mazumder (Dacca) is perhaps best known for his heroism during the Second World War, not least for being the only Indian imprisoned in the notorious German Colditz prison camp. There he endured torture at the hands of the Germans, suffered racism from the British officers and rejected the offer from Subhas Chandra Bose to join the Indian National Army.

A number of university representatives not only received western education in India, but also obtained degrees or other qualifications in Britain. At least eight (12%) studied at English universities, with Cambridge the clear favourite. Among them, A.M. Bose (Calcutta) was the first Indian to be classed as a wrangler. R.P. Paranjpye (Bombay) had an outstanding academic career in India and as a Government of India scholar at St John's College, Cambridge, where he emerged with the supreme distinction of senior wrangler. C.R. Reddy (Madras) was an exhibitioner at St John's, where he obtained a first class in the history tripos and also served as secretary and vice-president of the Union. Zia-ud-din Ahmed (Allahabad) went to Trinity College where he took an honours degree in mathematics, securing first place and honoured with the Sir Isaac Newton scholarship. After obtaining a DSc. in mathematics at Allahabad, Ganesh Prasad went to Cambridge as a Government of India scholar to pursue further studies. Mian Fazl-i-Husain (Punjab) took an MA at Cambridge. Prasanta Kumer Sen (Patna) obtained a first in part I of the moral sciences tripos, though Alfred Marshall, complaining that the exam was too easy, thought him an example of men 'who have got first classes who have not first class minds'.[78] At Oxford, Shadi Lal (Punjab) took top marks in the BCL examination, and Ahmad Fazlur Rahman (Dacca) obtained a BA (Hons) in history.

Several members also received professional training in England. Six (14% of the lawyers; 9% of all university representatives) were called to the Bar at the Inns of Court. Woomesh Chandra Bonnerjee (Calcutta) and Sachchidananda Sinha (Patna) were at the Middle Temple. A.M. Bose, while in the process of becoming the first Indian wrangler at Cambridge, simultaneously studied at the Inner Temple. Sarat Chandra Bose and Shyama Prasad Mookerjee were both called at Lincoln's Inn. Mian Fazl-i-Husain (Punjab) was called at Gray's Inn. The British-educated members also included Bidhan Chandra Roy (Calcutta), who took his medical training at St Bartholemew's Hospital (after overcoming resistance to the admission of an Indian student) and obtained postgraduate qualifications from the Royal College of Physicians and the Royal College of Surgeons. One could also include in this category the scientist Ruchi Ram Sahni (Punjab), who spent a period working in Ernest Rutherford's laboratory.

A sign of the close ties between university representatives, the institutions for which they sat and the academic community generally, 20 (29%) of the members served at some point as university vice-chancellors or rectors. Indeed, some fulfilled that role at more than one university. R.P. Paranjpye was vice-chancellor of two universities: Bombay, and

---

[77] Bobby Srinivas, 'Patriotism Made Easy!', *The Hitavada*, 16 Nov. 2005.

[78] *The Correspondence of Alfred Marshall, Economist, Vol. II: At the Summit, 1891–1902*, ed. John K. Whitaker (Cambridge, 1996), 357.

Lucknow. Sunder Lal was twice vice-chancellor at Allahabad, and later became the first vice-chancellor of Benares Hindu University. P.S. Sivaswami Iyer served as vice-chancellor of both Madras and Benares. C.P. Ramaswami Iyer, vice-chancellor of Annamali University in the 1950s, simultaneously became vice-chancellor of Benares in 1955 at the request of the Government of India.[79]

A good number of Indian university representatives were honoured for their contributions to public life. As David Cannadine has written, the creation of imperial honours was intended to link the British proconsular elite and the native elites of the territories under British rule. In India, it was thought by the British that such marks of distinction were especially valued.[80] But Cannadine's account of Indian honourees deals almost entirely with princes. The honours received by Indian university representatives illustrate how these awards were also distributed among the high-achieving but non-princely professional elites. Fifteen (22%) of the university members were knighted. Several of those knighted had previously received the lower order, the CIE (Companion of the Indian Empire), and a few other members were also so recognized. Five others (three of them also knighted) were designated Rai Bahadur, an honour equivalent to the OBE created by the British for Hindu and Christian Indians who have performed great service to the nation (Muslims and Parsis had a separate honour, Khan Bahadur). At least one university member, Sachchidananda Sinha (Patna), declined the offer of a knighthood as incompatible with his democratic ideals.

It is also important to note that, although university seats had been viewed from before their inception as a means of bringing responsible segments of the Indian population into official representative politics, a total of eight Europeans (12% of all university members) were elected for the universities of Madras and Allahabad. They, too, were accomplished in both the academic and legal realms. All of Madras' European representatives were missionary educators and nearly all were Scottish. Madras' first representative, the Rev. William Miller, principal of Madras Christian College, and later vice-chancellor of Madras University, is said to have 'defended college interests as an unobtrusive member of the legislative assembly'.[81] He was followed by G.H. Stuart, principal and professor of mathematics at Presidency College, Madras; and then by J.B. Bilderbeck (a non-Scot), professor of English and also principal of Presidency College.

This preponderance of Europeans in the early years of Madras' representation was in some senses accidental, especially since European members of the university's senate had a poor record of attendance.[82] In several cases, the Europeans came in as short-term replacements for incumbents who resigned. In the first election to represent the

---

[79] The others are as follows: Zia-ud-din Ahmad, Aligarh Muslim University; Bipin Krishna Bose, Nagpur; Bupendra Nath Bose, Calcutta; Thomas Conlan, Allahabad; Iqbal Narayan Gurtu, Allahabad; M.R. Jayakar, Poona; Earle Monteith Mcphail, Madras; William Miller, Madras; Asutosh Mookerjee, Calcutta (twice); Shayamaprasad Mookerjee, Calcutta; A.F. Rahman, Dacca; C.R. Reddy, Andhra University (twice); Bidhan Chandra Roy, Calcutta; Devaprasad Sarvadhikari, Calcutta; C.H. Setalvad, Bombay; Sachchidananda Sinha, Patna.

[80] David Cannadine, *Ornamentalism: How the British Saw Their Empire* (Oxford, 2001), ch. 7, esp. 88–90.

[81] Gerald Studdert-Kennedy, 'Miller, William (1838–1923)', *Oxford Dictionary of National Biography* (Oxford, 2004), online edn. http://www.oxforddnb.com/view/article/70299 21 Aug. 2008.

[82] The vicissitudes of the university's early representation, summarized in this and the next paragraph, are described in K.C. Markandan, *Madras Legislative Council: Its Constitution and Working between 1891 and 1909* (Delhi, 1965), 58–62; see also University of Madras, *Calendar for 1940–41*, vol. I, pt 1 (Madras, 1940), 103.

university, Miller polled an equal number of votes with an Indian candidate and was elected by the casting vote of the senate president. Roundly criticized for his inactivity, Miller resigned before the completion of his second term. Stuart was opposed by another European, the Indian electors having failed to rally around a single candidate. As director of public instruction, Stuart 'maintained the silence which his official position imposed upon him and gave his vote exactly as a servant of the Government'.[83] The awkwardness of this position eventually led him to resign his university seat, and Miller was reluctantly pressed into service again, including contesting the next election when neither of the candidates was deemed acceptable. Miller left again at the end of 1902 and his term was filled out by Bilderbeck, sitting as an additional official member.

The first Indian representative for Madras, P.S. Sivaswami Iyer, tied in voting with the Rev. Canon Snell, who as the more senior of the two men was given the casting vote by the vice-chancellor. After the result was challenged, the governor requested a new vote and Iyer was returned with a majority, Snell resigning in his favour without having been certified. After Sivaswami Iyer vacated his seat in 1907 on his appointment as advocate-general, Madras was represented by V. Krishnaswami Iyer and then briefly in 1909 by the Rev. Earle Monteith Macphail, who would later become, like Miller, principal of the Madras Christian College and vice-chancellor of the university. Macphail would return to the university seat from 1919 to 1921 when C.P. Ramaswami Iyer became advocate-general. They were preceded by another European, the Rev. George Pittendrigh, from Madras Christian College, who was elected in 1914 and re-elected in 1916.

The conditions under which Europeans were returned to represent the University of Allahabad appear somewhat different. The first representative was a well-known barrister, Walter Mytton Colvin. He was the younger brother of Sir Aukland Colvin, former lieutenant governor of the United Provinces (then called the North-Western Frontier Provinces until 1902), who had strongly criticized moves to include Indians from the professional and commercial classes in local self-government as constituting a threat to the maintenance of British superiority.[84] This may help account for the durability of Europeans in the early years of the University of Allahabad's representation. The younger Colvin was returned for two terms. He was followed by the university's former vice-chancellor, Thomas Conlan, a QC of the Allahabad high court and long-time member of the legislative council, who was re-elected twice before dying at the end of his third term in 1904. The attendance record of Europeans in the United Provinces legislative council was generally quite casual. Colvin and Conlan were more regular in their attendance than other European members, but they tended to remain quiet except on educational matters.[85] Later, the university returned another European, the Rev. A.W. Ward, a professor of mathematics and physics at Canning College, who was elected in 1918 but did not serve a full term.[86]

[83] Markandan, *Madras Legislative Council*, 60.

[84] B.R. Tomlinson, 'Colvin, Sir Auckland (1838–1908)', *Oxford Dictionary of National Biography* (Oxford, 2004), online edn. http://www.oxforddnb.com/view/article/32516 6 Aug. 2009.

[85] John Lowell Hill, 'Congress and Representative Institutions in the United Provinces, 1866–1901', Duke University PhD, 1966, pp. 264, 269–70, 287.

[86] University of Allahabad, *Calendar for the Year 1931* (Allahabad, 1931), 39.

While some university members were far more vocal and active than others, the performance of any member was constrained from the outset by the limited powers that were granted to the legislative councils. Under the 1892 system, the councils could not discuss non-provincial issues, their ability to debate on the budget was curtailed, legislative proposals were firmly directed by provincial and national governments, and the Indian opposition could always be outvoted by official and nominated members.[87] In addition, legislative councils met infrequently, further limiting non-official members' ability to have an impact on matters of substance. In the United Provinces, for instance, the legislative council met only 26 times between 1893 and 1901, an average of three meetings per year.[88]

Matters improved somewhat after 1919, but councils still had no power to enforce their decisions with respect to reserved subjects. In fiscal matters, councils could refuse or reduce items in the budget, but the governor was at liberty to restore them. On the other hand, the introduction of representative bodies and electoral politics under British rule, however gradual, selective and complex those processes were, came to play an important, and arguably definitive, role in shaping the particular characteristics of Indian democracy.[89] This was as true of representatives of universities as it was for those who sat in other constituencies. In spite of the structural limitations on provincial councils, the universities clearly returned people of capability whose subsequent records suggest that the experience was valuable for their formation as effective politicians.

5. *Conclusion*

In an article analysing the 1946 provincial legislative elections, the former Indian civil servant, F.O. Bell (who had served as district magistrate of Dacca during the elections, and thus *ex officio* returning officer for several constituencies), declared that his account would consider only the territorial constituencies, since 'the others are not constituencies of a mass democracy'.[90] University constituencies were, of course, among those that Bell dismissed, and his characterisation of such seats – written in the year that their abolition in Britain was secured by the Attlee government – was fully consistent with the main 20th-century British criticism of university representation as inconsistent with democracy. At a certain level, the histories of university representation in India and in the United Kingdom seem to follow the same general pattern. This suggests a common set of conditions that favoured the introduction of university seats. In both places, the growth of university representation in the later 19th and early 20th centuries resulted from contemporaneous processes of political reform and the extension of higher education.

These two processes were connected in the sense that university education was in one way or another seen to qualify its recipients as one form of 'capable citizenry' who could be considered for full political inclusion (though not, of course, extending to women

---

[87] Hill, 'Congress and Representative Institutions in the United Provinces', 318.

[88] Hill, 'Congress and Representative Institutions in the United Provinces', 285.

[89] Chiriyankandath, ' "Democracy" under the Raj', 40.

[90] F.O. Bell, 'Parliamentary Elections in Indian Provinces', *Parliamentary Affairs*, i (1948), 22.

until later). Just as the expansion of university representation in Britain was tied to the extension of the franchise downward on the social scale and the creation of a mass electorate, the impetus to establish university representation in India was explicitly tied to the gradual inclusion of Indians in new representative bodies.

It is also true that certain gross parallels of purpose underlay the extension of higher education in India and the United Kingdom in the later 19th and early 20th centuries. The new Indian universities were established within roughly the same time frame as the new universities in the English provinces, Ireland and Wales. In both locations, the motivations for creating these institutions stemmed from the perceived, and closely related, needs for a more highly skilled workforce and for imposing control over educational provision and standards. In Britain, questions of workforce needs and educational control tended to focus on scientific and technical knowledge, usually tied to regional industries. (The effective regulation of medical training had already been largely accomplished by the University of London.) In India, although scientific and technical training was not neglected, the universities' primary mission was to create 'native' administrative staff who could successfully operate within the systems of imperial governance and serve as the intermediaries between the ruling British and the mass of Indians that Macaulay and others who followed had called for.

In India as in Britain, opinions about the utility of university representation also came to be sharply divided. In both places, arguments in favour of university representation involved both the importance of incorporating learning into the political structure, and the role that a special university electorate could play in adding an element of stability within the widening scope of political participation. In one way or another, those opposed argued that university representation was at odds with representative advances. In India as in Britain, however, the political will to scrap the institution entirely was never adequately summoned up.

Although these generalized similarities reflect in interesting ways on how some kinds of political questions and developments were worked out in both metropole and empire simultaneously rather than sequentially, there are considerable differences between the British and Indian cases that are even more revealing. The modern growth of university representation in Britain as an adjunct to constitutional reform and a counterbalance to increasing democratisation provided a model to the Government of India when grappling with its own issues surrounding the extension of political rights. In the context of imperial rule, university representation was an established model available to those contemplating constitutional matters both at 'home' and in the empire – although conditions in India were almost unique in this respect. Once established in India, university representation in its colonial and metropolitan settings developed for the most part in parallel, though converging at points as British politicians (including university representatives) deliberated over successive measures for Indian political development.

The establishment of university constituencies in India was not simply a slavish imitation of Britain's constitutional peculiarity. In both countries, university representation responded to specific practical political concerns which may have resembled each other at some general level, but were different in both substance and implication. If university seats were a political mechanism that afforded some measure of reassurance when broadening the bases of formal political participation, the readiness with which Indian universities were incorporated into representative structures, even in cases where the institutions had not yet been established, demonstrates not the enthusiasm for university representation among those concerned with the administration of India, but rather their sense of the daunting rapidity and scale of introducing political reforms in the subcontinent. In this light, it is ironic to consider that both the 1914 review of Bombay University chaired by Manchester's vice-chancellor, Sir Alfred Hopkinson, and the 1917–19 Calcutta University commission chaired by Leeds' vice-chancellor, Sir Michael Sadler, reported on Indian universities that enjoyed a form of legislative representation at a time when the two northern English universities were as yet unrepresented.

University constituencies in India were established along with several other special franchises, and the number of distinctive electorates grew as the British administration attempted to balance or manage various social groups while expanding political partici-pation. In Britain, the process was largely the opposite. Although the gradual widening of political inclusion through successive reform acts was generally conceived of in terms of different social groups, there was also a simultaneous winnowing of older special franchises until the university and business owners' franchises were the only ones that remained. Unlike Britain, too, where universities were the only special franchise to return separate MPs, in India, each of the various constituencies represented on provincial councils elected their own designated members. At the level of legislative structures, therefore, the comparative position of university representation highlights the extent to which the widening of political inclusion in Britain proceeded along a largely integrative path, whereas the process in India was one of disaggregation and fracture.

Besides the multiplication of special constituencies, it should also be remembered that each legislative council had only one university seat, except for Bengal which had two. As university seats were created between 1892 and 1919, they were distributed among separate councils, rather than creating a larger body of members from similar constitu-encies as occurred at Westminster. In Britain, the number of university seats grew while the size of the house of commons remained roughly stable. In India, however, successive reforms enlarged the membership of the provincial councils to an extent that virtually swallowed up the university seats. In 1919, the seven provincial legislatures with univer-sity seats had a total of 779 members. After 1935, these provincial legislatures had a total of 1,307 seats.[91] Thus, where the eight university seats made up 1% of the total provincial council representation in 1919, comparable to the proportion of university seats in the house of commons from 1832 to 1867, by the 1937 general election, university seats made up only 0.6% of the total. The dilution of Indian university representation is even greater when compared to the total membership of all provincial councils (which grew in size and number between 1919 and 1935).

Finally there is the question of the basis of the electorate itself. The movement in Britain was to make the franchise less restrictive – from the original formulation under which only holders of MAs and higher degrees could vote, to the opening of the university electorates to all degree holders immediately after graduation. The only major controversy in the latter stage was whether it was appropriate and fair to require graduates to pay a modest fee for registration on the electoral rolls. In India, however, the question of the electorates was considerably more fraught. Whereas supporters of

---

[91] Figures from tables in Chiriyankandath, ' "Democracy" under the Raj', 45, 52.

university representation in Britain argued that a special franchise for graduates served as a helpful brake on democratisation, in India enfranchisement of graduates came to be viewed in the opposite way, as adding to the less reliable segments of the electorate since the university-educated class provided much of the leadership for those opposed to British rule. Thus, where the idea of the representation of learning in Britain shifted from focusing on the institutions to the graduate voters, in India it was argued that the representation of learning should attach not to the graduates but to the universities as institutions. The debate over the extent to which the university electorate should include graduates is a clear indication that the educational and political situation had developed well past the point of achieving Macaulay's co-opted, British-cultured, Indian intermediary elite.

Chapter 6. Imperial Comparisons

Outside the United Kingdom (including for these purposes Ireland), university representation came into being in a continuous and durable form in only 18th-century Virginia and early 20th-century India. But the idea of university representation was also actively discussed, and even in some cases implemented, in 19th-century Canada, Australasia and the Mediterranean. (The reasons why university representation did not appear in the other major zones of empire, Africa and the West Indies, are considered at the end of the chapter.) To the very limited extent that other scholars have taken account of these far-flung extensions of university representation, they have treated the cases in isolation rather than looking more broadly at the ways in which they were connected to related developments in Britain and across the empire.[1] Yet, the histories of university representation's more marginal instantiations constitute a necessary complement to, and reflect in important ways on, those of the more durable ones.

The significance of university representation as a trans-imperial phenomenon is more than simply the regularity with which it appeared over time and across the changing contours of the British empire from the beginning of the 17th century to the middle of the 20th century. It is also more than simply a distinctive part of a larger story about the colonial adaptation of Westminster parliamentary models and the evolving place of learning within colonial polities. For just as close study of university representation opens up new perspectives on significant constitutional and political processes in the United Kingdom, and on the methods and motivations of British rule in India, the ways that the idea of university representation played across the wider imperial ambit affords a rare opportunity to examine developing conceptions and practices of representation on a comparative basis across the broad range of the empire.

1. *Canada*

Following the independence of the 13 American colonies, of which the College of William and Mary's seat in the Virginia legislature was one casualty, the next effort to establish university representation on the continent occurred in Upper Canada (present-day Ontario). Interest in establishing a fully fledged university there dated back to the 1790s, but it took until 1827 for King's College (which would eventually become the University of Toronto in 1850) to be established by a royal charter granting it 'the style and privileges of an University'.[2] Self-government in Upper Canada was very limited in this period, and although the case for a university was pressed by some of the colony's

---

[1] The same holds true for studies of the establishment of universities in British settler societies generally. But see Stuart Macintyre's suggestive essay, 'The Same under Different Skies: The University in the United States and Australia', *Journal of Australian Studies*, xxxiii (2009), 353–69.

[2] J. George Hodgins, *Documentary History of Education in Upper Canada, Vol. I: 1790–1830* (Toronto, 1894), 222.

leading figures, London resisted the idea for some time. Locally, questions over the nature and purpose of the proposed university became major bones of contention between the colony's conservative anglican elite and its growing body of radical dissenting reformers.[3]

As would become the pattern elsewhere in the settler colonies, colonists' cultural ambitions, in the form of nascent higher education institutions, were entwined with the evolution of legislative structures. In 1819, while the Colonial Office was still resisting the idea of creating a university, the lieutenant governor, Sir Peregrine Maitland, recommended that Upper Canada's legislature consider, as part of a plan for increasing representation in the house of assembly, 'the propriety of providing for a distinct representation of the contemplated University, when founded, in conformity with the established practice in the mother country'.[4] Maitland was concerned to maintain Upper Canada as a loyal colony and to that end sought to suppress both radicalism and American influence. Accordingly, just as a university would serve as a bulwark of loyalism (lest colonists start finding their best options for higher education in the United States), its representation in the legislature would be a mainstay of conservative politics.

In accordance with Maitland's recommendation, members of the legislature acted to lay the necessary groundwork. In 1819, after the legislative assembly had passed the third reading of a bill to extend representation to certain new settlements, Robert Nichol, a leading opposition figure, moved a rider that 'whenever an University shall be established in the Province', the government should declare it 'to be a Town or Township [and] so constituted shall be represented by one Member' with an electorate consisting of those entitled to vote in convocation. Nichol's rider was defeated, but when the bill was sent up to the legislative council, his language was restored and sent back to the Assembly. The two Houses appointed conference committees, but there is no record that they ever met. The legislature was prorogued shortly thereafter, so the bill did not pass.[5]

The question of a seat for the university was taken up once again in the following year. A new bill to increase the representation of the commons in the provincial parliament was introduced in February 1820, repeating the language of the 1819 clause providing for the addition of one member of the Assembly to represent the university after it was established. The Commons and University Representation Bill, as it came to be known, moved rapidly through its second reading and committee stage. At the third reading, however, the university portion of the Bill was challenged by a motion 'that so much of the Bill as provides for the representation of a University be expunged'. But, where Nichol's rider had been voted down the year before, this time the idea of a university seat was upheld when the motion to expunge it was defeated. The bill was then sent to the legislative council and, following its favourable vote, was enacted.[6]

Seven years after the principle of university representation was established in law, King's College received its royal charter. Notwithstanding the 1820 legislation, the 1827

---

[3] Fred D. Schneider, 'The Imperial Factor and the "University Question" in Upper Canada', *Journal of British Studies*, xvii (1977), 82–104.

[4] Hodgins, *Documentary History*, 138. A full history of the idea of university representation in Canada may be found in Thomas Hodgins, 'A Member of Parliament for the University', *Canadian Magazine*, v (1895), 115–21.

[5] Hodgins, *Documentary History*, 138–42. *Journals of the Legislative Assembly of Upper Canada for the Years 1818, 1819, 1820, 1821*, Tenth Report of the Bureau of Archives for the Province of Ontario (Toronto, 1913), 168.

[6] Hodgins, *Documentary History*, 169–74. *The Journals of the Legislative Assembly of Upper Canada for the Years 1818, 1819, 1820, 1821*, 233.

charter for King's College did not, like William and Mary's charter, make explicit reference to the college's right to return a member to the Assembly. The charter only specified that King's College 'shall be deemed and taken to be an University' and that it and its convocation should enjoy all the same privileges as its counterparts in the United Kingdom.[7] No sooner had the charter been granted than the entire constitutionality of the 1820 Act which had promised King's College future representation came under sharp criticism from a committee of the Assembly, in which the Reform Party obtained a majority in 1928. Even more problematic for the university's future, however, was the public hostility to the charter's insistence that the university be an anglican establishment. Although the charter, drafted by the anglican clergyman (later first bishop of Toronto) John Strachan, required no religious tests for matriculation or degrees other than in divinity, this liberality was perceived to be vitiated by provisions that the Visitor was to be the anglican archbishop, the president was to be an anglican clergyman in holy orders and the council was to consist of members who subscribed to the Thirty-Nine Articles.

In the 17th and 18th centuries, the connection that Oxford, Cambridge, Trinity College Dublin, and William and Mary had with the Established Church was an important factor in their gaining representation. In 19th-century Canada, however, protests against the charter for King's College were connected with the more general Radical critique of elite anglican privilege. The weakening ties between church and state in Britain were evident in the greater recognition that barriers against religious plurality were counterproductive, as manifested in Britain's removal of disabilities against nonconformists in 1828 and catholics in 1829 as well as the founding of the explicitly secular University College London in 1826. As one Canadian appeal to the crown from the early 1830s complained – in much the same terms as contemporaneous critics in Britain who saw university seats as tantamount to a form of clerical representation – the grant of legislative representation to King's College meant the establishment of 'a nomination borough under the especial patronage of the Church and State'. In response, the colonial secretary, Lord Goderich, countered with the positive argument that university seats existed for the representation of learning broadly. He wrote that he 'could scarcely believe that any man, and, least of all, a man devoted to literary pursuits, would have denied the propriety of giving a representation to the principal seat of learning in the Province'.[8] At the same time, he was careful to distance his remarks from the proposed university constitution. The heated debates over the university's religious affiliation delayed its opening until 1837 after the sectarian clauses were finally eliminated.

This delay may well have prevented university representation, though enacted in principle, from becoming a reality in Canada. By the time King's College was formally inaugurated in 1842, the provinces of Upper and Lower Canada had been joined by the Union Act of 1840. In 1840, the university council had passed a resolution requesting that the lieutenant governor give effect to the 1820 Act and declare the university to be an electoral district once it was fully operational. But no action appears to have been

---

[7] The charter is printed as an appendix in *The Universities of Canada: Their History and Organization with an Outline of British and American University Systems: Appendix to the Report of the Minister of Education, 1896* (Toronto, 1896), 363–71.

[8] Quoted in Hodgins, 'A Member of Parliament', 119.

taken in response to the resolution. Although the 1840 Union Act and the subsequent 1853 Representation Act could be read to have allowed for the creation of a university constituency, the 1820 Act that had authorised university representation in the first place was explicitly repealed in 1859 when the statutes of Upper and Lower Canada were consolidated.

Although university representation existed on the books in Canada, it was ultimately easy to remove because reforming legislation never had to do away with established university seats or contend with the associated arguments about the virtues and contributions of university members. Nor was there a vocal constituency of graduates reluctant to lose their special franchise. In contrast, reform proposals in Britain around this time recognized the claims of London and the Scottish universities (backed by strong shows of support from their graduates) to take their place in parliament alongside Oxford, Cambridge and Dublin. In making provision for university representation before a university had actually been established – a phenomenon later replicated in Australia and India – the case of Upper Canada took the conservative colonial politics of university representation that had been already evident in Ireland and Virginia to a new and anticipatory level.

In a different key, when university representation in Britain became more embattled, some Canadian writers remarked wistfully on the value that university representation might bring to the Dominion's legislature. Concluding his 1895 account of Toronto's abortive representation, one author wrote that, apart from following the precedent of the imperial parliament in granting representation to universities, 'it will be conceded that the election to Parliament of University men, who have also the necessary political sagacity, would aid in producing Canadian statesmen of higher qualifications; in elevating the standard of public duty, and in infusing a purer political morality and a higher courtesy into our Parliamentary and national life'.[9] Another writer, reflecting on the 1917 report of the Speaker's Conference in Britain which proposed expanding the number of university seats to cover all such institutions, opined:

> How valuable might the new blood be, which University representation would introduce into our Dominion and provincial legislatures. And there should be the less objection seeing how thoroughly democratic in character Canadian Universities are. Why will not some Canadian politician qualify as a statesman by bringing in a bill in one of our numerous legislatures to introduce, in some measure, at any rate, the principle of University representation into Canada.[10]

2. Australasia

Around the same time that university representation was purged from the statutes in Canada and the case for enlarging it was being advanced in Britain, the processes of building legislatures and planting the seeds of higher education in the Australasian colonies spurred debates over whether the new universities should have a place in the

---

[9] Hodgins, 'A Member of Parliament', 121.

[10] [Anon.], 'By the Way', *The Canadian Law Times*, xxxvii (1917), 262.

new colonial parliaments. Nearly 40 years after Upper Canada adopted the principle of university representation, New South Wales followed suit. Indeed, uniquely among Australasian institutions, the University of Sydney even obtained a parliamentary seat, albeit for only a brief period. Similar, though ultimately unsuccessful, campaigns were also mounted to establish university seats in Victoria, Queensland and New Zealand.

As had been the case in Canada, the move to create a university in New South Wales was deeply intertwined with the interests of the conservative elite in building political and social institutions that would serve as a check on the advance of more democratic ideas.[11] Political dynamics in the settler colony were connected to the currents emanating from Britain and Europe. Where the Canadian situation was marked by the influence of post-revolutionary radicalism and the reform movement, conservative politicians in New South Wales (which was still adjusting to a free labour economy after ceasing to be a penal colony in 1840) were concerned about the inspiration their opposition drew from the democratic revolutions on the continent and the last revival of chartism in Britain. Led by William Charles Wentworth, these conservatives sought to establish self-government on terms that would contain democracy. Creating a university – even though presented as a secular institution for the public good – was pursued with the same objective in mind.

Wentworth proposed establishing a university in 1849 and the colony's narrowly based legislative council voted in favour the following year. The University of Sydney duly opened in 1852, the same year that the select committee chaired by Wentworth began preparing what would ultimately become the colony's constitution. The conservatives' vision of the university as an instrument for facilitating elite self-perpetuation brought the new institution into conflict with the rising and democratically minded liberals. Unlike the case of Upper Canada, however, the conflict was not bound up with questions of church and state. True, Wentworth had conceded to religious interests four places for clergy on the university's governing council. But following the abolition of the church of England's special privileges in 1836, and the subsequent provision of public funds for catholic and presbyterian churches, the principle of equal recognition for all churches was well established in New South Wales and accepted by the university's founders.

The conservatives associated with establishing the university set their sights on returning a member to the legislative council virtually from the outset. As the university senate recognized, the constitution-making process then under way presented an opportunity to secure representation. It passed a resolution:

> That a formal request should be made on behalf of the Senate to the Hon[ble] and learned Member for [the city of] Sydney [Wentworth] to add the University of Sydney to the constituencies to be proposed in his Bill, and that the Vice Provost be accordingly authorized to make such a request and to take any further measures which may be conducive to the attainment of the desired privilege.[12]

---

[11] The political background of Sydney's founding is described in greater detail in W.J. Gardner, *Colonial Cap and Gown: Studies in the Mid-Victorian Universities of Australasia* (Christchurch, NZ, 1979), 12–18; and in J.B. Hirst, *The Strange Birth of Colonial Democracy: New South Wales, 1848–1884* (Sydney, 1988), 9–11, 182–4.

[12] Univ. of Sydney Archives: Minutes of the Senate, 1851–7, 4 Apr. 1853.

The vice-provost, Sir Charles Nicholson, duly wrote to Wentworth,[13] but the July 1853 report of the select committee to prepare a constitution did not include any provisions for a university constituency.

As well as being a logical extension of the conservative aims that lay behind its creation, the university's quest for parliamentary representation was consistent with its assertive drive to acquire in short order all the privileges that university status entailed in the United Kingdom. In February 1858, Sydney was granted a royal charter following an unprecedented application from the senate to the privy council requesting that the university's degrees, not simply its corporate standing, be declared equal in status throughout the empire to that of universities in Britain.[14] Meanwhile, although London and the Scottish universities had been seeking representation for some time, only the most august universities of the empire – Oxford, Cambridge and Dublin – as yet had the privilege of returning members to parliament. While Virginia and more recently Canada afforded precedents for university representation in colonial legislatures, their example is not mentioned in any of the extant documents associated with Sydney's efforts.

In the same year that Sydney's charter was granted, manhood suffrage was introduced for elections to the recently established lower House of New South Wales' parliament. In addition, the 1858 Electoral Act provided for the creation of an extra seat for the university once there were 100 graduates who had taken the degrees of Master of Arts, Doctor of Laws or Doctor of Medicine.[15] The electorate, which would enjoy a plural vote, was to consist of the members of the senate, the faculty and holders of higher degrees. The Electoral Act had also created a special franchise for miners and businessmen in designated goldfields. But unlike the university vote, those covered by this provision could only cast ballots in either their goldfield or their residential district. Thus, the university franchise was doubly special.

There is evidence that university officials kept careful count of the number of eligible graduates in order to claim the privilege of returning a member at the first possible opportunity.[16] Yet, it took 18 years to reach the minimum threshold. Notwithstanding Sydney's early burst of energy in establishing itself and the privileges of its graduates, the university made very slow progress in actually educating students. By 1876 Sydney had awarded only 183 BA degrees. Of those graduates, 109 received MAs, which led to claims that the MA examinations in these years were merely nominal in order to get up to the electoral requirement (the number of doctorates in medicine and law being very small in this period).[17] If there is truth to the allegation, it serves as an instance of how the ambition to obtain representation affected the university's academic policies and standards.

When the requisite number of qualifying graduates was finally reached in mid 1876, a deputation was dispatched to the governor, Sir Hercules Robinson, to request that he

[13] Univ. of Sydney Archives: Minutes of the Senate, 1851–7, 2 May 1853.

[14] Clifford Turney, Ursula Bygott and Peter Chippendale, *Australia's First: A History of the University of Sydney, Volume 1: 1850–1939* (Sydney, 1991), 111–12.

[15] Electoral Act of 1858, 22 Vict. No. 20. See also *A Copy of the Electoral Bill Passed by the Legislature of New South Wales*, 2, 4, Parliamentary Papers, 1859, Session 1 (211), xvii, 343.

[16] Univ. of Sydney Archives: Minutes of the Senate, May 1871–Sept. 1878, 3 May 1876.

[17] Peter Chippendale, 'Members for the University: The University Constituency, 1858–1880', [Univ. of Sydney Archives] *Record* (2003), 7.

issue a writ for the return of a member (duly issued two weeks later).[18] Around the same time, the university's senate had been engaged in a discussion of the duties and responsibilities that should be associated with professorial rank. In advance of the scheduled election in September, the senate passed a by-law prohibiting professors from accepting seats in parliament.[19] The minutes do not indicate whether this measure stemmed from concerns about inordinate politicisation of academic life, or it merely reflected the senate's more general view that professors should not engage in teaching or business activities outside the university. (As noted below, a similar measure had been passed by the senate of Melbourne University in 1859, although this was in response to the actions of a particular faculty member. The issue resurfaced there in 1876.)

After its long wait, Sydney enjoyed university representation for only four years. In 1880, a new electoral act abolished the university's seat as part of a major redistribution of constituency boundaries.[20] It is impossible to say whether, if Sydney had developed more rapidly and reached the threshold number of graduates sooner, a longer record of representation in the legislature might have led more people to think that the university seat had value and should be retained. Certainly, appeals to the traditions of the mother country could not compensate for brevity of experience in New South Wales.

With respect to the value of the university seat, however, it is interesting to observe that, in contrast to the habitual complaints in Britain at this time about the general inadequacy of university members, both of the two men who sat for Sydney ultimately rose to the highest levels of young Australia's public life. William Charles Windeyer served as the New South Wales attorney-general until he was appointed to the colony's supreme court in 1879. In the 1880s, he also served as the university's vice-chancellor. Windeyer, who had become a member of the New South Wales legislature at an early age and enjoyed considerable success, had from the outset 'looked forward to the time when he would appeal to the electors of the University'.[21] Ironically, his high profile may have contributed to the vulnerability of his seat. During the debates over the Electoral Bill of 1877, one report noted in connection with efforts to remove the university constituency: 'As the present Attorney-General is the member for the University, the Opposition take a special delight in destroying his constituency'.[22]

The second occupant of the Sydney University seat, Edmund Barton, was also a distinguished figure in the history of New South Wales and of Australia. Barton had challenged Windeyer in 1876 and 1877 and lost by very small margins. He was finally returned in the 1879 by-election following Windeyer's elevation to the bench. Barton would become a leading figure in the federation movement and subsequently served as the Australian Commonwealth's first prime minister before taking a seat on the high court.[23]

[18] Univ. of Sydney Archives: Minutes of the Senate, May 1871–Sept. 1878, 5 July 1876.

[19] Univ. of Sydney Archives: Minutes of the Senate, May 1871–Sept. 1878, 6 Sept. 1876.

[20] On the debate over abolition of the university seat, see Marian Simms, *From the Hustings to Harbour Views: Electoral Institutions in New South Wales, 1856–2006* (Sydney, 2006), 27–8.

[21] Univ. of Sydney Archives, Personal Archives of W.C. Windeyer, P1: W.C. Windeyer, *Address to the Electors of the University of Sydney, Delivered at a Public Meeting of Electors Held August 18th, 1876* (Sydney, 1876), 16.

[22] *Argus*, 11 Aug. 1877, p. 5.

[23] H.E. Barff, *A Short Historical Account of the University of Sydney* (Sydney, 1902), 87–8; A.W. Martin and P. Wardle, *Members of the Legislative Assembly of New South Wales, 1856–1901* (Canberra, 1959), 11, 230–1.

Although Sydney's brief representation was embattled, its elimination was not a foregone conclusion. Indeed, the 1880 bill for electoral reform had not originally proposed to abolish the university seat. As the Liberal premier Sir Henry Parkes said, the bill sought 'to take the law as it stood, with the single exception of the Gold-fields, which were omitted as in former bills because it was a well-known fact that the diggers were on the ordinary electoral rolls of the colony'.[24] By that time, the qualifications for suffrage were very low and the population on the goldfields had declined markedly.[25] When questioned on the matter, Parkes allowed that the university vote was anomalous, but thought it a 'hard case' to remove it after it had been granted in principle for so many years and only recently become activated. But he left the matter open, and the proposal to eliminate special representation for the goldfields gave opponents of the university graduates' plural vote the opportunity to decry what they saw as a class-based and undemocratic institution. Critics also brought up the narrowness of the franchise, the fact that university electors could all vote elsewhere, and the 'slavish and wretched imitation of England'. In addition, opponents claimed that the university itself was immature, inadequate and suffering in public esteem.

The attacks on university representation in New South Wales were apparently consistent with the views of the general electorate. According to one report, 'There is no doubt that the general tone of public feeling is against University representation, which only finds its advocate among those who are believers in the virtues of culture'.[26] But as this claim of the critics' philistinism suggests, university representation was not wholly without its defenders. In August 1879, a leader in the *Sydney Daily Telegraph* had defended it at some length in terms familiar to proponents in the United Kingdom. In particular, the paper emphasized the idea that university members should be in theory more knowledgeable and less subject to the pull of popular sentiments, and that they represented a colony-wide electorate. Of more local salience was the perceived need among the 'true friends of Constitutional Government' for the rumbustious colonial parliament to be tempered by the representation of learning during a critical period of political development.[27] In the debates over the electoral bill, Barton sought to overcome the critics, citing among other things the precedent of the British reform bills that had extended university representation, and also promising to introduce a bill to broaden the university franchise to include all graduates. In the end, however, Barton and a very small number of allies failed to turn the tide.

In the neighbouring colony of Victoria, which formally separated from New South Wales in 1851, representation for the University of Melbourne never quite materialised, though not for want of effort. In a newly independent colony, flush with funds from the gold rush, and eager to establish its capital city as a first-rate colonial metropolis fully equal to Sydney, Melbourne's leading citizens and cultured political elite readily agreed

---

[24] My discussion of the 1879–80 debates over university representation is drawn from the *Sydney Morning Herald*, 16 Apr. 1880, p. 3, 30 Apr. 1880, p. 3, 18 June 1880, p. 3. See also Chippendale, 'Members for the University', 10–12.

[25] Hirst, *Strange Birth of Colonial Democracy*, 100–2, 162.

[26] *Argus*, 11 Aug. 1877, p. 5.

[27] Univ. of Sydney Archives, Personal Archives of W.C. Windeyer, P1/17/2: Clipping from the *Sydney Daily Telegraph*, 19 Aug. 1879.

in 1853 on the need for a university, which was established in 1855.[28] Although both nominated and elected elements of Victoria's legislative council were enlarged in 1853 and 1855, there appears to have been no view at that time towards creating a special constituency for the university. The 1855 Victorian constitution established a bicameral parliament, which was inaugurated in 1856.[29] Although initially there was a property qualification for the lower House electorate, this was quickly dropped in favour of manhood suffrage beginning in 1857. Unlike New South Wales at the same time, there was no additional provision for establishing a university seat. But the example of Sydney, as well as that of universities in the United Kingdom, was hardly lost on Melbourne.

Redmond Barry, the university's staunchly tory and autocratic chancellor, as well as the force behind the creation of many of Melbourne's civic institutions, conceived of a special franchise for graduates as an important part of his high-minded ambitions for the institution.[30] In this, he was no doubt influenced in part by the example of his own colonial university, Trinity College Dublin. The University of Melbourne made three unsuccessful attempts to gain a seat. Two occurred in 1858, when the Victorian parliament was considering a bill to increase the number of members. The timing of this bill coincided with the university's efforts to obtain letters patent (like those granted to Sydney) 'declaring that persons admitted to such degrees may be admitted in the United Kingdom and in the Colonies to equal rank and precedence with the Graduate of any University of the United Kingdom'.[31] As already observed in the case of Sydney, obtaining equal privileges for graduates was seen to include the privilege of returning members to the legislature.

Accordingly, the university's council asked the vice-chancellor, William Clark Haines, who had just vacated the colony's premiership, to try and arrange for the university to get the franchise when it had 100 higher degree graduates. In April 1858, Haines introduced a clause to this effect in the legislative assembly. Haines said he thought 'that there was a very general desire to follow the practice of the Imperial Legislature in this respect by the direct representation of intelligence in that House'. At this point, the new premier, John O'Shanassy, interjected 'No!' Haines, for his part, approached the matter with great diffidence. He simply introduced the clause for university representation and, when it was contested, said that although he was indisposed to withdraw the clause so that he would not appear lukewarm to the interests of the university, he also had no desire to detain the House with any lengthened debate. Opponents argued that it was premature to consider creating a seat for the university, and lacking any strong advocacy from Haines, the clause was rejected without a division.[32]

The *Argus*, the conservative newspaper that would be a consistent supporter of university representation, deplored Haines' 'indisposition to press on a discussion of the merits of his clause' and failure to respond to the objections, which the paper thought

---

[28] For the political background, see Gardner, *Colonial Cap and Gown*, 18–26.

[29] For the early history of Victoria's legislature and franchise arrangements, I have drawn upon Raymond Wright, *A People's Counsel: A History of the Parliament of Victoria, 1856–1900* (Melbourne, 1992), and Kathleen Thompson and Geoffrey Serle, *A Biographical Register of the Victorian Parliament, 1859–1900* (Canberra, 1972).

[30] Ernest Scott, *A History of the University of Melbourne* (Melbourne, 1936), 106–7.

[31] Univ. of Melbourne Archives: Minutes of Council, 26 July 1858; see also Minutes of Council, 17 May 1858.

[32] *Argus*, 23 Apr. 1858, p. 5.

weak. (The liberal-leaning and more influential *Age*, on the other hand, took a more critical view of the university in general.) In a leader, the *Argus* sought to make up for Haines' perceived shortcomings and put forward its own case for giving Melbourne a seat: 'The University sustains more important relations to the educational systems of the colony, and to the spread of intelligence amongst the masses of the people than there seemed any disposition to recognize, or than can be measured by the number of its actual students and graduates'.[33] For its part, the university's council tersely paid 'a passing compliment to Mr Haines' in its annual report, and expressed 'a hope that on a future occasion the claims of the academic body will be deemed entitled to greater consideration'.[34]

The second effort occurred in November, during the third reading of the Electoral Districts Alteration Bill. Colin Campbell, an early supporter of establishing a university and a member of its council, moved the addition of a clause that, this time, would give a member to the university when it had 200 graduates. He argued that, since the constitution of the country was about to be settled, 'the colony should follow the course that had been pursued in the mother country'. The right of returning a member to the assembly, he argued, would not merely be a 'grateful acknowledgement of the intellect and learning of a noble institution', but (as Walter Buchanan had argued the year before on behalf of the Scottish universities) would also have a beneficial effect on the university by encouraging more Victorians to send their sons there.[35]

An 'animated discussion' followed. Members objected to altering the population basis of representation, as well as to establishing plural voting for an already privileged population. One member thought it wrong to increase the number of members at the very last moment. The partisan character of university constituencies was another cause for objection: 'So far from believing that the member for the University would not be a party member, he believed, from what they saw in England, that he would be nothing else'. In refutation, another member noted the less exclusive and less party-spirited character of the Scottish universities. Campbell, having already proposed doubling the threshold of graduates, was also willing to do away with plural voting and deprive university voters of all other franchises (as would be attempted in Britain several times during the early 20th century). Although Campbell said he was convinced that the mind of the House was with him, his motion was defeated by 16 votes to nine.[36]

When the Bill went up to the legislative council in December, Thomas T. A'Beckett, also a member of the university's council, reintroduced the 100-graduates version of the clause to give the university a representative. A'Beckett, like Campbell, showed more spirit than Haines had done in the previous attempt. He argued that representation on the basis of population placed the educated on the same level as the wholly uneducated. Other members of the legislative council objected on principle to the proposal of a clause that had been decisively rejected in the assembly. One member suggested that, long before the university had produced a hundred higher degree graduates, there would be another bill to increase the size of the legislature. Another member thought

---

[33] *Argus*, 23 Apr. 1858, p. 4. An even stronger criticism of Haines appears on 20 Oct. 1858, p. 4.

[34] *Argus*, 23 Nov. 1858, p. 7.

[35] *Argus*, 13 Nov. 1858, p. 6.

[36] *Argus*, 13 Nov. 1858, pp. 4, 6.

introducing a political element would be injurious to the university and also claimed erroneously that university representation in England was only instituted to give residential college fellows the vote.[37]

Again, the clause was rejected without a division, and again the *Argus* lamented the legislative council's failure to 'secure a constituency of the best possible kind, and in behalf of which the most zealous democrat might well make an exception to his favorite rule'. Looking to the English precedent, the paper listed the great occupants of university seats, and pointed out that Britain's abortive reform bills of the 1850s carried provisions to give members to the universities that were still unrepresented. With respect to Victoria, the *Argus* asserted, the university was a great national institution, and regretted that amid so much discussion of representing the urban, agricultural and mining interests, the representation of learning should go unheeded.[38]

The university, for its part, was very unhappy about the outcome, as recorded (at some length) in the council's annual report to the governor:

> The failure has been to the Council an occasion of particular concern inasmuch as having so frequently to acknowledge the liberality of the Parliament they had hoped to find conceded to the University a recognised political position similar to that so long enjoyed by the University of the mother country and to that recently granted to their University by the Parliament of New South Wales and also because from the graceful concession of such a privilege they had expected much good to flow as it would have sustained the connection with the University of her graduates, prevented that severance of them from her which now when their education is terminated must take place, have further enlisted the sympathies of the public in the welfare of the University and permitted the representation of the elements of Literature and Science to take a share in the deliberation for the good government of the country.[39]

This lament not only reiterated Barry's case for university representation but also distils all the reasons a new colonial university might seek to emulate the privilege bestowed upon the great universities of the mother country: a mark of full university standing, parity with the neighbouring (rival) university, strengthening the graduates' institutional ties and protecting the interests of the university (and of learning and culture more generally) from a colonial population that may not appreciate the utility of higher learning. Conservatives feared the consequences of introducing manhood suffrage for elections to the lower House, and the council (which had a very restrictive franchise) was already blocking democratic measures emanating from the assembly. In this context, the concerns about the tyranny of the majority that were being aired in the pages of the *Argus* dovetailed with Barry's vision of the university as a bulwark of social hierarchy.[40]

Some years passed before the next, and last, attempt to secure representation for Melbourne in 1876 when the Victorian parliament was considering an Electoral Act Amendment Bill, and also coincidentally the year that Sydney returned its first

---

[37] *Argus*, 3 Dec. 1858, pp. 5–6.

[38] *Argus*, 6 Dec. 1858, p. 4.

[39] Univ. of Melbourne Archives: Minutes of Council, 30 May 1859.

[40] See Stuart Macintyre, *A Colonial Liberalism: The Lost World of Three Victorian Visionaries* (Melbourne, 1991), 25–36.

representative. Members of the legislature are reported to have been irritated by the university's intensive lobbying effort.[41] In early September, the university's senate resolved that Melbourne 'ought like other universities to be represented in Parliament', and a committee was appointed to work with the council to draw up a petition for presentation to both houses of the legislature.[42] Shortly thereafter, petitions were duly submitted to both houses of the Victorian parliament seeking amendment of the electoral bill to confer upon Melbourne graduates the right to return a member to the legislative assembly.

After noting that in addition to Oxford, Cambridge and Dublin, which had been allowed representation 'for centuries', London and the Scottish universities had recently been given a similar privilege, the petition asked:

> That the graduates of the University of Melbourne, having been placed by Her Majesty's letters patent on an equality with the graduates of the most learned universities of the United Kingdom, may fairly hope to acquire at the hands of the parliament of Victoria a recognition similar to that which in the Parliament of England the graduates of the universities within the United Kingdom receive.

The petition further noted that Melbourne had more graduates than the already enfranchised Sydney. In addition (again, akin to the case that had been made for the Scottish universities), the petition argued that the privilege of returning a member would encourage greater numbers of matriculated students to take degrees.[43]

In committee, Townsend Macdermott, a barrister and graduate of Trinity College Dublin representing Ballarat East, moved a clause giving the university a representative elected on a franchise extending to all holders of Melbourne degrees. The debate on Macdermott's clause lasted for two nights and covered many of the arguments for and against university representation that have already been described in the British context.[44] In support were the precedents (both in the 'mother country' and New South Wales), the litany of distinguished occupants of university seats and the expectation that the university would return members of 'liberal views and educational attainments who would be likely to take a distinguished part in the work of legislation'. One member even quoted from Newman's *Idea of a University*.

Against Macdermott's motion it was argued that the constituency was too small (though some members conceded that they might support a university seat when the body of graduates would be larger), that it would be bad to introduce party politics into the university, that creating a special franchise under conditions of manhood suffrage elevated one segment of society over the rest, that graduates could be elected to regular seats and did not need a special constituency in order to contribute to the colony's public life, and (with irony) that one might just as well give a special vote to the

---

[41] Scott, *History of the University of Melbourne*, 110; and R.W. Selleck, *The Shop: The University of Melbourne, 1850–1939* (Melbourne, 2003), 169.

[42] Univ. of Melbourne Archives, Registrar's Correspondence UM447: 685/1876 Representation in Parliament.

[43] Univ. of Melbourne Archives: Minutes of Council, 7 Sept. 1876. See also *Argus*, 13 Sept. 1876, p. 6.

[44] This account is based on the report in *Argus*, 11 Oct. 1876, pp. 9–10, and the leader of the same date, p. 4.

professional classes. There were also long-standing reservations about William Edward Hearn, a politically active Melbourne professor who had long sought a seat in the legislative assembly and hoped to be the university's first member.[45] Hearn's candidacy had led the university council to 'secure the isolation of the professors' through a resolution to change the charter so that 'the Professors shall not . . . sit in Parliament, nor become members of any political association'.[46]

In addition to these familiar arguments, there was, as happened in the case of Sydney, a particular Australian twist in the way that the question of the university's class identity entered the debate. One democratically minded charge against the idea of a seat for the university was that it would give added representation to the wealthier classes. In response, Macdermott claimed that those who persevered in obtaining degrees were 'the sons of small shopkeepers, schoolmasters, and men of that class'. Another member said that Melbourne was 'essentially a middle class institution' and, in contrast to the wealthy who tend to avoid the demands of a student's life, those who have succeeded 'spring from the poorer classes'. At this level, the debate was over whether the university was a facilitator of colonial meritocracy or an engine for replicating the privileges and distinctions of the British social elite.

Class, or rather classlessness, could also enter into arguments in favour of the Melbourne seat when seen in 'national' terms. According to the writer of a letter that appeared in the *Argus* in August, in light of the establishment of the state school exhibitions and the proposals to abolish students' fees, Victoria had 'recognized the principle of opening the gates of the University to all sections of the community'. As a result, enfranchising Melbourne would go beyond the situation in the mother country in which university members 'cannot be supposed to have many sympathies in common with the country at large'. Rather, the university 'with us is a truly national institution, and as a constituency would be likely to return a truly national representative, enlightened and unprejudiced by class or local bias'.[47]

At another level, the realities of colonial democracy generated support for university representation as a means of tempering what was seen as a debased political culture with a parliamentary proponent of higher values and ideals. The *Melbourne Punch*, for example, articulated an interesting version of the argument that university representation provided a unique benefit to the body politic, either directly or virtually. In the case of Dublin, the constituency was said to have a special 'national' role because its graduates were spread across the whole of Ireland. Later, there was also the more general proposition that university constituencies were the only means by which graduates working abroad could at least in theory vote. In the context of Victoria's status as a comparatively new and growing colony, with a political tone set by 'men whom nature designed for grooms and peddlers, but whom Democracy selects to make its laws', the *Melbourne Punch* observed:

---

[45] On the arguments over Hearn's candidacy for the Murray district in 1859, see *Argus*, 20 Jan. 1859, p. 5; 25 Jan. 1859, p. 4.

[46] Univ. of Melbourne Archives: Minutes of Council, 20 and 21 Jan. 1859. Subsequently, the professors of the university sent a memorial to the governor requesting he withhold his assent to the change in the statutes. The governor requested that the council review the memorial. Minutes of Council, 23 May 1859.

[47] *Argus*, 21 Aug. 1876, p. 5.

that there are hundreds of educated men in the country, unconnected with the University, who are wholly unrepresented in the assembly, men smarting under the sense of wrong engendered by being taxed – say rather robbed – under an infamous fiscal system, which breeds prostitutes and larrikins, just as maggots breed in putrid meat, and they would feel themselves represented for the first time by an educated independent gentleman taking his seat as the chosen of the best intellect in the colony.[48]

In this view, university representation offered a kind of virtual representation for the educated.

The *Argus* took a similar position, expressed with scarcely greater restraint. When Macdermott's clause was defeated by 32 votes to 22, the newspaper called the outcome a 'churlish act' and pointed to the important role this special franchise had to play in a democratic system: 'The tendency to appeal to passion or to prejudice, and not to reason, in politics is daily becoming more pronounced in character and more pernicious in consequence'. Accordingly, it was all the more urgent and necessary to ensure 'the introduction of a new and purer element into public life – of an element which would be placed above the temptation to "soil" itself by the "dirty" warfare that is waged by purely professional politicians'. These sentiments anticipate justifications for preserving university representation in Britain with the advent of manhood suffrage, though without the same apprehensions over the prospect of a working-class majority. Also familiar was the *Argus*' claim that 'It is a well-founded reproach, so often brought against democratic systems, that they repeal and exclude such men from all participation in politics, and thrust them aside to make room for the accommodating adventurer, the cunning jobber, and the unscrupulous demagogue'.[49]

The elimination of university representation in New South Wales only three years later deprived Melbourne of the neighbouring precedent and any appeals to institutional and inter-colonial rivalries. Yet, it was also the case that, though never obtaining a seat for the university in the legislative assembly, graduates were not wholly without special status in relation to the Victorian parliament. Along with substantial property holders, lawyers, medical practitioners, ministers and officers in the armed services, graduates were included as a category in the more limited franchise for the legislative council, which was so constituted to serve as a conservative counterweight to the democratic lower House.[50] This throws into further relief how the debates over a seat for the University of Melbourne expressed the inherent tension in the colony between democratic populism and elitist traditionalism.

With respect to Australia's third university, Adelaide, there does not appear to have been an effort to obtain legislative representation. This may be due to the fact that, by the time the university was established in 1874, South Australia (a progressive-minded settlement from the outset) was under a very liberal constitution that had been in place for some years. Thus, South Australia lacked the context of conservative anxieties about democratic advances that had earlier played an important role in arguments for university

---

[48] 'University Representation', *Melbourne Punch*, 12 Oct. 1876, p. 144.

[49] *Argus*, 13 Oct., 1876, p. 4.

[50] See Geoffrey Serle, 'The Victorian Legislative Council, 1856–1950', *Historical Studies, Australia and New Zealand*, vi (1954), 186–203.

representation in New South Wales and Victoria. Yet the story of university representation in Australia does extend further, albeit tenuously, to Queensland. There, the effort
to establish a university took several decades after the colony split off from New South
Wales in 1859.[51] For this frontier colony's dispersed population, a university seemed like
a privileged luxury when practical necessities arguably demanded that resources be
channelled towards basic infrastructure needs like the expansion of railways and primary
education. Ultimately, the University of Queensland only came to be established at the
end of 1909. Still, even though no university was yet in existence or even being actively
developed, later 19th-century proponents of higher education in the colony nevertheless
sought to ensure the entitlement of a future institution to be represented in the
Queensland parliament.

Queensland separated from New South Wales the year after the 1858 Electoral Act had
allowed for the eventual creation of a seat for Sydney University. Because the new
colony's constitution was essentially carried over from New South Wales, university
representation was part of Queensland's constitutional heritage and appeared in subsequent legislation. During 1870–1, a variety of electoral bills were brought forward, but
the nearly even balance of government and opposition made it extremely difficult for
measures to be passed. Finally, following a dissolution and election in 1871, the Queensland parliament passed an elections act which conferred manhood suffrage after six
months' residence and provided that no man could hold two votes in one electorate. In
addition, however, 'a strange provision of this law', as one chronicler recalled, 'was that
the University of Queensland, *when established*, and when it could produce 100 superior
graduates, was to return a member' to the legislative assembly.[52]

Of course, given the colony's character and stage of development, some politicians
sought to make sure that the idea of a university seat was approached with due caution,
not least those who had struggled to enact electoral reform. During the second reading
of the Elections Bill, John Malbon Thompson, who had unsuccessfully advanced earlier
bills along similar lines, stated that, 'With regard to the clause referring to Universities,
he had left it as it was in the original bill, but if they were simply to have a grammar
school turned into a university it would be necessary to see that it possessed the
necessary status before being afforded the privilege proposed. At present, however, it was
not necessary'.[53] In response to complaints about the clause, however, the premier, Arthur
Palmer, said 'he would simply point out that this clause was in the present Electoral Act
and there was no intention on the part of the Government to alter the electoral
districts'.[54] Ultimately, the provision for giving representation to a future university
passed with only slight opposition.[55] The *prospective* provision for representation
of a university that had not yet been fully established followed the example (if
known) of Upper Canada, and anticipated the similar arrangements for some planned
Indian universities in the 1920s. Further, it bears consideration that, like many other

---

[51] For the early history of the University of Queensland, see Malcolm I. Thomas, *A Place of Light and Learning: The University of Queensland's First Seventy-Five Years* (St Lucia, 1985), ch. 1.

[52] Charles Arrowsmith Bernays, *Queensland Politics during Sixty (1859–1919) Years* (Brisbane, 1919), 287, emphasis in original.

[53] *Brisbane Courier*, 30 Nov. 1870, p. 3.

[54] *Brisbane Courier*, 19 Apr. 1871, p. 3.

[55] *Brisbane Courier*, 20 Apr. 1871, p. 2.

efforts to give representation to colonial universities (existing or not), this took place well before new higher education institutions in the United Kingdom sought to be enfranchised.

The idea of creating a university in the colony was first brought up in 1877, when the lawyer, liberal reformer and subsequently chief author of Australia's federal constitution, Samuel Griffith, introduced 'A Bill to facilitate and encourage higher education, and to make provision for the establishment of a University in the Colony of Queensland' – an attempt that did not proceed beyond its first reading.[56] Several years later, the Elections Bill of 1885, introduced after Griffith had become Queensland's premier, also included a clause for permitting the planned university to return one member to parliament once the number of its graduates reached 100. In addition to the usual motivations for seeking to establish a university seat, the Bill's provision for university representation was also influenced by the 1885 Redistribution Act in Britain, which had preserved university seats there. But, unlike the situation in the mother country, a by-product of the politics of enlarging the electorate at 'home', the outcomes in Queensland were determined, as in New South Wales and Victoria, by the forces of young colonial democracy. Although opposition had been fairly modest in debates over earlier bills, in 1885 the university representation clause was roundly criticized. One member opened the attack by objecting to the size of the university constituency, repudiating 'the idea that because a man had received a university education he was equal to a hundred other electors'. The interjection from another member that 'they represent intelligence' is reported to have 'raised a laugh of doubt'. A third member condemned the university franchise as 'too Conservative for a democratic country', and the cross-bench objection to university representation found support from other members.[57]

In committee, Thomas McIlwraith, the leader of the Conservative opposition, said the clause was 'one of the fancy clauses which the Premier should allow to go at once to save time'. Griffith is reported to have said 'with a rueful face' that 'he was sorry to part with the clause which had been on the statute book since separation, but was afraid it would have to go'. Although the premier sought to withdraw the clause, one member forced a division 'on the ground not that he believed in having a member for a university, but that he wished to show the government had not heart in backing up their own opinions'. The clause was struck out by 28 votes to three.[58] In Queensland, therefore, university representation died well before there was ever a university to be represented. The case of university representation in Queensland, taken together with those in New South Wales and Victoria, not only shows the correspondence between certain pre-federation constitutional outcomes across the Australian colonies, but also demonstrates a shared set of prevailing assumptions about the relationship between the legislative and educational development of the colonies.

Across the Tasman Sea, higher education in New Zealand emerged in a somewhat different form. In pre-federation Canada and Australia, each province or colony pursued independent plans for creating colleges and universities. A similar process, marked by regional cultural ambitions and rivalries, began in New Zealand with the provinces of

[56] Bernays, *Queensland Politics*, 424.
[57] *Brisbane Courier*, 22 July 1885, p. 5.
[58] *Brisbane Courier*, 5 Aug. 1885, p. 5.

Otago and Canterbury taking the lead.[59] But the territorial politics of New Zealand led to a very different outcome with the passage of the University of New Zealand Act in 1870, which created the framework for a national institution composed of regional university colleges. In 1874, Otago (which had been founded in 1869) and Canterbury (1873) became the first members of the federation, later joined by Auckland (1883) and Wellington (1897). Although the creation of the national university owed much to inter-regional politics, it was also part of the more general diminishment of provincial authority in this period that culminated in the creation of a unitary state at the beginning of 1877. Notwithstanding the different origin, structure and context of the University of New Zealand, the politicians who had worked to bring it into being, like the earlier proponents of higher education in Canada and Australia, also subsequently bent their efforts to obtain a seat for the new institution in the colony's house of representatives.[60]

As early as 1875, the Canterbury politician, educational reformer and member of the university's council, William Rolleston, had raised the idea during a debate on the Qualification of Electors Bill. He argued that the representation of interests was as important as the representation of numbers, and that a wide view needed to be taken of extending the franchise. 'Education, if represented in the House, would have a beneficial influence on the House and the country. He suggested that the Government should consider the question of the New Zealand University being represented in that House'.[61] As happened elsewhere, however, opponents of the idea argued that the new university had not yet reached a necessary state of maturity. For the government, the justice minister, C.C. Bowen, said he 'doubted whether the University was yet established on such a footing as to warrant them giving it representation in Parliament'. Yet, as a strong proponent of education with numerous ties to Canterbury's schools and college, Bowen showed that his general sympathies were in keeping with Rolleston's. 'In due time', he said, 'the Government would be prepared to consider the matter'.[62]

Like its counterparts in the United Kingdom and Australia, the University of New Zealand sought to advance the cause of representation when franchise reform was in prospect. In 1880, with the government expected to bring in a new representation bill, the university's senate had resolved 'That in the event of a Bill for the Redistribution of Seats being likely to be brought before Parliament, the Chancellor be requested to call the attention of the Government to the claims of the University to a member'.[63] Accordingly, the chancellor, Henry John Tancred, who like Rolleston had played a major part in the effort to establish a higher education system in New Zealand, wrote to the minister of education to advocate for a university seat. Tancred made the familiar argument that, through their representatives, university constituencies make especially informed and enlightened contributions to legislative deliberation: 'I need hardly remind you that this body would form a constituency representing the highest intellectual power

[59] Gardner, *Colonial Cap and Gown*, 26–34.

[60] The starting point for this investigation of efforts to obtain representation for the University of New Zealand is J.C. Beaglehole, *The University of New Zealand: An Historical Study* (Auckland, NZ, 1937), 141–2 n.

[61] *Evening Post* [New Zealand], 28 Sept., 1875, p. 2.

[62] *The Star*, 17 Sept. 1875, p. 2.

[63] Archives New Zealand, ADAU 8740 UNZ1/3, Univ. of New Zealand: Minutes of Senate, 1880–4, p. 48.

in the Colony: and that each year there would be an increased number of electors drawn from that population who may be supposed to take the most intelligent view of public affairs'.[64] In September 1880, Joseph Augustus Tole, a member of the house of representatives, announced his intention to move an amendment that would enable the university to return a member to the house of representatives as soon as it had a body of 200 graduates.[65]

In early 1881, in advance of the new session of parliament and with the representation bill still in the works, the university's registrar, William Miles Maskell, renewed contact with the minister of education, reiterating Tancred's main arguments, 'namely that such Representation is given elsewhere and that the member for the University would probably represent a constituency able probably to take the most intelligent view of public affairs, this constituency increasing year by year'. Maskell further added that the number of graduates then stood at 129, 36 by examination and 93 admitted *ad eundem gradum*.[66] Later that year, the chancellor wrote once more to the minister about the university's case for representation.[67]

Ultimately, the 1881 Representation Act replaced the constituency system based on the number of propertied male electors plus a special franchise for miners, with a distribution of seats based on population. Some interesting light is shed on the question of university representation in relation to the wider political milieu around this time by the results of the 1878 census, in which only one of the 648 university men resident in New Zealand described himself as a member of the house of representatives. As a newspaper account observed, it is 'either a sign that the University debating class affords but a poor training for Parliamentary life, or else that debating power is by no means an infallible passport to New Zealand political life'. It was a sign, the same article noted, that 'a laborer who knows how to handle a pick and shovel is more sought after in the colony than an individual whose only recommendation is that he is able to write "BA" or "MA" after his name'.[68]

The census also indicated that three women were affiliated with the University of New Zealand, two of them holding BAs. Since women's suffrage was granted in New Zealand in 1893, the question of women graduates' electoral rights in a university constituency was an implicit, if apparently unaddressed, complication in the effort to secure representation in the 1880s. Although university representation had failed to make legislative headway, it was not the result of a blanket opposition to special representation. In 1884, the New Zealand parliament debated bills for the representation of both Maori and seamen. Perhaps it was these measures that prompted the convocation and its senate to pass resolutions to renew the university's application to the government for the right to elect a member to the house of representatives.[69] Although, as in the past, the

[64] Archives New Zealand, ADAU 8746 UNZ 13/7★7, Univ. of New Zealand, Entry Books of Outward Letters, 13 Dec. 1879–15 Mar. 1881, p. 236: Tancred to Minister of Education, 7 May 1880.

[65] *Otago Witness*, 4 Sept. 1880, p. 22.

[66] Archives New Zealand, ADAU 8746 UNZ 13/8★8, Univ. of New Zealand, Entry Books of Outward Letters, 15 Mar. 1881–26 Sept. 1883, p. 98: Maskell to Minister of Education, 17 May 1881.

[67] Archives New Zealand, ADAU 8746 UNZ 13/8★8, Univ. of New Zealand, Entry Books of Outward Letters, 15 Mar. 1881–26 Sept.1883, pp. 217–18: Tancred to Minister of Education, 10 Aug. 1881.

[68] *Evening Post* [New Zealand], 25 Mar. 1880, p. 2.

[69] Archives New Zealand, ADAU 8746 UNZ 13/9★9, Univ. of New Zealand, Entry Books of Outward Letters, 26 Sept. 1883–14 Dec. 1886, p. 289: Maskell to Minister of Education, 19 June 1884.

substance of these resolutions was communicated to the minister for education, there appears to have been no further consideration of legislation to give the university a seat in parliament.

As a group, the Australasian cases, like that of Canada, demonstrate how the idea of university representation was regularly advanced as political development and aspirations for intellectual and cultural life in the settler societies coincided. Because the lay members of the universities' governing councils who advanced proposals for university representation were active in public life, the issue was inevitably tangled up with the colonies' internal political struggles. At an institutional level, university representation was a mark of status fully consistent with the ambitions in Toronto, Sydney, Melbourne, Queensland and New Zealand to create universities that 'will equal, in the means of instruction, the most favoured Institutions in the Mother Country'.[70] Yet, institutionally, socially and politically, the universities' base of support was too weak for the successful establishment of university representation. At the time they sought representation, the universities were either recently inaugurated or simply proposed, and thus they lacked any public stature within the colonies. Where universities did exist, their small number of graduates provided neither a natural lobby within their legislatures nor an influential base of public support. At the same time, democratic development proceeded at a more rapid pace than in Britain, and limited the opportunities for adapting university representation as a constitutional safeguard.

3. The Mediterranean

In contrast to the important but ultimately slight record of university representation in the settler colonies of Canada and Australasia, the Mediterranean offers a more robust and more varied picture of the ways that university representation accompanied Britain's imperial activities and ideas of British constitutionalism. In Sicily, for instance, university representation featured as part of two short-lived British-style constitutions in the early 19th century. The political and constitutional history of the island in this period is tangled in the extreme, and this account is necessarily confined to noting briefly the essential facts necessary to understand the circumstances under which university seats for a short while came into existence.

The appearance of university representation in Sicily occurred during the Napoleonic Wars. Sicily had great strategic value for British operations in the Mediterranean, especially for the campaign in Spain, and British forces were stationed on the island from 1806. With the Italian peninsula under French control, Sicily was sundered from its regal union with Naples and the Bourbon king, Ferdinand (III of Sicily, IV of Naples), had moved to Palermo along with his Neapolitan court. Ferdinand antagonised the local nobles, who had historically exercised considerable autonomy, with extraordinary new taxation and the imprisoning of some of the barons who protested against it.

In 1811, Lord William Bentinck (later a reforming governor-general of India) was given concurrent appointments as commander-in-chief in the Mediterranean and British envoy

---

[70] From the 1837 'Report of the President of the King's College Council on the Expediency of Putting the University into Operation', in Hodgins, *Documentary History*, 94.

to the court of the Two Sicilies. With growing public disorder and a variety of diplomatic intrigues afoot, Bentinck's brief was to keep Sicily stable, and solidly in the British column.[71] A whig reformer sympathetic to the wider cause of Italian unification, Bentinck persuaded the Sicilian nobles, and London, to support a sweeping transformation of the existing feudal parliament originally established by the Normans. In 1812, the Sicilians promulgated a constitution largely along British lines.[72] Bentinck is often described as guiding the process out of a belief that all the world's ills could be solved by emulating the British constitution. In fact, Bentinck had grave doubts about the Sicilians' capabilities, but he acquiesced to their Anglophilic enthusiasm for British precedents.[73] Consistent with the Westminster model, this included establishing representation for the universities of Palermo and Catania in the parliament's lower House, the Camera de Comuni.[74]

Between 1813 and 1815, three parliaments were convened under the new constitution, but, quickly riven by factionalism and anti-constitutional resistance, they were by no means a success.[75] Parliament was dissolved for the last time in 1815, and the Sicilian constitution was effectively scrapped with the restoration of the Kingdom of the Two Sicilies under the Treaty of Vienna. In spite of its shortcomings in practice, and the fact that it had required firm British support to work at all, the 1812 constitution was subsequently held dear by supporters of Sicilian independence as the island's legitimate but illegally suspended constitution. In the ensuing years, Sicilians revolted against Naples on several occasions, and succeeded for a brief period in 1848–9.

In the wake of the 1848 revolt, a provisional government called both houses of the parliament, based on the 1812 constitution but with some modifications, to adapt to changes affecting representation over the intervening 33 years. The representation of the universities of Catania and Palermo was duly restored, with one and two seats, respectively.[76] In addition, a seat was also provided for the University of Messina, which had been founded in 1548 but was closed in 1678 and only recently resurrected in 1838. (In 1847 it had been closed once more on account of the independence protests in the city that preceded the wider revolt.) Sicily remained independent for only 16 months before the Neapolitan forces proceeded to reduce the island. British and French navy vessels on the scene enforced a cessation of hostilities. Although Naples promised certain concessions to the Sicilians, despotic rule under the Bourbons resumed in short order and endured until Italian unification.

If university representation in Sicily was as short-lived as the island's British-inspired liberal constitutions, in Malta the Mediterranean also provides one of the more durable instances of university representation in the empire.[77] Like Sicily, Malta came under

[71] For entertainment and detail, it is difficult to improve upon H.M. Lackland, 'Lord William Bentinck in Sicily, 1811–12', *EHR*, xlii (1927), 371–96.

[72] C.W. Crawley, 'England and the Sicilian Constitution of 1812', *EHR*, lv (1940), 251–74.

[73] John Rosselli, *Lord William Bentinck and the British Occupation of Sicily, 1811–1814* (Cambridge, 1956), esp. 44, 49, 53.

[74] *Costituzione di Sicilia Stabilita nel Generale, Straordinario Parlamento del 1812* (Palermo, 1813), 13.

[75] See H.M. Lackland, 'The Failure of the Constitutional Experiment in Sicily, 1813–1814', *EHR*, xli (1926), 210–35.

[76] *Statuto Costituzionale del Regno di Sicilia* (1848), 6; *Sicily and England: A Sketch of Events in Sicily in 1812 & 1848, Illustrated by Vouchers and State Papers* (1849), 91.

[77] Rex writes that universities were represented in the Spanish Cortes after 1812. Millicent Barton Rex, *University Representation in England, 1604–1690* (1954), 13. Examination of the constitution of that year reveals

British protection during the war against the French. The University of Malta had been founded in 1769, though its origins lie in the founding of a Jesuit college in the late 16th century. Thus, once Malta became part of the British empire in 1800, the university, by far the oldest outside the United Kingdom, could lay claim to a kind of institutional standing that the colonial colleges could not. According to the university's historian, 'It is in the British period that the University first begins to come to life',[78] in part because of a series of reforms over the course of the 19th century that attempted to bring its statutes and regulations into some conformity with those of British universities.[79] Beyond mere conformity with the British system, however, the perceived need to develop institutions that would instil British values and loyalty into the 'responsible' segments of society was as keen in Malta as it was in Ireland or in India. Lord Glenelg, secretary of state for war and the colonies, for one believed 'that an improvement in the education of the higher and middle classes [in Malta] would facilitate the admission of natives to employments in the civil government'.[80]

University representation was first introduced to Malta with the 1887 constitution, which created an expanded council of government with a non-official majority. Of the 20 council members (not including the governor, who presided), six were officials, ten were elected by general electors and four represented special groups: the clergy, the nobility and landed proprietors, the merchants and the university graduates. Voters for the special constituencies were also general electors and thus had a plural vote.[81] As would be the case in the Indian provincial councils, 'Part of the elected membership was thus based on the corporate principle giving expression to functional interest'.[82] In a letter of 14 December 1887 transmitting the letters patent for the new constitution to Malta's governor, General Sir J.L.A. Simmons, Sir Henry Holland, secretary of state for the colonies, wrote:

These four members will occupy the same position in the Constitution as the members for the Universities occupy in the Parliament of this country; the graduates

---

[77] *(continued)* no such provision. Further, it has been argued that, notwithstanding the British alliance with Spain and its military presence in the peninsula at that time, the Spanish constitution of 1812 was influenced to a far greater extent by French ideas than by English ones. See C.W. Crawley, 'French and English Influences in the Cortes of Cadiz, 1810–1814', *Cambridge Historical Journal*, vi (1929), 176–208. Rather, the 1812 constitution, which came to be briefly revived at various points, suppressed forms of privileged representation and was based strictly on egalitarian principles of territory and property. See Carlos Dardé and Manuel Estrada, 'Social and Territorial Representation in Spanish Electoral Systems, 1809–1874', in *How Did they Become Voters? The History of Franchise in Modern European Representation*, ed. Raffaele Romanelli (The Hague, 1998), 139–42.

Rex is correct that the Spanish constitution of 1876, which would remain in force until 1923, provided for university representation in the senate of the Cortes. Half of the 360-member senate consisted of elected representatives, 30 of which came from the corporations of state including one each from ten universities (the other corporate interests represented were nine archbishoprics, six academies and five regional economic associations). This had nothing to do with English influence, but rather organic theories of representation, or *krausistas*, popular among certain mostly conservative intellectual and political circles. See Aurora Garrido, 'Electors and Electoral Districts in Spain, 1874–1936', in *How Did they Become Voters?* ed. Romanelli, 208–10.

[78] Andrew P. Vella, *The University of Malta: A Bicentenary Memorial* (Malta, 1969), 107–8.

[79] See Vella, *University of Malta*, 64–8, 76–88.

[80] As noted in an 1838 report by John Austin and George Cornewall Lewis, who had been appointed to inquire into the affairs of Malta. Quoted in Vella, *University of Malta*, 77.

[81] *Further Correspondence Respecting the Constitution and Administration of Malta*, 80, Parliamentary Papers, 1888 [Cmd 5308], lxxiii, 535.

[82] J.J. Cremona, *The Maltese Constitution and Constitutional History since 1813* (San Gwann, Malta, 1994), 16.

of our Universities being entitled to give a vote for their own special members, in addition to the votes which they may have in the electoral districts in which they reside, or in which they possess a property qualification.[83]

Growing conflict between elected and official members led to the collapse of the constitution in 1903, after which Malta was governed as a crown colony. In 1919, a national assembly convened to frame a new constitution, and letters patent were issued in 1921 to create a diarchal system of government like that introduced in India a few years earlier. Under this regime, representation of the university graduates (along with the clergy, nobility, chamber of commerce and trade union council) moved to a new corporatist senate – not dissimilar to the upper Houses in Spain after 1876 (see note 77), and Ireland after 1937 (see Conclusion). Plural voting was again adopted as in the 1887 constitution. In his letter of 9 April 1921, transmitting the orders in council for the new constitution to Lord Plumer, the governor of Malta, Leopold Amery, parliamentary under-secretary at the Colonial Office, wrote that he had sought, in structuring the senate, to combine suggestions 'which found most favour with the persons and bodies who have been consulted'.[84] Following the ordeal of extended siege during the Second World War, Malta's 1947 constitution both introduced universal suffrage and dispensed with the senate to create a unicameral legislature.[85]

Whereas the histories of university representation in the settler colonies of North America and Australasia can be seen to have a family resemblance, the Maltese situation was much closer to that in India. This may help explain something of the durability of university representation in the Indian and Maltese cases in contrast to the overall failure to establish university seats in the settler colonies. In Malta, like in India, British rule was an imperial overlay on what was understood to be a developed civilization with a strong cultural heritage. As a staunchly catholic people with mixed Mediterranean ancestry, the Maltese were as non-British as the Indians, although the British naturally held them in higher regard as Europeans than they did the Indians. Malta, like India, had enormous strategic value for the British and thus necessitated a higher degree of control. The British could not rely on the same kinds of 'racial' affinities that they could in the settler colonies, which were encouraged to develop self-government at the earliest practicable opportunity. Further, both Malta and India were far more densely populated than the settler colonies. With the British presence a small minority, the need for native participation in administration was at a premium. Britain created the universities in India and reformed the University of Malta along British lines to meet this need. University representation in both lands was one logical way to connect the requirements of British rule with the effort to incorporate those educated in emulation of the British into the political structures.

---

[83] *Further Correspondence Respecting the Constitution and Administration of Malta*, 77, Parliamentary Papers, 1888 [Cmd 5308], lxxiii, 535.

[84] *Papers Relating to the New Constitution of Malta*, 93, Parliamentary Papers, 1921 [Cmd 1321], xxiv, 581.

[85] When, in 1955–6, the idea of uniting Malta with the United Kingdom was under serious consideration, university representation had been discontinued in Britain, so reviving a seat for the University of Malta would have been inconsistent with the available definitions of parliamentary constituencies.

4. Conclusion

As the cases of India, North America, Australasia and the Mediterranean demonstrate, university representation in the empire, like in Britain, was for the most part contemplated or enacted at periods in which the advancement of higher education coincided with episodes of constitutional development or reform. The case of Sicily is somewhat anomalous in this respect, but underscores the strong identification of university representation within the practice of British constitutionalism.

Elsewhere in the empire, what seem to have been the requisite elements for university representation to have been at least considered were not all present. The Bahamas, for instance, has a tradition of continuous British-style parliamentary government from 1728, but higher education institutions were not present until the middle of the 20th century (and the major institution, the University of the West Indies, was based in Jamaica). Similarly, the development of legislatures and the growth of higher education in African colonies did not intersect in the ways that elsewhere raised the possibility of university representation. When the Cape Colony's first legislative council was set up in 1834, the precursor to University of Cape Town, the South African College, had only recently (1829) been established as a boys' high school. When a new constitution created a full bicameral parliament in 1853, there were still another 20 years before the separation of the college's tertiary division, which then only developed into a fully fledged university at the end of the century. Representation in both the early council (with non-official members appointed from the chief landed proprietors and principal merchants) and then the parliament (with franchises based on owner occupation, rental payments and wage earnings) focused on economic status with no special consideration for learning.[86]

Of course, British attitudes towards the development of self-government and higher learning elsewhere in Africa were substantially different from their views on these processes in the colonies of white settlement, and even in India where there was a pressing need for an intermediary administrative class. Even those who thought Africans were not inherently inferior beings but simply existed at an earlier state of civilization than Europeans saw political and educational development as long-term propositions. Indeed, British policy, to the extent there could be said to be one before 1945, did not even aim at developing African educational institutions into fully fledged universities until quite late in the colonial period.[87]

In Sierra Leone, the Fourah Bay College in Freetown had been founded by missionaries in 1826, but had a rocky early existence and was not on the path to becoming a significant higher education institution until its affiliation with Durham University in 1876, several years after the first (narrowly constructed) legislative council was established

---

[86] Information about the Cape legislatures is drawn from Ralph Kilpin, *The Romance of the Colonial Parliament: Being a Narrative of the Parliament and Councils of the Cape of Good Hope from the Founding of the Colony by Van Riebeeck in 1652 to the Union of South Africa in 1910* (1930); and J.L. McCracken, *The Cape Parliament, 1854–1910* (Oxford, 1967). Analysis of the occupations of members of both the house of assembly and the legislative council between 1854 and 1908 reveals no clear affiliation to learning as such (although there were a small number of lawyers and doctors). McCracken, *Cape Parliament*, 54–60.

[87] For summary information on higher education in British Africa, I have relied on Y.G.-M. Lulat, *A History of African Higher Education from Antiquity to the Present: A Critical Synthesis* (Westport, CT, 2005), esp. 207–23.

in 1863. The college was not included in the representation under the 1924 constitution.[88] In the 20th century, Achimota College (1924) in Ghana and the Higher College at Yaba (1932) in Nigeria were founded with the expectation that they might one day develop into universities, but that this would take some time. Thus these institutions did not exist when the small advisory legislative council of the Gold Coast was created in 1850, and its enlarged successor from 1916, or when the Nigerian legislative council was established in 1922.[89] Similar to Nigeria, the first Ugandan legislative council, made up of seven Europeans, plus one representative of the Indian community, was established in 1921, a year before the founding of Makerere College, which would not be elevated to the status of a university college (under London) with an expectation of ultimately achieving full university status until the late 1930s.[90]

Even such brief consideration of where and why university representation did not occur in the empire indicates not only the formal conditions under which it might arise (the timing and level of constitutional and higher educational developments) but also the interlocking character of British and settler assumptions about constitutionalism, race and the socio-political functions of universities. More broadly, the surprising prevalence of university representation as a constitutional principle that was at least debated and sometimes implemented in numerous parts of the empire clearly has a collective significance that cannot be observed when examining each case alone.

First, especially when examined alongside developments in India, these cases demonstrate that university representation, so often viewed as a distinctly British constitutional peculiarity, must also be understood as a wide-ranging imperial institution. The question of university representation links developments in colonies across a variety of historical and administrative circumstances, regardless of whether Britain was imposing its rule, or allowing colonies to advance towards de facto independence. At the same time, the comparative study of how university representation was thought of, argued about and (where it existed) functioned, reveals critical differences among different categories of colony. The history of university representation in the empire also reveals important connections with what was occurring in Britain itself by showing how constitutional and educational developments in the metropole took place within a larger trans-imperial set of constitutional and educational formations in the 19th and early 20th centuries. University representation was an imperial phenomenon, not an imperial policy. It served different ends and represented somewhat different things in each part of the empire, and the impetus behind it could come from both above and below. Embodying a mixture of tradition and innovation wherever it appeared, university representation is at once a substantive example and deeply emblematic of a mixed-up modernity shared by both imperial centre and colony.

---

[88] Christopher Fyfe, *A History of Sierra Leone* (Oxford, 1962).

[89] Joan Wheare, *The Nigerian Legislative Council* (1950).

[90] G.F. Engholm, 'The Development of Procedure in Uganda's Legislative Council', *Parliamentary Affairs*, ix (1955), 338–52.

Conclusion

University representation, though generally recognized (if at all) as a quaint oddity, was in fact an institution of real significance within, and a link between, the broader frameworks of politics and education, both in Britain and across the empire. Because some of that significance resonated in the world after 1950, the first part of this Conclusion functions as an epilogue of sorts by describing some of the legacies of university representation. It focuses on three exemplary cases that highlight the continuity of significant themes described in the preceding chapters: the continued, and contested, existence of university seats in Ireland; the transmuted provisions for the representation of learning in the new constitutional structures of post-independence India; and the persistence in the United Kingdom of arguments about representation similar to those which surrounded the university franchise. Significantly, in all three of these cases, the legacy of university representation bears on the upper rather than the lower branch of each legislature.

Looking back on the whole sweep of university representation's history, a major theme that emerges is its mutability as both a practice and a concept. This can be seen in the ways that it responded to changing political and educational contexts, and how it came to be understood in terms quite different from the institutional and religious motivations that had caused it to be created in the first place. University representation's mutability is further revealed in its adaptation to a variety of imperial situations, and more generally in its complex relationship to political modernisation. Another set of considerations revolved around the sometimes vexed question of what exactly university representation stood to represent. Finally, there is the issue of why university representation was able to continue in its seemingly anomalous existence for so long, and what conditions contributed to its end.

1. *Afterlives*

In both the United Kingdom and India, university representation ceased to exist in 1950. It had ended in Malta three years earlier. Ireland, however, was an exception. Legislatively separated from the United Kingdom in 1921, both parts of Ireland were insulated from the attempts during the interwar years to abolish university representation. The seat for Queen's University Belfast established at Westminster may have been abolished in 1950, but the university continued to be represented by four members in the devolved Northern Ireland parliament at Stormont until 1969 when the seats were reassigned to new territorial constituencies. Three years later, the legislature was suspended and Britain resumed direct rule. Although from early on in the government of the reforming prime minister Terence O'Neill (1963–9) 'there was a considerable measure of agreement that the University seats were an anachronism' and it 'was not easy to find logical arguments to defend the retention of University seats', securing their end took some time because there was no mandate from the unionists to do so (even though they were losing influence with the Queen's electorate) and it was deemed 'politically inadvisable to concede on a Labour Party Motion points which had hitherto been strongly and successfully resisted'.[1] Consistent with the way that university representation was always bound up with larger political and constitutional issues, the O'Neill government also proceeded cautiously out of concern that replacing the university seats would bring pressure from both the opposition and Westminster for an array of other changes.[2]

Under the Republic of Ireland's 1937 constitution, the seats for Trinity College Dublin and the National University of Ireland that had earlier been transferred to the Irish Free State parliament were retained, but (as in Malta's 1921 constitution) they were relocated from the Dáil to the vocationally oriented Seanad Éireann, in which each institution continues to hold three seats. Ironically, therefore, the place where university representation endures today is the place of its earliest imperial extension. In present-day Ireland, the question of whether special representation for university graduates is an elitist privilege that should be abolished, or whether voting rights should be extended equally to graduates from all tertiary institutions in the Republic (as provided for in a 1979 constitutional amendment but never implemented), continues to be debated.[3] In recent years, proposals for reform of the Seanad have included converting the two university panels into a single six-member constituency in which all third-level graduates would be able to vote.[4] While in some ways extending the principle of combined university constituencies instituted in Britain and India, such pure representation of graduates divorced from any institutional identification would be a new variant of university representation. The question of Seanad reform has also involved calls for the abolition of the expensive and (except for the university seats) undemocratic upper House.[5] Should the unicameralists succeed, the demise of university representation's last survival will not have occurred in response to direct opposition. Rather, like the elimination of university representation in virtually all cases, it will be a casualty of a larger constitutional process.

In India, for example, except for the seats set aside for the untouchables in response to historic disabilities, the constitution's framers did away with special constituencies in the central and state governments. Even so, the ideal of university representation with respect to the quality and special contributions of members, and as the representation of learning, was not entirely lost. The constitution gave India's president the power to nominate 12 people with 'special knowledge or experience of literature, science, art, or social services' to seats in the upper House.[6] In addition, there was further special status given to the representation of learning in the superior chambers of the state legislatures, in which some members are elected by graduates of three years' standing from any

[1] Public Record Office of Northern Ireland (PRONI), CAB/4/1277/8: Northern Ireland Cabinet Minutes, 4 Nov. 1964.

[2] See, e.g., PRONI, CAB/4/1307/12: Northern Ireland Cabinet Minutes, 2 June 1965; and CAB/4/1355/15: Northern Ireland Cabinet Minutes, 19 Oct. 1966.

[3] For a summary of the role of university representation in the Republic of Ireland, current views on its utility and recent proposals for reform, see Seanad Éireann Committee on Procedure and Privileges, Sub-committee on Seanad Reform, *Report on Seanad Reform* (2004), 9, 12, 20, 23, 26, 33, 44–5.

[4] See, e.g., *Irish Times*, 28 Nov. 2007, p. 1; 29 Nov. 2007, p. 9.

[5] See, e.g., *Irish Times*, 20 Oct. 2009, p. 12.

[6] M.R. Palande, *Introduction to Indian Administration* (5th edn, Bombay, 1951), 290.

university in India and teachers at secondary and post-secondary educational institutions within the state (only six Indian states are currently bicameral).[7] At both the federal and state levels, then, India has implicitly reproduced a set of rationales for the representation of learning in relation to sustaining a vast and young democracy in a developing country.

In Britain, although the Conservatives' short-lived and, as it turned out, rhetorical commitment to restoring university seats in the early 1950s could be seen as the last gasp, new circumstances produced new arguments for the value of university representation. The alienation and unrest of university students in the late 1960s led A.P. Herbert, who had been one of Oxford's last MPs, to opine:

> There are many good reasons why the University representation should be restored. An immediately topical one is the link that it would provide between the great and growing world of students and Parliament. After the troubles of 1968 and 1969, the House of Commons lumberingly wound itself up and sent a Select Committee round the Universities to find out what was going on and report. If the University Members had still existed they would have been doing the job long before.[8]

Yet, Herbert's view is perhaps a rather idealised one in light of the historical record of university MPs' limited effectiveness in the affairs of their institutions.

In 1982, Lord Cranborne briefly, and quixotically, revived the effort to restore university representation. Having won a place in the ballot for private members' bills, Cranborne announced his intention to fulfil Churchill's abandoned pledge of 1950. Perhaps his inspiration was not wholly Churchillian, but rather animated as well by a kind of Cecil family piety to bring back the university seats that Lord Salisbury had so staunchly defended in 1885.[9] The first reading of Cranborne's bill occurred on 2 February 1983. The second reading was scheduled for 4 February, but on that day the bill was not high on the list of those under consideration and it was never discussed. At the end of the sitting, when the time came for the second reading, members objected on the ground that no discussion had taken place. No further date was named, which meant that the bill was effectively dropped.[10]

The great irony of the abolition of university representation in Britain is that it occurred when higher education started to become an increasingly important concern of the state. The 1944 Education Act laid the basis for state-provided financial support for university students' fees and maintenance. Combined with reforms in the schools sector, the number of students in higher education began to rise substantially in the immediate post-war decades. The pressure this put on the tertiary system had already set in train the creation of new universities when the Robbins commission's 1963 report declared higher education to be a vital national interest requiring considerable further expansion,

---

[7] Palande, *Introduction to Indian Administration*, 395.

[8] Alan Herbert, *A.P.H.: His Life and Times* (1970), 31.

[9] Cranborne may also have been influenced by Humberstone's assertion that his ancestor, Sir Robert Cecil, played an important role in the original creation of university seats. Rex, however, found no evidence to support this claim and gives full credit for the innovation to Sir Edward Coke. See T. Lloyd Humberstone, *University Representation* (1951), 19; Millicent Barton Rex, *University Representation in England, 1604–1690* (1954), 38, n. 26.

[10] *The Times*, 1 Dec. 1982, 7 Feb. 1983; Martin Davies, House of Commons Information Office, email correspondence with author, 1 Nov. 2006.

especially in the realms of science and technology, to maintain Britain's competitive position in the world. With the stakes and the costs thus raised, parliament and the treasury became even more directly involved in higher education, and a minister responsible for the sector became a fixture of government, first within the ministry of education, then the department of education and science, then the department of education and skills and, most recently, the department of business, innovation and skills. Denuded of their MPs, universities lacked a parliamentary voice with which to respond to the increasing levels of government intervention and politicisation. The expansion of higher education in the later 20th century provided the basis of some organised response to government policies outside parliament in the form of the National Union of Students (founded in 1922) and in a number of constituencies where academics and university students have come to make up a significant portion of the electorate.[11] But at best, like the university representatives of the past, these groups can have only marginal effects on the government's higher education agenda.

Looking to the house of lords, it is tempting to try and identify cases of virtual university representation in the post-1950 period, since a number of university chancellors given peerages could be said to have measured up to the ideals of learning and independence often claimed for university representation. Although most British university chancellors since the Second World War have come from the ranks of royals, local grandees or (more recently) celebrities, there are several others who in another era might have been thought very suitable candidates for university seats. Oxford stands out in this respect with its last three chancellors: Lords Macmillan of Stockton (although he came to the peerage at the very end of a long career as chancellor), Jenkins of Hillhead and Patten of Barnes. Sheffield's chancellor, Lord Butler of Saffron Walden, would also fit this category. Yet, in contrast to university seats in the Commons, which were somewhat prized and ideally set aside for a special type of member, the chancellorships, like the peerages themselves, can also be seen as consolation prizes for political failure. Amid political scandal, Macmillan resigned the premiership ostensibly because of a health scare, but regretted it for the remainder of his long life. Rab Butler, Roy Jenkins and Chris Patten were all widely admired politicians of great ability, accomplishment and expectations, but all were sidelined in one way or another. Aside from professional politicians of this ilk, Cambridge offers the example of the physiologist and Nobel laureate, E.D. Adrian. (The historian G.M. Trevelyan served as chancellor of Durham, but most likely refused the offer of a peerage.) The broadcaster and author Melvyn Bragg, now Lord Bragg of Wigton and chancellor of the University of Leeds, speaks regularly on questions relating to education, arts and culture.

The creation of life peerages in 1958 created new opportunities for learning generally to be represented in the Lords. A sterling example was the biochemist Alexander Todd, a Nobel laureate, master of Christ's and president of the Royal Society, who received a life peerage in 1962. Achievement in the sciences has, of course, featured prominently in the honours lists. As this suggests, however, to the extent that life peerages have enabled the Lords to incorporate the representation of learning, it is field-based rather than institutional in character.

[11] See Melanie Newman and Rebecca Atwood, 'Students Told: "Terrify Main Parties or be Screwed Over" ', *Times Higher Education*, 22 Apr. 2010, pp. 6–7; Rebecca Atwood, 'Shaped by the Fees Fight: New Leader Sets Agenda after Landslide Victory', *Times Higher Education*, 22 Apr. 2010, p. 11.

The idea that university representation might more appropriately be shifted to the Lords never developed in any serious way in Britain (unlike Ireland and Malta), and the Blair government's efforts to complete the work of reforming the house of lords it began in 1999 included no proposals to establish seats for universities. Even so, debates over the role of appointed members in a modernised second chamber employed concepts and language that would not have been unfamiliar to those who had argued over the merits of university representation (or, for that matter, close boroughs):

> To its critics, today's House of Lords, filled with appointed life peers, a rump of the old hereditary members, a smattering of bishops and senior judges in the shape of serving law lords, represents an unelected bloc that is fundamentally at odds with the principles of democracy. To its defenders, the appointed chamber allows expert peers, untroubled by the short-term requirements of elections to scrutinize and, if necessary, delay laws in the long term interests of the public.[12]

As in the earlier case of university representation, supporters of the plan for Lords reform justified the idea of bypassing regular electoral pressures by the promise of strengthening the legislature with highly talented individuals or species of disinterested experts who might otherwise be unable or unwilling to participate.[13] Critics, on the other hand, saw the proposals as inconsistent with general principles of representative democracy and likely to favour the installation of party placemen who could not succeed at the polls.[14] In the same way, university representation had been viewed as either a source of safe seats or a special parliamentary asset.

In the longer view, therefore, university representation needs to be understood within the context of enduring constitutional tensions in modern British political history. Along with rotten boroughs and Lords reform, the concern in each case was to preserve or create mechanisms by which, it was argued, the contributions of especially talented individuals to parliamentary deliberations could be secured when they might otherwise be discouraged from seeking election through the usual process. Additionally, these mechanisms came to be thought of as a useful counterbalance to the excesses that purely popular electoral procedures might produce. At the same time, objections in all three cases focused on the inequitable, unrepresentative and undemocratic nature of these arrangements. With respect to university representation – from Lord John Russell's early ideas about the independent character of university voters to later claims about the independence of university MPs – the persistent belief that it would harness learning to the political process without partisanship was never adequately justified, notwithstanding the service of a number of exceptional individuals.

---

[12] Ben Russell, 'After 10 Years, How Close is Labour to Reforming the House of Lords? The Big Question', *The Independent*, 6 Feb. 2007, p. 30.

[13] See Meg Russell, *Reforming the House of Lords: Lessons from Overseas* (Oxford, 2000), 301–7. At various points, Russell takes note of the independent role of the university senators in the primarily vocational Irish Seanad created in 1937 (esp. 73, 80, 81, 98, 151–52), though the Irish model is not among those she considered most relevant to the future of the Lords.

[14] On proposals for the Lords, see Vernon Bogdanor, 'Why the Lords Doesn't Need More Politicians: An Elected Upper House Would Turn into a Retirement Home for Failed Party Hacks', *Sunday Telegraph*, 11 Feb. 2007, p. 24.

2. *Significance*

University representation was created in order to protect the corporate interests of Oxford and Cambridge following a period of intense political and religious uncertainty under the Tudors. It carried on throughout the turmoil of the 17th century, and became even more constitutionally embedded during the political stabilisation that followed. Thus, university representation did not simply endure as the Westminster parliamentary system gradually took shape around it in the 17th and 18th centuries. Rather, it was incorporated within the body of political ideas and structures that emerged over the course of this period. During these two centuries, England also became the centre of an empire, and university representation travelled along with imperial rule and colonial settlement, playing its distinctive part in the extension of English political forms and religious interests in Ireland and North America.

The intertwined domestic–imperial duality of university representation continued to develop in the 19th and 20th centuries. In the United Kingdom, to which Ireland had been uneasily joined, the growth of university representation was the point at which the processes of political reform and the expansion of higher education connected. The growth of university representation between 1868 and 1918 was not the anachronism that critics claimed. By encompassing a broader range of older and new centres of higher learning, university representation's significance shifted from protecting a more narrowly defined set of institutional and religious concerns to manifesting a new dynamic of modernising cross-currents in both politics and society.

The new university constituencies that were established in 1868 were in no way inconsistent with the broadening but still limited electorate under a variety of franchises. And as the modern party system took shape in the later 19th century, it is hardly surprising that party influences would make their mark on university constituencies. Although it was increasingly criticized, university representation survived and grew further in 1918, in part because of the degree to which it was entangled with larger issues like franchise reform, plural voting and the representation of women. On another level, in an era of political transition, providing extra votes for segments of the polity – in this case, the highly educated – thought most likely to be invested in the stability of the existing order had a clear political logic that seems far more compelling than the justifications made for including representatives with special capacities and perspectives. Apart from whatever merits might be argued for it, the politics of reform and the timing of external events favoured the continued existence of university representation in the face of increasing hostility. It narrowly escaped harm in the early 20th century during the great parliamentary struggle between Liberals and Conservatives, and subsequently only survived because of the outbreak of the Great War. It seems fitting, therefore, that university representation's extinction occurred in the aftermath of another world war.

In the empire, as in Britain, each iteration of university representation or attempt to establish it arose at a point of confluence between political and educational developments. But the dynamics in each case varied greatly depending on the character of the imperial territory in question. In the settler colonies of Canada and Australasia, efforts to create universities grew out of the intertwined political and cultural aspirations of local conservative elites, and promoting the representation of learning in their assemblies stemmed from their twin desires to counter the rising spirit of democracy and to moderate the perceived philistinism of incipient colonial self-rule. In the colonists' debates over the merits of establishing university seats, the extent to which university representation was understood as a normative feature of Westminster constitutionalism was readily apparent. Even the critics did not dismiss university representation as an exotic deviation; rather, they argued that it was inappropriate in their particular colonial contexts and inconsistent with the new polities that were taking shape.

In India and Malta, the situation was rather different from that in the settler colonies, although many of the same impulses were present in one form or another. The representation of universities served as one element in structures of self-government based around the representation of interest groups and communities. The directly imposed and sustained nature of British rule in these places supported longer-lived versions of university representation than in the settler colonies, where the idea was at best only fleetingly realized. The Indian and Maltese cases demonstrate how the British saw university representation as a way of ensuring that any limited form of self-government they granted would include people whose British-influenced education would lend stability to the experiment. In this respect, notwithstanding important differences in the nature of the power relationships, the outlook of the Government of India and the British administration in Malta was clearly related to the ways that conservative elites in Canada and Australasia looked to universities and their parliamentary representation to sustain their own social and political order against the more radical forces at work.

University representation's sporadic appearances in Maltese politics must also be seen as one part of the long-term experiment of bringing a Mediterranean society into some rough conformity with British norms, culminating in 1955–6 with the stillborn attempt to join Malta to the United Kingdom as a fully fledged *départment d'outre-mer*. But the scope and longevity of university representation in India provide the basis for special comparison with the British experience. After 1857, the central dilemma of British policy in India was, on the one hand, whether or how to modernise and, on the other, the extent to which traditionalism should be reaffirmed. The creation of railway and telegraph systems and, indeed, legislative bodies, counted among the most apparent manifestations of British commitment to modernisation. The creation of universities to organise higher learning and provide suitably educated Indian administrators can also be seen in this light. Simultaneously, 'ornamentalism' attested to a vision of adhering to tradition, though it was a largely invented tradition intended to deepen the hold of British power.[15]

In the political realm, therefore, university representation in India, as in Britain, can be understood as a modern institution that was introduced within a particular political context – a growing but still limited franchise – and was made possible by the creation of universities to meet the new needs of society and the state. But the unintended consequence was to provide an entrée into politics for one of the groups that would ultimately prove instrumental in the effort to undermine British rule. In these ways, the history of university representation in India, especially in comparison to contemporaneous developments in Britain, provides an exemplary instance of the theoretical and practical complexities involved in modernising projects.

---

[15] David Cannadine, *Ornamentalism: How the British Saw their Empire* (Oxford, 2001).

Like other aspects of the British constitution, conceptions of who or what was represented by university seats never resolved itself into a fixed principle or set of principles. Rather, they varied over time and covered a wide range of possibilities, including the institutions (as akin to boroughs, or as centres of talent), those who were educated by them (or specific subsets of graduates), 'learning' generally, specific kinds of learning (arts versus professional), religion, and national or regional interests. In the eyes of critics, these conceptions also involved, variously, privilege, inequality, slavish imitation of the mother country, and graduates who were unfit or unworthy. This was further complicated by the plurality of the franchise that obtained in most cases, leading to questions of whether and for whom the representation was actually needed in practice.

In Britain, wider debates about broadening electoral participation from the 1830s until 1918 revolved around notions about the types of people who were fit to exercise the vote. The growth of university representation over this period can almost be understood as a parallel, institutional version of these more general ideas. Anticipating a second measure of reform, both the Scottish universities and London sought to demonstrate their fitness for enfranchisement, just as the 'capable citizenry' had shown to Gladstone's satisfaction that they should come 'within the pale of the constitution'.[16] Similarly, the civic universities demonstrated value to the nation during the Great War, which opened the way for their enfranchisement in a manner analogous to the experience of workers, women and veterans below normal voting age. In all cases, national contributions and the readiness to assume the obligations of parliamentary representation were routinely claimed by the universities and their supporters.

At the same time, like social groups that did not yet have the vote, the complex and gradual constitutional processes that took shape after 1832 established the *expectation* that the franchise would be granted sooner rather than later. Accordingly, as new universities started coming into their own towards the end of the 19th century, they argued that they should not continue to be held in an inferior status. This culminated in 1918 with what could be termed 'full university suffrage'. But this was hardly 'one-university-one-vote' given the entirely unsystematic terms on which university constituencies were organised. The simultaneous advent of an essentially full democratic franchise fundamentally altered the conditions in which university representation had managed to flourish. Even opening up the multiple-seat university constituencies to the single transferable vote could not make them more relevant to the new polity.

The relationship between conceptions of university representation and of representation more generally varied across imperial settings. In the settler colonies, the spread of this part of the British parliamentary model ultimately proved incompatible with the more advanced democratic sentiments that prevailed among those who succeeded in giving shape to the local constitutional order. In Canada, popular objections to the religious basis of the proposed King's College prevented the university from establishing itself in time to claim the legislative seat to which it had been entitled by statute before the constitutional reconfiguration associated with the union of the two Canadian provinces tacitly closed the door on university representation. In Australasia, the vigorous assertion of democratic principles and the rapid advance to manhood suffrage for the settler population, especially when combined with the practical and economic impera-

---

[16] See H.C G. Matthew, *Gladstone, 1809–1874* (Oxford, 1986), 139.

tives of colonial development and the struggles over how far to replicate British traditions and structures, severely curtailed the possibilities for the representation of (at best barely established) universities.

In India, the place of university representation within the context of broader ideas about representation was different from that in both the settler colonies and Britain. Seats for Indian universities were initially conceived of as part of the groundwork being laid for the development of representative institutions. The universities were initially looked to as 'reliable' electorates – that is, ones that would behave according to British models, not so much from the fact that the constituencies had a family relationship to those at Westminster, but rather by virtue of shared understandings derived from western education and the institutions' close ties to the structures of imperial rule. Yet, the subsequent formation of bodies for some measure of self-government under the Raj placed the university constituencies in a different relationship as one variety of many specialised corporate or communal constituencies. In part, as the universities increasingly returned members with antagonistic political positions, the British sought to identify more reliably conservative interests to help uphold the existing order. Meanwhile, the Government of India and the universities themselves sought to limit the basis of their representation to the governing bodies in order to mitigate the influence of nationalistic graduates.

Looking at these overlapping interests of university institutions and the general political order in different settings helps to answer the question of why university representation survived as long as it did. In India, independence from British rule and the commitment to a democratic constitution (to which a number of former university representatives contributed) provided the kind of sweeping change required to undo institutional structures that, once established, are always difficult to get rid of under normal circumstances. Similarly, constitutional changes in Canada and New South Wales also occasioned the elimination of university representation.

Uprooting university representation in Britain also occurred in a moment of dramatic political and social, if not quite constitutional, change. Given the difficulty opponents of university representation encountered in their sundry efforts to eliminate university seats, it is possible that it might have continued even longer but for the unusual intensity of democratic impulses produced by wartime experience and given effect by the 1945 Labour government supported by an overwhelming majority in the Commons. The durability of university representation may be attributed to the paradox that lay at its core. On the one hand, while giving seats to universities may have sprung in part from effective lobbying by those institutions and their supporters, among politicians of all persuasions the university franchise was increasingly understood in the 19th and 20th centuries as a safeguard (though hardly the only one) against the democratic trend of politics.

Although the tories reaped the electoral benefits, university representation was hardly their cause alone. From Russell and Mill to Rathbone, more progressively minded politicians and thinkers argued for the importance of learning as a special criterion for representation. On the other hand, if the high politics of extending university representation seemed to run against the grain of democratising reforms, the state also provided the sources of modernisation, albeit less directly, via government policies for reforming the ancient universities and encouraging the creation of new centres of learning that broadened the social reach and educational purposes of higher education. Extending the representation of universities beyond the old anglican monopolies to institutions serving new, non-elite social strata and geographical catchments was fully in keeping with progressive developments in higher education and new views about the role of universities in a modern (or modernising) society.

When Sir Edward Coke succeeded in obtaining letters patent for Oxford and Cambridge to return burgesses to parliament, he could never have imagined how his innovation in the structure of representation would develop over time, the extent to which it would spread throughout the British Isles and to an empire of then inconceivable dimensions, the seemingly contradictory functions it would come to perform within the political system, or the panoply of imperfect justifications that would come to be offered for its continued existence. This is because the history of university representation provides a pathway through the profound transformations of British politics, and their reflection in the wider world, from 1603 to 1950 – from royal absolutism to full parliamentary democracy; from a traditional and religiously ordered society to a modern secularised one; from the early glimmerings of the scientific revolution to the threshold of the post-industrial information age; from the beginnings of global supremacy to the end. All these changes and more were reflected in, and are illuminated by, the history of university representation.

Appendix 1: A Timeline of University Representation

	England & Wales	Scotland	Ireland	North America	Mediterranean	India	Australasia
1603	Oxford and Cambridge granted the privilege of returning two burgesses each to parliament. First burgesses elected.						
1613			Dublin (Trinity College) granted the privilege of returning two burgesses to the Irish parliament. First burgesses elected.				
1653	Nominated Parliament: university representation merged into three-member county constituencies.						
1654	Under the Instrument of Government, Oxford and Cambridge represented by one member each.		Dublin's separate representation abolished in united Commonwealth Parliament.				
1658	Second Protectorate Parliament: university seats moved to new upper House.						
1660	Restoration: Oxford and Cambridge resumed returning two burgesses to the house of commons.		Irish parliament re-established; Dublin's seats restored.				
1693				William and Mary's royal charter granted the college, once fully established, the privilege of returning a member to the Virginia house of burgesses.			
1715				W&M attempted but failed to seat a representative.			
1718				W&M returned a member.			
1720				W&M returned a member.			

1730	Following the 1729 transfer of property from the temporary corporation to the college; W&M began to return members on a continuous basis.
1776	W&M's representation ended with start of American revolution. — Malta came under British protection.
1800	Act of Union. 100 MPs for Irish constituencies added to house of commons.
1812	Irish parliament dissolved; Dublin's representation transferred to Westminster and reduced to one member. — Sicily adopted British-style constitution; parliament included seats for universities of Palermo and Catana.
1815	Sicilian parliament dissolved.
1820	Upper Canada Assembly approved representation of proposed King's College (Toronto).
1826	University of London (later University College London) established. — Royal commission on the Universities and Colleges of Scotland (reported in 1831).
1827	University of Durham established. — King's College granted royal charter.
1832	Under the Great Reform Act, Dublin's representation restored to two seats; MAs now eligible to vote.
1836	Federated University of London created.
1837	Sectarian clauses of King's College charter removed.
1840	Union Act: joined provinces of Upper and Lower Canada.
1842	King's College inaugurated.

Appendix 1: (*Continued*)

	England & Wales	Scotland	Ireland	North America	Mediterranean	India	Australasia
1845			University colleges established at Belfast, Cork and Galway.				
1848					Following Sicily's liberal revolution, provisional government called a parliament based on 1812 constitution: universities of Palermo, Catania and Messina represented. Lasted 16 months.		
1850			Queen's University of Ireland established, federating colleges at Belfast, Cork and Galway.				New South Wales legislative council voted to turn Sydney College into a university (opened in 1852).
1851	Owens College (Manchester) established.						
1852	Royal commissions on reform of Oxford and Cambridge. Resulted in acts (1854, 1856) enabling nonconformists to matriculate and take degrees.						
1853							University of Melbourne established (opened in 1855).
1857						Universities established at Bombay, Calcutta and Madras.	

1858	Universities (Scotland) Act: reconstructed universities' constitutions.
	University of Sydney received royal charter.
	NSW Electoral Act provided for representation for University of Sydney when it has 100 graduates.
	Failed attempt by University of Melbourne to gain representation.
1859	Statutes of Upper and Lower Canada consolidated: repealed 1820 act providing for university representation.
	University of Sydney gained a seat in NSW legislative council.
1861	Indian Councils Act: established provincial councils.
1864	Postal voting introduced for university constituencies.
1867–8	Second Reform Act (1867): University of London gained one seat in the house of commons.
	Representation of the People (Scotland) Act (1868): Scottish university constituencies established: Edinburgh and St Andrews (one seat); Glasgow and Aberdeen (one seat).
1870	Federated University of New Zealand established, with colleges at Auckland, Christchurch (Canterbury), Dunedin (Otago) and Wellington.
1871–2	Queensland elections bills allowed for representation of a university once it is established.
1875	Mason Science College (later University of Birmingham) founded.
	NZ Qualification of Electors Bill: question of university representation raised in debates.

Appendix 1: *(Continued)*

	England & Wales	Scotland	Ireland	North America	Mediterranean	India	Australasia
1876							Failed attempt by University of Melbourne to gain representation.
1877	Universities of Oxford and Cambridge Act created commissions for carrying out various statutory reforms.						
1878						College (later university) established at Rangoon.	
1880			Royal University of Ireland succeeded Queen's University; added catholic colleges.				NSW Electoral Act abolished University of Sydney's seat.
1881							NZ Representation Act: question of university representation raised during debates; Act placed representation on population basis.
1882						University of Punjab established.	
1884	Victoria University established, included Owen's College, University College at Liverpool, Yorkshire College of Science at Leeds.						
1885	Reform and Redistribution Acts: university representation preserved by compromise.						
1887					Constitution of Malta provided for representation of the University of Malta in the council of government.	University of Allahabad established.	Queensland Elections Bill provided for representation of future university once it reaches 100 graduates.

Year	Britain (England/Wales)	Scotland & Malta	Ireland	India & Empire
1892				Indian Councils Act: university constituencies added to councils of Calcutta, Bombay, Madras and United Provinces.
1893	University of Wales established, including colleges at Aberystwyth, Bangor and Cardiff.			
1900	Mason College received charter and became University of Birmingham. Other 'civic' universities followed suit.			
1903		Maltese constitution collapsed: run as a crown colony.		
1909				Indian Councils Act: enlarged councils. University of Punjab gained representation. University of Patna established.
1913	Plural Voting Bill			
1917				
1918	Representation of the People Act: two seats created for Combined English Universities and one for University of Wales; women graduates over 30 obtained university franchise; all qualified Oxford and Cambridge graduates entitled to vote; proportional representation for multi-member constituencies.	Representation of the People Act: Scottish university constituencies combined into single three-member constituency; members to be elected by proportional representation.	Redistribution of Seats (Ireland) Act: seats created for Queen's University Belfast (one) and the National University of Ireland (one). All Dublin graduates entitled to vote; members to be elected by proportional representation.	
1919				Government of India Act: provincial university constituencies retained; franchise to be extended to planned universities of Dacca and Nagpur.

Appendix 1: (*Continued*)

	England & Wales	Scotland	Ireland	North America	Mediterranean	India	Australasia
1920			Ireland partitioned, with regional parliaments in north and south: universities represented in each body.			University of Dacca established.	
1921					New Maltese constitution provided for university representation in the senate.		
1922			Irish Free State established: members for Dublin and NUI transferred from Westminster; each entitled to return three members to new Dominion Parliament.				
1923						University of Nagpur established. Burma incorporated into the Raj; University of Rangoon gained representation.	
1928	University of Reading added to Combined English Universities constituency.						
1930						Indian statutory commission report: maintained university seats.	
1935						Government of India Act: maintained university seats; Madras and United Provinces constituencies enlarged to include multiple universities. Burma separated from British India.	
1937			Republic of Ireland established: university seats transferred to senate.				

Year		
1939		Provincial governments suspended in five provinces with university constituencies: Bihar, Bombay, Central Provinces, Madras and United Provinces.
1947	New Maltese constitution dispensed with senate; university representation eliminated.	British India partitioned into independent states of India and Pakistan. Indian constituent assembly resolved to abolish university representation.
1948	Representation of the People Act: abolished university constituencies with the next general election.	
1950	University seats abolished at Westminster.	Constitution of India took effect: university seats in state legislatures abolished.
1950–1	Tory Party included restoration of university seats in election platform (dropped from 1955 platform).	
1955		University constituencies ended in Pakistan.
1969	QUB seats in Northern Ireland parliament abolished and replaced with territorial constituencies.	
1979	Republic of Ireland amended constitution to create additional senate seats for other tertiary institutions; never implemented.	
1982	Lord Cranborne's abortive private members' bill to restore university seats.	

Appendix 2: Representation of Universities in the English, Irish and United Kingdom Parliaments (by Decade), 1603–1950

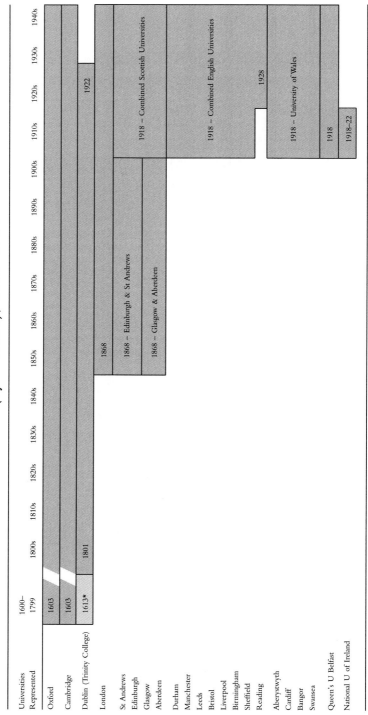

★ Granted representation in the Irish parliament in 1613; transferred to UK parliament by 1800 Act of Union

Appendix 3: University Representatives in the Parliaments of England, Great Britain and the United Kingdom, 1603–1950

Parliament	Oxford	Cambridge	Dublin	London	Edinburgh & St Andrews Combined Scottish (from 1918)	Glasgow & Aberdeen	Combined English	Wales	Belfast	National U Ireland
1604–11	**Dunne, Sir Daniel** **Crompton, Sir Thomas** (d 1608) **Byrd, Sir William** (fr 1608)	**Mountlowe, Henry** **Steward, Nicholas**	*Represented in Irish Parliament from 1613 to 1800 (see Appendix 4)*							
1614	Dunne, Sir Daniel **Bennett, Sir John**	**Bacon, Sir Francis** **Sandys, Sir Miles**								
1621–2	Bennett, Sir John (expelled 1621) **Edmondes, Sir Clement** **Danvers, Sir John** (fr 1621)	**Naunton, Sir Robert** **Gooch, Barnaby**								
1624–5	**Calvert, Sir Geroge** **Wake, Sir Isaac**	Naunton, Sir Robert Gooch, Barnaby								
1625	Danvers, Sir John **Edmondes, Sir Thomas**	Naunton, Sir Robert **Morton, Sir Albertus**								
1626	Danvers, Sir John Edmondes, Sir Thomas (unseated) **Stewart, Sir Francis** (fr 1626)	**Coke, Sir John** **Eden, Thomas**								
1628–9	Danvers, Sir John **Marten, Sir Henry**	Coke, Sir John Eden, Thomas								
1640	Danvers, Sir John **Windebanke, Sir Francis**	Eden, Thomas **Lucas, Henry**								
1640–2	**Roe, Sir Thomas** (d 1644) **Selden, John**	Eden, Thomas (d 1645) Lucas, Henry **Bacon, Nathaniel** (fr 1645)								
1653 *Nominated Parliament*	**Goddard, Jonathan**	**Sadler, John**								

Appendix 3: (*Continued*)

Parliament	Oxford	Cambridge	Dublin	London	Edinburgh & St Andrews Combined Scottish (from 1918)	Glasgow & Aberdeen	Combined English	Wales	Belfast	National U of Ireland
1654–5	**Owen, John**	**Cromwell, Henry**								
1656–8	**Fiennes, Nathaniel**	**Cromwell, Richard**								
1659	**Hale, Sir Matthew** **Mills, John**	**Thurloe, John** **Sclater, Thomas**								
1660	**Clayton, Thomas** Mills, John	**Crouch, Thomas** **Montague, William**								
1661–79	**Finch, Sir Heneage** (p 1674) **Hyde, Lawrence** **Thynne, Thomas** (fr 1674)	Crouch, Thomas **Fanshawe, Sir Richard**								
1679	**Finch, Herneage** **Edisbury, John**	**Exton, Sir Thomas** **Vernon, James**								
1679–81	**Jenkins, Sir Leoline** **Perrot, Charles**	Exton, Sir Thomas **Temple, Sir William**								
1681	Jenkins, Sir Leoline Perrot, Charles	Exton, Sir Thomas **Brady, Robert**								
1685–7	Jenkins, Sir Leoline (d 1685) Perrot, Charles **Clarke, Sir George** (fr 1685)	Exton, Sir Thomas Brady, Robert								
1689–90	**Finch, Herneage** **Clarges, Sir Thomas**	**Sawyer, Sir Robert** **Newton, Isaac**								
1690–5	Finch, Heneage Clarges, Sir Thomas	Sawyer, Sir Robert (d 1692) **Finch, Edward** **Boyle, Henry** (fr 1692)								
1695–8	Finch, Heneage **Trumbull, Sir William**	Boyle, Henry **Oxenden, George**								
1698–1700	**Musgrave, Sir Christopher** **Glynne, Sir William**	Boyle, Henry **Hammond, Anthony**								
1701	Finch, Heneage Musgrave, Sir Christopher	Boyle, Henry Newton, Isaac								
1701–2	**Bromley, William** Finch, Herneage (fr 1701)	Boyle, Henry **Annesley, Arthur**								

1702–5	Bromley, William Finch, Heneage (to 1703) **Whitelocke, Sir William** (fr 1703)	Boyle, Henry Annesley, Arthur
1705–7	Bromley, William Whitelocke, Sir William	Annesley, Arthur **Windsor, Dixie**
1707–8	Whitelocke, Sir William Bromley, William	Annesley, Arthur Windsor, Dixie
1708–10	Whitelocke, Sir William Bromley, William	Annesley, Arthur Windsor, Dixie
1710–13	Whitelocke, Sir William Bromley, William	Windsor, Dixie **Paske, Thomas**
1713–15	Whitelocke, Sir William Bromley, William	Windsor, Dixie Paske, Thomas
1715–22	Bromley, William Whitelocke, Sir William (to 1717) **Clarke, George** (fr 1717)	Windsor, Dixie Paske, Thomas (to 1720) **Willoughby, Thomas** (fr 1720)
1722–7	Bromley, William Clarke, George	Windsor, Dixie Willoughby, Thomas
1727–34	Bromley, William (to 1732) Clarke, George **Hyde, Henry** (fr 1732)	**Townshend, Thomas Finch, Edward**
1734–41	Hyde, Henry Clarke, George (to 1736) Bromley, William (1737) **Butler, Edward** (fr 1737)	Townshend, Thomas Finch, Edward
1741–7	Hyde, Henry Butler, Edward (to 1745) **Palmer, Peregrine** (fr 1745)	Townshend, Thomas Finch, Edward
1747–54	Hyde, Henry (to 1750) **Newdigate, Sir Roger** (fr 1751) Palmer, Peregrine	Townshend, Thomas Finch, Edward

Appendix 3: (Continued)

Parliament	Oxford	Cambridge	Dublin	London	Edinburgh & St Andrews Combined Scottish	Glasgow & Aberdeen Combined Scottish (from 1918)	Combined English	Wales	Belfast	National U of Ireland
1754–61	Newdigate, Sir Roger Palmer, Peregrine	Townshend, Thomas Finch, Edward								
1761–8	Newdigate, Sir Roger Palmer, Peregrine (to 1762) **Bagot Walter** (1762–8) **Dolben, Sir William** (1768)	Townshend, Thomas Finch, Edward								
1768–74	**Page, Francis** Newdigate, Sir Roger	Townshend, Thomas **Yorke, Charles** (to 1770) **De Grey, William** (fr 1770; j 1771) **Croftes, Richard** (fr 1771)								
1774–80	Page, Francis Newdigate, Sir Roger	Croftes, Richard **Manners, Charles** (p 1779) **Mansfield, James** (fr 1779)								
1780–4	Page, Francis Dolben, Sir William	Mansfield, James **Townshend, Lord John**								
1784–90	Page, Francis Dolben, Sir William	**earl of Euston** **Pitt, William**								
1790–6	Page, Francis Dolben, Sir William	earl of Euston Pitt, William								
1796–1800	Page, Francis Dolben, Sir William	earl of Euston Pitt, William								
1801–2	**Scott, Sir William** (fr 1801) Dolben, Sir William	earl of Euston Pitt, William	**Knox, George**							
1802–6	Scott, Sir William Dolben, Sir William	earl of Euston Pitt, William (d 1806)	Knox, George							
1806–7	Scott, Sir William **Abbot, Charles**	earl of Euston **Petty, Lord Henry**	Knox, George							
1807–12	Scott, Sir William Abbot, Charles	earl of Euston (p 18ll) **Gibbs, Sir Vicary** **Lord Palmerston** (fr 1811)	**Foster, John Leslie**							

1812–18	Scott, Sir William Abbot, Charles (p 1817) **Peel, Robert** (fr 1817)	Lord Palmerston **Smyth, John H.**	**Plunkett, William C.**
1818–20	Peel, Robert Scott, Sir William	Lord Palmerston Smyth, John H.	Plunkett, William C.
1820–6	Peel, Robert Scott, Sir William (p 1821) **Heber, Richard** (fr 1821)	Lord Palmerston Smyth, John H. (to 1822) **Bankes, William J.** (fr. 1822)	Plunkett, William C.
1826–30	Peel, Robert (to 1829) **Estcourt, Thomas** (fr 1829) **Inglis, Sir Robert** (fr 1829)	Lord Palmerston **Copley, John Singleton** (j 1827) **Tindal, Sir Nicholas** (fr 1827; j 1829) **Cavendish, William** (fr. 1829)	**Croker, John Wilson**
1831–2	Inglis, Sir Robert Estcourt, Thomas	**Goulburn, Henry** **Peel, William Yeats**	**Lefroy, Thomas L.**
1833–4	Inglis, Sir Robert Estcourt, Thomas	Goulburn, Henry **Manners-Sutton, Charles**	Lefroy, Thomas L. **Shaw, Sir Frederick**
1835–7	Inglis, Sir Robert Estcourt, Thomas	Goulburn, Henry Manners-Sutton, Charles (p 1835) **Law, Charles Evan** (fr 1835)	Lefroy, Thomas L. Shaw, Sir Frederick
1837–41	Inglis, Sir Robert Estcourt, Thomas	Goulburn, Henry Law, Charles Evan	Lefroy, Thomas L. Shaw, Sir Frederick
1841–7	Inglis, Sir Robert Estcourt, Thomas	Goulburn, Henry Law, Charles Evan	Shaw, Sir Frederick **Jackson, Joseph** (j 1842) **Hamilton, George A.** (fr 1843)
1847–52	**Gladstone, William** Inglis, Sir Robert	Goulburn, Henry Law, Charles Evan (to 1850) **Wigram, Loftus** (fr 1850)	Hamilton, George A. **Napier, Joseph**

Appendix 3: (*Continued*)

Parliament	Oxford	Cambridge	Dublin	London	Edinburgh & St Andrews Combined Scottish (from 1918)	Glasgow & Aberdeen Combined Scottish (from 1918)	Combined English	Wales	Belfast	National U of Ireland
1852–7	Gladstone, William Inglis, Sir Robert (to 1854; d 1855) **Heathcote, Sir** **William** (fr 1854)	Goulburn, Henry (d 1856) Wigram, Loftus (to 1856) **Walpole, Spencer** (fr 1856)	Hamilton, George A. Napier, Joseph							
1857–9	**Mowbray, Sir John** Heathcote, Sir William	Wigram, Loftus Walpole, Spencer	Hamilton, George A. Napier, Joseph (j 1858) **Lefroy, Anthony** (fr 1858)							
1859–65	Mowbray, Sir John Heathcote, Sir William	Walpole, Spencer **Selwyn, Charles**	Lefroy, Anthony **Whiteside, James**							
1865–7	**Hardy, Gathorne** Heathcote, Sir William	Walpole, Spencer Selwyn, Charles	Lefroy, Anthony Whiteside, James (j 1866) **Walsh, John Edward** (1866–7) **Chatterton, Hedges** (1867)							
1868–74	Hardy, Gathorne Mowbray, Sir John	Walpole, Spencer Selwyn, Charles (to 1868) **Hope, A.J. Beresford** (fr 1868)	Lefroy, Anthony (to 1870) **Warren, Robert** (1867–8) **Plunket, David Robert** (fr 1870) **Ball, John Thomas** (fr 1868)	**Lowe, Robert**	**Playfair, Lyon**	**Moncreiff, James** (to 1869) **Gordon, Edward S.** (fr 1869)				
1874–80	Hardy, Gathorne (to 1878) Mowbray, Sir John **Talbot, John Gilbert** (fr 1878)	Walpole, Spencer Hope, A.J. Beresford	Ball, John Thomas (to 1875) Plunket, David Robert **Gibson, Edward** (fr 1875)	Lowe, Robert	Playfair, Lyon	Gordon, Edward S. (p 1876) **Watson William** (fr 1876)				
1880–5	Talbot, John Gilbert Mowbray, Sir John	Walpole, Spencer (to 1882) Hope, A.J. Beresford **Raikes, Henry** (fr 1882)	Plunket, David Robert Gibson, Edward	**Lubbock, Sir** **John**	Playfair, Lyon	**Campbell, James** **Alexander**				
1886	Talbot, John Gilbert Mowbray, Sir John	Raikes, Henry Hope, A.J. Beresford	Plunket, David Robert **Holmes, Hugh**	Lubbock, Sir John	**Macdonald,** **John H.A.**	Campbell, James Alexander				

1886–92	Talbot, John Gilbert Mowbray, Sir John	Raikes, Henry (d 1891) Hope, A.J. Beresford (d 1887) **Jebb, Sir Richard C.** (fr 1891) **Stokes, George G.** (fr 1887)	Lubbock, Sir John	Plunket, David Robert Holmes, Hugh (to 1887) **Madden, Dodgson** (fr 1887)	Macdonald, John H.A. (to 1888) **Darling, Moir** Todd (1888–90) **Pearson, Sir Charles** (fr 1890)	Campbell, James Alexander				
1892–5	Talbot, John Gilbert Mowbray, Sir John	Jebb, Sir Richard C. **Gorst, Sir John Eldon**	Lubbock, Sir John	Plunket, David Robert **Carson, Sir Edward**	**Pearson, Sir Charles**	Campbell, James Alexander				
1895–1900	Talbot, John Gilbert Mowbray, Sir John (d 1899) **Anson, Sir William** (fr 1899)	Jebb, Sir Richard C. Gorst, Sir John Eldon	Lubbock, Sir John	Carson, Sir Edward **Lecky, W.E.H.**	Pearson, Sir Charles (to 1896) **Priestley, William O.** (fr 1896)	Campbell, James Alexander				
1900–6	Talbot, John Gilbert Anson, Sir William	Jebb, Sir Richard C. Gorst, Sir John Eldon	**Foster, Sir Michael**	Carson, Sir Edward Lecky, W.E.H. (d 1903) **Campbell, James** (fr 1903)	**Tuke, Sir John Batty**	Campbell, James Alexander				
1906–10	Talbot, John Gilbert Anson, Sir William	**Butcher, Samuel Henry** **Rawlinson, John Frederick**	**Magnus, Sir Philip**	Carson, Sir Edward Campbell, James (fr 1903)	Tuke, Sir John Batty	**Craik, Sir Henry**				
1910	**Lord Hugh Cecil** Anson, Sir William	Rawlinson, John Frederick Butcher, Samuel Henry	Magnus, Sir Philip	Carson, Sir Edward Campbell, James (fr 1903)	**Finlay, Sir Robert**	Craik, Sir Henry				
1910–18	Lord Hugh Cecil Anson, Sir William (to 1914) **Prothero, Rowland** (fr 1914)	Rawlinson, John Butcher, Samuel H. (d 1910) **Larmor, Sir Joseph** (fr 1911)	Magnus, Sir Philip	Carson, Sir Edward Campbell, James (fr 1903)	Finlay, Sir Robert (j 1916) **Johnston, Christopher** (1916–17) **Cheyne, Sir William** (fr 1917)	Craik, Sir Henry				
1918–22	Lord Hugh Cecil Prothero, Rowland (to 1919) **Oman, Sir Charles** (fr 1919)	Rawlinson, John Larmor, Sir Joseph	Magnus, Sir Philip	**Woods, Sir Robert** **Samuels, Arthur** (to 1919) **Jellett, William M.** (fr 1919)	Cheyne, Sir William **Cowan, Dugald** Craik, Sir Henry		**Fisher, H.A.L.** **Conway, Sir Martin**	**Lewis, John Herbert**	**Whitla, William**	**MacNeill, Eoin** (did not take seat)
1922–3	Lord Hugh Cecil Oman, Sir Charles	Rawlinson, John **Butler, James**	Magnus, Sir Philip	*Representation transferred to Irish Free State*	**Berry, Sir George** Cowan, Dugald Craik, Sir Henry		Fisher, H.A.L. Conway, Sir Martin	**Lewis, Thomas**	Whitla, William	*Representation transferred to Irish Free State*

Appendix 3: (Continued)

Parliament	Oxford	Cambridge	Dublin	London	Combined Scottish (Edinburgh & St Andrews / Glasgow & Aberdeen) (from 1918)	Combined English	Wales	Belfast	National U of Ireland
1923–4	Lord Hugh Cecil Oman, Sir Charles	Rawlinson, John **Butler, Sir George**		Magnus, Sir Philip	Berry, Sir George Cowan, Dugald Craik, Sir Henry	Fisher, H.A.L. Conway, Sir Martin	**Davies, George Lloyd**	**Sinclair, Thomas**	
1924–9	Lord Hugh Cecil Oman, Sir Charles	Rawlinson, John (to 1926) Butler, Sir George **Withers, Sir John** (fr 1926)		**Graham-Little, Sir Ernest**	Berry, Sir George Cowan, Dugald Craik, Sir Henry (d 1927) **Buchan, John** (fr 1927)	Fisher, H.A.L. (r 1926) Conway, Sir Martin **Hopkinson, Sir Alfred** (fr 1926)	**Evans, Ernest**	Sinclair, Thomas	
1929–31	Lord Hugh Cecil Oman, Sir Charles	Withers, Sir John **Wilson, Godfrey**		Graham-Little, Sir Ernest	Berry, Sir George Cowan, Dugald Buchan, John	Conway, Sir Martin **Rathbone, Eleanor**	Evans, Ernest	Sinclair, Thomas	
1931–5	Lord Hugh Cecil Oman, Sir Charles	Withers, Sir John **Pickthorn, Sir Kenneth**		Graham-Little, Sir Ernest	Cowan, Dugald (d 1933) Buchan, John **Skelton, Noel** **Morrison, George** (fr 1934)	**Craddock, Sir Reginald** Rathbone, Eleanor	Evans, Ernest	Sinclair, Thomas	
1935–45	Lord Hugh Cecil (to 1937) **Salter, Sir Arthur** (fr 1937) **Herbert, A.P.**	Pickthorn, Sir Kenneth Withers, Sir John (to 1940) **Hill, Archibald** (fr 1940)		Graham-Little, Sir Ernest	Skelton, Noel (d 1935) Morrison, George (r 1945) **Kerr, Sir John** **Macdonald, Ramsay** (fr 1936, d 1938) **Anderson, Sir John** (fr 1938) **Boyd-Orr, Sir John** (fr 1945)	Craddock, Sir Reginald (d 1937) Rathbone, Eleanor **Harvey, Thomas**	Evans, Ernest (j 1943) **Gruffydd, William** (fr 1943)	Sinclair, Thomas (r 1940) **Savory, Douglas Lloyd** (fr 1940)	
1945–50	Salter, Sir Arthur Herbert, A.P.	Pickthorn, Sir Kenneth **Harris, Henry Wilson**		Graham-Little, Sir Ernest	Kerr, Sir John Anderson, Sir John Boyd-Orr, Sir John (r 1946) **Elliot, Walter** (fr 1946)	Eleanor Rathbone (d 1946) **Lindsay, Kenneth** **Strauss, Henry** (fr 1946)	Gruffydd, William	Savory, Douglas Lloyd	

Note: Bold type indicates the first time a name appears.
Key:
d = died
j = judicial appointment (incl. lord chancellor)
p = peerage
r = resigned

Appendix 4: Burgesses for the University of Dublin (Trinity College) in the Irish House of Commons, 1613–1800

Parliament	Members	Notes
1613–15	**Temple, William**	
	Doyne, Charles	
1634–5	**Ware, Sir James**	
	James Donellan	
1639–49	Ware, Sir James	
	Gilbert, William	
1654–9	*Commonwealth Parliament: No Representation*	
1661–6	Ware, Sir James	
	Butler, Lord John	
1689	**Coghlan, Joseph**	
	Meade, Sir John	
1692–3	**Wynche, Sir Cyril**	
	Molyneux, William	
1695–9	**Aldworth, Richard**	
	Molyneux, William	Died 1698
	Crowe, William	Elected to replace Molyneux in 1698
1703–13	**Robinson, Sir William**	Died 1712
	Southwell, Edward	
1713–14	**Coghill, Marmaduke**	
	Elwood, John	
1715–27	Coghill, Marmaduke	
	Dopping, Samuel	Died 1720
	Hopkins, Edward	Elected to replace Dopping in 1721
1727–60	Coghill, Marmaduke	Died 1739
	Molyneux, Samuel	Died 1728
	Elwood, John	Elected to replace Molyneux in 1728; died 1740
	Tisdall, Philip	Elected to replace Coghill in 1739
	Acheson, Sir Archibald	Elected to replace Elwood in 1741
1761–8	**Clement, William**	
	Tisdall, Philip	
1769–76	**Molyneux, Capel**	
	Tisdall, Philip	
1776–83	**Hely-Hutchinson, Richard**	Switched to sitting for Sligo (for which he was also returned in 1776) in 1778
	Hussey-Burgh, Walter	Vacated seat in 1782 when appointed chief baron of the exchequer; died 1783
	Fitzgibbon, John	Elected in 1778 to replace Hely-Hutchinson
	Parsons, Sir Laurence	Elected in 1782 to replace Hussey-Burgh
1783–90	Parsons, Sir Laurence	
	Browne, Arthur	
1790–7	**Hely-Hutchinson, Francis**	
	Browne, Arthur	
1797–1800	**Knox, George**	Became MP for University of Dublin in UK parliament
	Browne, Arthur	
1801	*Irish Parliament dissolved under the Act of Union. Dublin University continued to be represented by one member at Westminster.*	

Note: Bold type indicates the first time a name appears.

Appendix 5: Members for the College of William and Mary in the Virginia House of Burgesses, 1700–76

Assembly	Name	Notes
1700–2	[Cowles, Thomas]	sheriff of James City Co.; not seated by Blair's objection?
1703–5	–	
1705–6	–	
1710–12	–	
1712–14	–	
1715	[Beverley, Peter]	former Speaker; not permitted by House to take seat
1718	**Custis, John**	
1720–2	**Jones, Thomas**	
1723–6	–	hiatus pending the 1729 Transfer
1727–34	**Nicholas, George**	'gentleman'; writ ordered in 1830 following Transfer; died 1734
1736–40	**Randolph, John**	Speaker; died 1737
	Barradall, Edward	attorney-general; from 1738; replaced John Randolph
1742–7	Barradall, Edward	attorney-general; died 1744
	Randolph, Beverley	from 1744; son of John Randolph
1748–9	Randolph, Beverley	
1750	Randolph, Beverley	
1752–5	**Randolph, Peyton**	son of John Randolph
1756–8	Randolph, Peyton	
1758–61	**Wythe, George**	
1761–5	**Page, Mann II**	
1765	**Blair, John Jr**	grand-nephew of James Blair
1766–8	Blair, John Jr	
1769	Blair, John Jr	
1769–71	Blair, John Jr	appointed clerk of the council in 1771
	Page (Rosewell), John	from 1771, replaced Blair
1772–4	Page (Rosewell), John	appointed to council 1773
	Randolph, John	from May 1774; attorney-general; son of John Randolph
1775–6	Randolph, John	

Notes: Bold type indicates the first time a name appears. Square brackets indicate elected but not seated.

Appendix 6: Allocation of Seats under the Government of India Act, 1935, for the Lower House in Each Provincial Legislature

Provinces	Total Seats	Total of General Seats	General Seats Reserved for Scheduled Castes	Seats for Representatives of Backward Areas and Tribes	Sikh Seats	Mohammedan Seats	Anglo-Indian Seats	European Seats	Indian Christian Seats	Seats for Representatives of Commerce, Industry, Mining and Planting	Landholders Seats	University Seats	Seats for Representatives of Labour	Seats for Women				
														General	Sikh	Mohammedan	Anglo-Indian	Indian Christian
Madras	215	146	30	1	–	28	2	3	8	6	6	1	6	6	–	1	–	1
Bombay	175	114	15	1	–	29	2	3	3	7	2	1	7	5	–	1	1	–
Bengal	250	78	30	–	–	117	3	11	2	19	5	2	8	2	–	2	–	–
United Provinces	228	140	20	–	–	34	1	2	2	3	6	1	3	4	–	2	–	–
The Punjab	175	42	8	–	31	84	1	1	2	1	5	1	3	1	1	2	–	–
Bihar	152	86	15	7	–	39	1	2	1	4	4	1	3	3	–	1	–	–
Central Provinces & Berar	112	84	20	1	–	14	1	1	–	2	3	1	2	3	–	–	–	–
Assam	108	47	7	9	–	34	–	1	1	11	–	–	4	1	–	–	–	–
North-West Frontier Province	50	9	–	–	3	36	–	–	–	–	2	–	–	–	–	–	–	–
Orissa	60	44	–	5	–	4	–	–	1	1	2	–	1	2	–	–	–	–
Sind	60	18	6	–	–	33	–	2	–	2	2	–	1	1	–	1	–	1
Totals	1,585	808	151	24	34	452	11	26	20	56	37	8	38	28	1	10	1	1

In Bombay seven of the general seats shall be reserved for Marathas.

In the Punjab one of the Landholders seats shall be a seat to be filled by a Tumandar.

In Assam and Orissa the seats reserved for women shall be non-communal seats.

Adapted from B.R. Ambedkar, *Pakistan, or the Partition of India* (2nd edn, Bombay, 1946), 444.

Appendix 7: University Members in Indian Provincial Legislative Councils, 1893–1955

Session	Member	Notes
Bombay		
1893–5	**Yajinik, Javerilal Uniashanker**	
1895–7	Yajinik, Javerilal Uniashanker	
1897–9	**Chandavarkar, Narayan Ganesh**	
1899–1901	Chandavarkar, Narayan Ganesh	
1901–3	**Krishna, Sir Bhalchandra**	
1903–5	**Setalvad, Chimanlal Harilal**	
1905–7	Setalvad, Chimanlal Harilal	
1907–9	Setalvad, Chimanlal Harilal	
1910–12	Setalvad, Chimanlal Harilal	
1913–16	Setalvad, Chimanlal Harilal	Resigned in 1915
	Samarth, Narayan Mudhav	
1917–19	**Paranjpye, Raghunath Purushottam**	
1919–21	Paranjpye, Raghunath Purushottam	
1921–3	Paranjpye, Raghunath Purushottam	
1923–5	**Jayakar, Mukund Ramaro**	
1927–9	**Munshi, Kanaiyalal Maneklal**	Resigned in 1928 over Bardoli Satyagraha, then re-elected
1929–36	Munshi, Kanaiyalal Maneklal	
1937–46★	Munshi, Kanaiyalal Maneklal	
1947–50	**Ker, Bal Gangadhar**	
Calcutta		
1893–5	**Bonnerjee, Woomesh Chandra**	
1895–7	**Bose, A.M.**	
1897–9	**Banurji, Kalicharan**	
1899–1901	**Mookerjee, Asutosh**	
1901–3	Mookerjee, Asutosh	
1903–5	**Bose, Bhupendranath**	
1905–7	Bose, Bhupendranath	
1907–9	**Sarvadhikari, Devaprasad**	
1910–12	Sarvadhikari, Devaprasad	
1913–16	Sarvadhikari, Devaprasad	
1916–20	Sarvadhikari, Devaprasad	
1921–3	**Ghose, Rai Bahadur Jogendra Chunder**	
1923–5	**Bose, Bejoy Krishna**	
1927–9	**Bose, Sarat Chandra**	
1929–36	**Mookerjee, Shyamaprasad**	
1937–46	Mookerjee, Shyamaprasad	
1946–8	Mookerjee, Shyamaprasad	
1948–50	**Roy, Bidhan Chandra**	
Madras (from 1937 includes Andhra and Annamalai)		
1893–5	**Miller, Rev. William**	
1895–7	Miller, Rev. William	Resigned in 1897
	Stuart, G.H.	
1897–9	Stuart, G.H.	Resigned in 1898
	Miller, Rev. William	
1899–1901	Miller, Rev. William	
1901–3	Miller, Rev. William	Resigned in 1902
	Bilderbeck, J.B.	
1904–5	**Iyer, P.S. Sivaswami**	
1905–7	Iyer, P.S. Sivaswami	

Appendix 7: (*Continued*)

Session	Member	Notes
1907–9	**Ayyer, Sri V. Krishnaswami**	
	Macphail, Rev. Earle Monteith	
1909–12	**Iyer, T. V. Sheshatiri**	
1913–14	Iyer, T. V. Sheshatiri	
1914–16	**Pittendrigh, Rev. George**	
1916–19	Pittendrigh, Rev. George	
1919–21	**Ayyar, Sri C. P. Ramaswami**	
	Macphail, Rev. Earle Monteith	From 1920
1921–3	**Iyengar, S. Srinivasa**	Resigned in 1922, in protest over arrest of Congress leaders
	Reddy, Cattamanchi Ramalinga	
1923–5	**Satyamurti, Sri S.**	
1926–30	Satyamurti, Sri S.	
1930–7	**Aiyar, T.S. Ramaswami Aiyar**	
1937–46★	**Rajagopalachari, Sri Chakravarti**	
1946?–50	**Bhashyam, K.**	

Allahabad (United Provinces Universities from 1937; includes Agra and Lucknow)

1893–5	**Colvin, Walter Mytton**	
1896–8	Colvin, Walter Mytton	
1898–1900	**Conlan, Thomas**	
1900–2	Conlan, Thomas	
1902–4	Conlan, Thomas	
1904–6	**Lal, Sir Sunder**	
1907–9	Lal, Sir Sunder	
1909	Lal, Sir Sunder	
1910–12	Lal, Sir Sunder	
1913–15	Lal, Sir Sunder	Resigned in 1915
	Banerji, Satish Chandra	Died a month after election
	Hussain, Syed Karamat	
1916–18	Lal, Sir Sunder	
1918–20	**Ward, A.W.**	
	Ahmad, Zia-ud-din	From 1919
1921–3	**Gurtu, Iqbal Narain**	
1924–6	**Prasad, Ganesh**	
1927–30	**Gurtu, Iqbal Narain**	
1930–6	**Prasad, Munshi Gajadhar**	
1937–46★	**Zaheer, Syed Husain**	
1946–50	**Kidwai, Rafi Ahmad**	Resigned in 1947
	Misra, Ram Dhar	

Punjab

1909–12	**Lal, Rai Bahadur Shadi**	
1912–13	Lal, Rai Bahadur Shadi	
1913–14	Lal, Rai Bahadur Shadi	
1914–16	**Chatterjee, Sir P.C.**	
1916–20	**Fazl-i-Husain, Mian**	
1921–3	**Lal, Manohar**	
1924–6	**Sahni, Lala Ruchi**	
1927–30	Lal, Manohar	
1930–7	Lal, Manohar	
1937–46	Lal, Manohar	
1947–9★★	unoccupied	
1951–5★★	**Shuja-ud-Din, Khalifa**	

Patna

1921–3	**Sen, Prasanta Kumer**	
1923–6	**Sahay, Shri Narayan**	

Appendix 7: (*Continued*)

Session	Member	Notes
1926–30	Sahay, Baldeva	
1930–6	**Hafeez, Maulavi Saiyid Muhammad**	
1937–46★	**Sinha, Sachchidananda**	
1946–50	Sinha, Sachchidananda	
Nagpur		
1921–3	**Bose, Bipin Krishna**	
1923–6	**Golwalker, M.K.**	
1926–30	Golwalker, M.K.	
1930–6	**Mangalmurti, D.T.**	
1937–46★	**Khaparde, Balkrishna Ganesh**	
1947–50	**Hasan, Syed Minhajul**	
Dacca		
1924–6	**Rahaman, A.F.**	
1927–9	**Chanduri, Maharaja Sashikanta Acharyya**	
1929–36	**Mazumdar, Birendra Nath**	Resigned in 1930
	Gosh, Rai Bahadur Sasanka Kumar	
1937–46	**Rahman, Fazlur**	
1947–54★★	unoccupied	

★ Provincial constitution suspended November 1939.
★★ In Pakistan.
Note: Bold type indicates the first time a name appears.

Bibliography

1. Manuscript, Archival and Related Collections

Archives New Zealand
    University of New Zealand, Minutes of Senate, 1880–4, ADAU 8740 UNZ1/3;
        ADAU 8746 UNZ13/7★7; UNZ13/8★8, UNZ13/9★9.
British Library
    India Office Records, IOR/L/PJ/9/14.
    Morley, John Collection, MSS Eur D573/9 and 11.
Jebb, R.C. Correspondence, in private hands, currently being edited for publication by
    Dr C.A. Stray, Swansea University.
The National Archives
    Beaverbrook Papers, BBK/H/253.
National Library of Wales
    Lewis, J. Herbert Papers, D79.
    'University of Wales By-Election 1943', http://www.llgc.org.uk/ymgyrchu/
        Pleidleisio/Is/1943/index-e.htm 3 Nov. 2006.
Newnham College, Cambridge, Newnham College Archives
    Newnham College Political Society Minute Book, 1894–5.
Public Record Office of Northern Ireland
    Northern Ireland Cabinet Minutes, CAB/4/1277/8; CAB/4/1307/12; CAB/4/1355/
        15.
Royal Institution of Great Britain
    Bragg, Sir Lawrence Papers, W.L. BRAGG/56A/514.
    Bragg, William Henry Papers, W.H. BRAGG/10A/35 and 36.
University of Birmingham Library, University of Birmingham Archive
    Minutes of the Committee of the Guild of Graduates.
    Minutes of Council.
    Minutes of the Guild of Graduates.
University of Bristol Library, Special Collections
    National Liberal Club Papers, Election Addresses, DM.668.
University of Edinburgh Library, Special Collections Division
    Miscellaneous Materials Relating to Glasgow University, Gen. 566/5.
University of Leeds Library, University of Leeds Archive
    Administrative Records: Parliamentary Representation.
    Microfilm Reels 133.F42; 134.F1.
    Minutes of Convocation.
    Minutes of Inter-Convocation Conference Held at the University of Manchester, 13
        July 1918.
    Minutes of Standing Committee of Convocation.

University of Liverpool, Archive of the University of Liverpool
  Letter Books of the Principal Later the Vice-Chancellor, nos. XX, XXV.
  Records of Convocation, S3681.
  Vice-Chancellor, P712/6; S2339; S2344.
University of London, Senate House Library, University of London Archives
  Convocation and Committees, UoL/CN 1/1/1; UoL/CN 1/1/3; UoL/CN 1/1/12;
    UoL/CN 1/1/13.
  Senate, UoL/ST 3/2/6.
University of Manchester, The John Rylands University Library
  Convocation Archive, CON/2/3.
  University of Manchester Council Archive, Minutes of Council.
  University of Manchester Court Archive, Minutes of Court.
  University of Manchester Senate Archive, Minutes of Senate.
  Vice Chancellor's Archive, VCA/6/24; VCA/7/138 (1); VCA/7/138 (2).
University of Melbourne, University of Melbourne Archives
  Minutes of Council.
  Registrar's Correspondence UM447, 685/1876 Representation in Parliament.
University of Oxford, Bodleian Library
  Fisher, H.A.L. Papers, MS Fisher 63.
University of Sheffield Library, University of Sheffield Administrative Archive
  Minutes of Council.
University of Sydney, University of Sydney Archives
  Minutes of the Senate.
  Windeyer, W.C., Personal Archives, P1.

2. Government and Related Publications

Calcutta University Commission, 1917–19, *Report*, iii, pt I: *Analysis of Present Conditions* (Calcutta, 1919).
Calendar of State Papers, Colonial Series, Vol. 18: America and the West Indies, 1700, ed. Cecil Headlam (1910).
Constituent Assembly Debates [India] (12 vols, Faridabad, 1946–50), iv.
Costituzione di Sicilia Stabilita nel Generale, Straordinario Parlamento del 1812 (Palermo, 1813).
Government of India, Department of Social Welfare, Ministry of Education and Social Welfare, *Toward Equality: Report of the Committee on the Status of Women in India* (New Delhi, 1974).
Hansard, *Parliamentary Debates* [United Kingdom] (3rd, 4th, 5th ser.).
Journals of the House of Burgesses of Virginia, 1712–1714, 1715, 1718, 1720–1722, 1723–1726, ed. H.R. McIlwaine (Richmond, 1912).
Journals of the House of Burgesses of Virginia, 1727–1734, 1736–1740, ed. H.R. McIlwaine (Richmond, 1910).
Journals of the House of Burgesses of Virginia, 1742–1747, 1748–1749, ed. H.R. McIlwaine (Richmond, 1909).
Journals of the House of Burgesses of Virginia, 1758–1761, ed. H.R. McIlwaine (Richmond, 1908).

Journals of the House of Burgesses of Virginia, 1761–1765, ed. John Pendleton Kennedy (Richmond, 1907).

Journals of the House of Burgesses of Virginia, 1766–1769, ed. John Pendleton Kennedy (Richmond, 1906).

Journals of the House of Burgesses of Virginia, 1770–1772, ed. John Pendleton Kennedy (Richmond, 1906).

Journals of the Legislative Assembly of Upper Canada for the Years 1818, 1819, 1820, 1821,Tenth Report of the Bureau of Archives for the Province of Ontario (Toronto, 1913).

Parliamentary Papers (United Kingdom)

A Bill to Abolish the Representation in Parliament of the Universities of the United Kingdom, Parliamentary Papers, 1894 (166), viii, 569.

Bill to Extend the Parliamentary Franchise to Men and Women and to Amend the Registration and Electoral System (Electors and Representation of the People: Absent and Infirm Voters), Parliamentary Papers, 1912–13 (109), v, 85.

A Bill Further to Amend the Laws Relating to the Representation of the People in England and Wales, Parliamentary Papers, 1854 (17), v, 375.

Conference on Electoral Reform: Letter from Mr Speaker to the Prime Minister, Parliamentary Papers, 1917–18 [Cmd 8463], xxv, 385.

Conference on Electoral Reform and Redistribution of Seats: Letter from Mr Speaker to the Prime Minister, Parliamentary Papers, 1943–4 [Cmd 6534], iii, 213.

Conference on the Reform of the Second Chamber: Letter from Viscount Bryce to the Prime Minister, Parliamentary Papers, 1918 [Cmd 9038], x, 569.

'*A Copy of the Electoral Bill Passed by the Legislature of New South Wales*', Parliamentary Papers, 1859 Session 1 (211), xvii, 343.

Draft Rules under the Government of India Act Required to Give Effect to the Notification Issued under Section 52A(1) of the Act of 27th October 1921, by the Governor-General of India in Council, with the Sanction of His Majesty, Constituting Burma as a Governor's Province under the Act, Parliamentary Papers, 1922 [Cmd 1672], xvi, 521.

East India (Constitutional Reforms – Elections), Return Showing the Results of Elections in India, 1923, Parliamentary Papers, 1924 [Cmd 2145], xxviii, 497.

East India (Constitutional Reforms – Elections), Return Showing the Results of Elections in India in 1929 and 1930, Parliamentary Papers, 1930–1 [Cmd 3922], xxiv, 363.

East India (Constitutional Reforms – Elections), Return Showing the Results of Elections in India, 1937, Parliamentary Papers, 1937–8 [Cmd 5589], xxi, 205.

East India (Constitutional Reforms: Lord Southborough's Committee), Vol. I: Report of the Committee Appointed by the Secretary of State for India to Enquire into Questions Connected with the Franchise and Other Matters Relating to Constitutional Reforms, Parliamentary Papers, 1919 [Cmd 141], xvi, 449.

East India (Constitutional Reforms: Lord Southborough's Committee), Vol. III: Views of the Government of India upon the Reports of Lord Southborough's Committees, Parliamentary Papers, 1919 [Cmd 176], xvi, 865.

Further Correspondence Respecting the Constitution and Administration of Malta, Parliamentary Papers, 1888 [Cmd 5308], lxxiii, 535.

Government of India Act, 1935: Report of the Committee Appointed in Connection with the Delimitation of Constituencies and Connected Matters, Vol. I, Parliamentary Papers, 1935–6 [Cmd 5099], ix, 1.

Government of India Act 1935: Report of the Committee Appointed in Connection with the Delimitation of Constituencies and Connected Matters, Volume II: Proposals for the Delimitation of Constituencies, Parliamentary Papers, 1935–6 [Cmd 5100], ix, 331.

Government of India's Despatch on Proposals for Constitutional Reform, Dated 20th September, 1930, Parliamentary Papers, 1930–1 [Cmd 3700], xxiii, 679.

Papers Relating to the New Constitution of Malta, Parliamentary Papers, 1921 [Cmd 1321], xxiv, 581.

Parliament Bill, 1947: Agreed Statement on Conclusion of Conference of Party Leaders, February–April 1948, Parliamentary Papers, 1947–8 [Cmd 7380], xxii, 1001.

Report of the Commissioners Appointed to Inquire into the Arrangements in the Inns of Court and Inns of Chancery, for Promoting the Study of the Law and Jurisprudence, Parliamentary Papers, 1854–5 [Cmd 1998], xviii, 345.

Report on Indian Constitutional Reforms, Parliamentary Papers, 1918 [Cmd 9109], viii, 113.

Report of the Indian Franchise Committee, Vol. I, Parliamentary Papers, 1931–2 [Cmd 4086], viii, 489.

Report of the Indian Statutory Commission, Vol. 1: Survey, Parliamentary Papers, 1929–30 [Cmd 3568], xi, 1.

Report of the Indian Statutory Commission, Vol. 2: Recommendations, Parliamentary Papers, 1929–30 [Cmd 3569], xi, 443.

Report from the Joint Select Committee on the Government of India Bill, Parliamentary Papers, 1919 (203), iv, 1.

Report Made to His Majesty by a Royal Commission of Inquiry into the State of the Universities of Scotland, Parliamentary Papers, 1831 (310), xii, 111.

Return Showing, for Each Parliamentary Constituency in the United Kingdom, the Numbers of Parliamentary and Local Government Electors on the First Register Compiled under the Representation of the People Act, 1918, Parliamentary Papers, 1918 (138), xix, 925.

Provincial Papers: Documents and Records Relating to the Province of New Hampshire, Vol. VII: From 1764 to 1776, ed. Nathaniel Buton (Nashua, NH, 1873).

Seanad Éireann Committee on Procedure and Privileges, Sub-committee on Seanad Reform, *Report on Seanad Reform* (2004).

Statuto Costituzionale del Regno di Sicilia, 1848.

The Universities of Canada: Their History and Organization with an Outline of British and American University Systems: Appendix to the Report of the Minister of Education, 1896 (Toronto, 1896).

3. Institutional Publications

College of William and Mary, *The Officers, Statutes and Charter of the College of William and Mary* (Philadelphia, PA, 1817).

University of Allahabad, *Calendar for the Year 1931* (Allahabad, 1931).

University of Bombay, *The Calendar for the Year 1907–1908*, vol. I (Bombay, 1907).

University of Calcutta, *Calendar for the Year 1908*, pt 2 (Calcutta, 1908).

University of Dacca, *The Calendar for the Sessions 1929–30, 1930–31, 1931–32, 1932–33, 1933–34, 1934–35* (Dacca, n.d).

University of Madras, *Calendar for 1940–41*, vol. I, pt 1 (Madras, 1940).

University of Nagpur, *Nagpur University Calendar for 1941–42* (Mylapore, 1941).

University of the Punjab, *The Calendar of the University of the Panjab for the Year 1940–41* (Lahore, 1940).

University of Rangoon, *University of Rangoon Calendar for 1934–35* (Rangoon, 1935).

4. Newspapers

Argus [Melbourne].
Brisbane Courier.
Evening Post [New Zealand].
Irish Times.
John Bull.
Melbourne Punch.
Otago Witness.
Saturday Review.
The Star [New Zealand].
Sydney Morning Herald.
The Times.
Times Educational Supplement.
Times of India.

5. Printed Primary Sources

[Anon.], 'By the Way', *The Canadian Law Times*, xxxvii (1917), 261–2.

[Anon.], 'PR in University Elections: How the System Worked', *Representation: The Journal of the Proportional Representation Society*, xlii (1924), 30–2.

[Anon], 'Some Opinions on Questions of University Representation', *The Arena*, iii (1913), 246–7.

Billington-Greig, Teresa, 'The Sex-Disability and Adult Suffrage', *Fortnightly Review*, lxxxiv (1908), 258–71.

Blackstone, William, *Commentaries on the Laws of England, Vol. I: Of the Rights of Persons* (Chicago, 1979).

Bose, Subhas Chandra, *Correspondence, 1924–1932* (Calcutta, 1967).

Buchanan, Walter, *The Parliamentary Representation of the Scottish Universities: Being the Substance of a Paper Read at a Meeting of the Scottish Literary Institute Held at Glascow on the 24th of April 1857* (Edinburgh, 1857).

Burke, Edmund, 'Speech at the Conclusion of the Poll' [3 November 1774], in *The Writings and Speeches of Edmund Burke, Vol. 3: Party, Parliament, and the American War, 1774–1780*, ed. W.M. Elofson and John A. Woods (Oxford, 1996).

Childs, William MacBride, *Making a University: An Account of the University Movement at Reading* (1933).

Coleridge, Samuel Taylor, *The Collected Works of Samuel Taylor Coleridge, Vol. 10, On the Constitution of Church and State*, ed. John Colmer (Princeton, NJ, 1976).

The Correspondence of Alfred Marshall, Economist, Vol. II: At the Summit, 1891–1902, ed. John K. Whitaker (Cambridge, 1996).

Curzon, George Nathaniel, *Lord Curzon in India: Being a Selection from His Speeches as Viceroy & Governor-General of India, 1898–1905* (1906).

Elmy, Elizabeth C. Wolstenholme, 'Justice between the Sexes', *Westminster Review*, clxix (1908), 29–40.

Fisher, H.A.L., *An Unfinished Autobiography* (1940).

_____ et al., *British Universities and the War: A Record and Its Meaning* (1917).

Freeman, Edward A., 'University Elections', *Contemporary Review*, xliii (1883), 16–30.

Furniss, Harry, *Pen and Pencil in Parliament* (1897).

Heywood, James, *Academic Reform and University Representation* (1860).

Hodgins, J. George, *Documentary History of Education in Upper Canada, Vol. I: 1790–1830* (Toronto, 1894).

Humberstone, T. Lloyd, 'University Representation in Parliament', *The Arena*, iii (1913), 243–6.

Lorimer, James, 'University Representation', *North British Review*, xx (1854), 361–88.

Macaulay, Thomas Babington, 'Minute on Education in India', reproduced in *Politics and Empire in Victorian Britain: A Reader*, ed. Antoinette M. Burton (New York, 2001), 18–20.

MacNeill, J.G. Swift, 'Hibernia Irredenta: I – Mr Lecky and Irish Affairs', *Fortnightly Review*, lix (1896), 18–39.

_____ 'A Lusus Parliamenti: Dublin University Representation, 1801–1922', *Fortnightly Review*, cxiv (1923), 486–97.

Macpherson, Stuart, 'Patna University Convocation: New Vice-Chancellor's Address', *The Ravenshavian*, xv (1930), 17–21.

Macpherson, William Charteris, *The Baronetage and the Senate: The House of Lords in the Past, the Present, and the Future* (1893).

Mill, John Stuart, *Considerations on Representative Government* (1861).

Politics and Empire in Victorian Britain: A Reader, ed. Antoinette M. Burton (New York, 2001).

Rogers, Charles, *Leaves from My Autobiography* (1876).

Russell, Lord John, *An Essay on the History of the English Government and Constitution from the Reign of Henry VII to the Present Time* (2nd edn, 1823).

Sicily and England: A Sketch of Events in Sicily in 1812 & 1848, Illustrated by Vouchers and State Papers (1849).

Smith, J. Parker, 'University Representation' [pt 1], *The Law Magazine and Review*, 5th ser., ix (1883), 21–41.

Smith, J. Parker, 'University Representation' [pt 2], *The Law Magazine and Review*, 5th ser., ix (1884), 143–58.

6. Books, Articles, Theses and Electronic Publications

Allen, Adrian R., *University Bodies: A Survey of Intra- and Supra-university Bodies and Their Records* (Liverpool, 1990).

Ambedkar, B.R., *Pakistan, or the Partition of India* (2nd edn, Bombay, 1946).

Ames, Ellis [Paper on the Qualification for Voting in the Massachusetts Province Charter, December 1868], *Proceedings of the Massachusetts Historical Society*, x (1867–9), 370–5.

Atwood, Rebecca, 'Shaped by the Fees Fight: New Leader Sets Agenda after Landslide Victory', *Times Higher Education*, 22 Apr. 2010, p. 11.

Baker, J.H., *The Third University: The Inns of Court and the Common-Law Tradition* (1990).

Banerjee, Dilip, *Election Recorder* (Calcutta, 1990).

Barff, H.E., *A Short Historical Account of the University of Sydney* (Sydney, 1902).

Beaglehole, J.C., *The University of New Zealand: An Historical Study* (Auckland, NZ, 1937).

Beales, Derek, 'Parliamentary Parties and the "Independent" Member, 1810–1860', in *Ideas and Institutions of the Victorians: Essays in Honour of George Kitson Clark*, ed. Robert Robson (1967).

Bell, F.O., 'Parliamentary Elections in Indian Provinces', *Parliamentary Affairs*, i (1948), 20–9.

Bernays, Charles Arrowsmith, *Queensland Politics during Sixty (1859–1919) Years* (Brisbane, 1919).

Blewett, Neal, 'The Franchise in the United Kingdom, 1885–1918', *Past & Present*, no. 32 (1965), 27–56.

Blomfield, J.H, 'The Vote and the Transfer of Power: A Study of the Bengal General Election, 1912–1913', *Journal of Asian Studies*, xxi (1962), 163–81.

Bogdanor, Vernon, 'Why the Lords Doesn't Need More Politicians: An Elected Upper House Would Turn into a Retirement Home for Failed Party Hacks', *Sunday Telegraph*, 11 Feb. 2007, p. 24.

Bourne, Kenneth, *Palmerston: The Early Years, 1784–1841* (1982).

Burton, Antoinette, 'Tongues Untied: Lord Salisbury's "Black Man" and the Boundaries of Imperial Democracy', *Comparative Studies in Society and History*, xlii (2000), 632–61.

Butler, D.E., *The Electoral System in Britain, 1918–1951* (Oxford, 1953).

Cannadine, David, *The Decline and Fall of the British Aristocracy* (New Haven, CT, 1990).

———— *Ornamentalism: How the British Saw Their Empire* (Oxford, 2001).

———— 'Parliament: Past History, Present History, Future History', in *Making History Now and Then: Discoveries, Controversies and Explorations* (Basingstoke, 2008).

Carleton, Don, *A University for Bristol: An Informal History in Text and Pictures* (Bristol, 1985).

Cecil, Lady Gwendolen, *Life of Robert Marquis of Salisbury* (4 vols, 1921–32).

Charan, Umeshwari, *Responsible Government: A Case Study of Bihar, 1919–1937* (New Delhi, 1985).

Charlton, H.B, *Portrait of a University, 1851–1951: To Commemorate the Centenary of Manchester University* (Manchester, 1951).

Chase, Frederick, *A History of Dartmouth College and the Town of Hanover New Hampshire, Vol. 1* (Cambridge, 1891).

Chippendale, Peter, 'Members for the University: The University Constituency, 1858–1880', [University of Sydney Archives], *Record* (2003), 7–12.

Chiriyankandath, James, ' "Democracy" under the Raj: Elections and Separate Representation in British India', *Journal of Commonwealth and Comparative Politics*, xxx (1992), 39–63.

Choudhury, G.W., 'The First Constituent Assembly of Pakistan, 1947–1954', Columbia University PhD, 1956.

Chowdhury, Najima, *The Legislative Process in Bangladesh: Politics and Functioning of the East Bengal Legislature, 1947–58* (Dacca, 1980).

Clark, Anna, 'Gender, Class, and the Nation: Franchise Reform in England, 1832–1928', in *Re-reading the Constitution: New Narratives in the Political History of England's Long Nineteenth Century*, ed. James Vernon (Cambridge, 1996).

Clark, J.C.D., *English Society, 1688–1832: Religion, Ideology, and Politics during the Ancien Régime* (2nd edn, Cambridge, 2000).

Colley, Linda, *Taking Stock of Taking Liberties: A Personal View* (2008).

Cooter, Roger, 'The Rise and Decline of the Medical Member: Doctors and Parliament in Edwardian and Interwar Britain', *Bulletin of the History of Medicine*, lxxviii (2004), 59–107.

Cottle, Basil and J.W. Sherborne, *The Life of a University* (Bristol, 1951).

Crawley, C.W., 'French and English Influences in the Cortes of Cadiz, 1810–1814', *Cambridge Historical Journal*, vi (1929), 176–208.

_____ 'England and the Sicilian Constitution of 1812', *English Historical Review*, lv (1940), 251–74.

Cremona, J.J., *The Maltese Constitution and Constitutional History since 1813* (San Gwann, Malta, 1994).

Cross, Cecil Merne Putnam, *The Development of Self-Government in India, 1885–1914* (Chicago, IL, 1922).

Dardé, Carlos and Manuel Estrada, 'Social and Territorial Representation in Spanish Electoral Systems, 1809–1874', in *How Did They Become Voters? The History of Franchise in Modern European Representation*, ed. Raffaele Romanelli (The Hague, 1998).

Dixon, W. Macneile, *Trinity College, Dublin* (1902).

Dyhouse, Carol, *No Distinction of Sex? Women in British Universities, 1870–1939* (1995).

Easthope, Reginald, 'Durham University Society: History of the Society', University of Durham, http://www.dur.ac.uk/dusada/history.htm 3 Nov. 2006.

Ehrman, John, *The Younger Pitt* (3 vols, 1969–96).

Engholm, G.F., 'The Development of Procedure in Uganda's Legislative Council', *Parliamentary Affairs*, ix (1955), 338–52.

Forbes, Geraldine, *Women in Modern India* (Cambridge, 1996).

Fyfe, Christopher, *A History of Sierra Leone* (Oxford, 1962).

Gandhi, J.S., 'Past and Present: A Sociological Portrait of the Indian Legal Profession', in *Lawyers in Society: The Common Law World*, ed. Richard L. Abel and Philip S.C. Lewis (Berkeley, CA, 1988).

Gardner, W.J., *Colonial Cap and Gown: Studies in the Mid-Victorian Universities of Australasia* (Christchurch, NZ, 1979).

Garrard, John, *Democratization in Britain: Elites, Civil Society and Reform since 1800* (Basingstoke, 2002).

Garrido, Aurora, 'Electors and Electoral Districts in Spain, 1874–1936', in *How Did They Become Voters? The History of Franchise in Modern European Representation*, ed. Raffaele Romanelli (The Hague, 1998).

Gash, Norman, *Politics in the Age of Peel: A Study in the Technique of Parliamentary Representation, 1830–1850* (1953).

____ *Mr Secretary Peel: The Life of Sir Robert Peel to 1830* (Cambridge, MA, 1961).

Ghosh, Suresh Chandra, 'The Genesis of Curzon's University Reform: 1899–1905', *Minerva*, xxvi (1988), 463–92.

Gibson, Hamilton, *Concise Chronological History of Dartmouth College* (Hanover, NH, 1919).

Godsen, P.H.J.H. and A.J. Taylor, *Studies in the History of a University, 1874–1974* (Leeds, 1975).

Greene, Jack P., 'Foundations of Political Power in the Virginia House of Burgesses, 1720–1776', *William and Mary Quarterly*, 3rd ser., xvi (1959), 485–506.

Hall, Catherine, Keith McClelland and Jane Rendall, *Defining the Victorian Nation: Class, Race, Gender and the Reform Act of 1867* (Cambridge, 2000).

[Harris, Theodore Wilson], 'The University Vote' [review of Rex, *University Representation*], *Times Literary Supplement*, 8 Oct. 1954, p. 634.

Harrison, Brian, *Separate Spheres: Opposition to Women's Suffrage in Britain* (1978).

Hartog, P.J., 'The Indian Universities', *Annals of the American Academy of Political and Social Science*, cxlv (1929), 138–50.

Hayes, William A., *The Background and Passage of the Third Reform Act* (New York, 1982).

Henry, Wm Wirt, 'House of Burgesses, 1766 to 1775', *Virginia Magazine of History and Biography*, iv (1897), 380–6.

____ 'Members of the House of Burgesses', *Virginia Magazine of History and Biography*, viii (1901), 245–60.

Herbert, Alan, *A.P.H.: His Life and Times* (1970).

Heron, Denis Caulfield, *The Constitutional History of the University of Dublin* (Dublin, 1847).

Hill, John Lowell, 'Congress and Representative Institutions in the United Provinces, 1866–1901', Duke University PhD, 1966.

Hirst, J.B., *The Strange Birth of Colonial Democracy: New South Wales, 1848–1884* (Sydney, 1988).

A History of the University of Cambridge, ed. Christopher N.L. Brooke (4 vols, Cambridge, 1989–2004).

The History of the University of Oxford, Vol. 4: Seventeenth-Century Oxford, ed. Nicholas Tyacke (Oxford, 1997).

The History of the University of Oxford, Vol. 6: Nineteenth-Century Oxford, Part 1, ed. M.G. Brock and M. C. Curthoys (Oxford, 1997).

The History of the University of Oxford, Vol. 8: The Twentieth Century, ed. Brian Harrison (Oxford, 1994).

Hitchner, Dell G, 'The Labour Government and the House of Commons', *Western Political Quarterly*, v (1952), 417–44.

Hodgins, Thomas, 'A Member of Parliament for the University', *The Canadian Magazine*, v (1895), 115–21.

Hoeveler, J. David, *Creating the American Mind: Intellect and Politics in the Colonial Colleges* (Lanham, MD, 2002).

Humberstone, T. Lloyd, 'University Representation in Parliament – I', *Parliamentary Affairs*, i (1947), 67–82.

____ 'University Representation in Parliament – II', *Parliamentary Affairs*, i (1947), 78–93.

____ 'University Representation in Parliament – II', *Parliamentary Affairs*, i (1948), 78–88.

_____ *University Representation* (1951).

Ives, Eric, Diane Drummond and Leonard Schwartz, *The First Civic University: Birmingham, 1880–1980: An Introductory History* (Birmingham, 2000).

Jenkin, Thomas P., 'The British General Election of 1950', *Western Political Quarterly*, iii (1950), 179–89.

Jones, Andrew, *The Politics of Reform, 1884* (Cambridge, 1972).

Karkaria, R.P, *The Late K.T. Telang and the Present Political Movement in India, Reprinted from the 'Calcutta Review'* (Bombay, 1895).

Kelly, Thomas, *For Advancement of Learning: The University of Liverpool, 1881–1891* (Liverpool, 1981).

Kilpin, Ralph, *The Romance of the Colonial Parliament: Being a Narrative of the Parliament and Councils of the Cape of Good Hope from the Founding of the Colony by Van Riebeeck in 1652 to the Union of South Africa in 1910* (1930).

Kirkpatrick, John E., 'The Constitutional Development of the College of William and Mary', *William and Mary Quarterly*, 2nd ser., vi (1926), 96–108.

Knights, Ben, *The Idea of the Clerisy* (Cambridge, 1979).

Lackland, H.M, 'The Failure of the Constitutional Experiment in Sicily, 1813–1814', *English Historical Review*, xli (1926), 210–35.

_____ 'Lord William Bentinck in Sicily, 1811–12', *English Historical Review*, xlii (1927), 371–96.

Lawrence, Jon, 'The Transformation of British Public Politics after the First World War', *Past & Present*, no. 190 (2006), 185–216.

Literature and Social Reform in Colonial Orissa: The Legacy of Sailabala Das (1875–1968), ed. Sachidananda Mohanty (New Delhi, 2006).

Lowe, Roy, 'The Expansion of Higher Education in England', in *The Transformation of Higher Learning, 1860–1930: Expansion, Diversification, Social Opening, and Professionalizing in England, Germany, Russia, and the United States*, ed. Konrad H. Jarausch (Chicago, IL, 1983).

Lowell, A. Lawrence, *The Government of England* (2 vols, New York, 1908).

Lulat, Y.G.-M., *A History of African Higher Education from Antiquity to the Present: A Critical Synthesis* (Westport, CT, 2005).

Macintyre, Stuart, *A Colonial Liberalism: The Lost World of Three Victorian Visionaries* (Melbourne, 1991).

_____ 'The Same under Different Skies: The University in the United States and Australia', *Journal of Australian Studies*, xxxiii (2009), 353–69.

Madden, A.F, ' "Not for Export": The Westminster Model of Government and British Colonial Practice', *Journal of Imperial and Commonwealth History*, viii (1979), 10–29.

Mahaffy, John Pentland, *An Epoch in Irish History: Trinity College, Dublin, Its Foundation and Early Fortunes, 1591–1660* (1903).

Malet, Charles Edward, *A History of the University of Oxford* (3 vols, 1924).

Malten, Helen, *Steel City Scholars: The Centenary History of the University of Sheffield* (2005).

Markandan, K.C., *Madras Legislative Council: Its Constitution and Working between 1891 and 1909* (Delhi, 1965).

Martin, Briton Jr, 'Lord Dufferin and the Indian National Congress, 1885–1888', *Journal of British Studies*, vii (1967), 68–96.

Martin, Ged., *Bunyip Aristocracy: The New South Wales Constitution Debate of 1853 and Hereditary Institutions in the British Colonies* (Sydney, 1986).

Matthew, H.C.G., *Gladstone, 1809–1874* (Oxford, 1986).

_____, R.I. McKibbin and J.A. Kay, 'The Franchise Factor in the Rise of the Labour Party', *English Historical Review*, xci (1976), 723–52.

McCallum, R.B. and Alison Readman, *The British General Election of 1945* (Oxford, 1947).

McCracken, J.L., 'Irish Parliamentary Elections, 1727–68', *Irish Historical Studies*, v (1947), 209–30.

_____ *The Cape Parliament, 1854–1910* (Oxford, 1967).

McCully, Bruce Tiebout, *English Education and the Origins of Indian Nationalism* (New York, 1940).

McDowell, R.B. and D.A. Webb, *Trinity College Dublin, 1592–1952: An Academic History* (Cambridge, 1982).

Meisel, Joseph S., *Public Speech and the Culture of Public Life in the Age of Gladstone* (New York, 2001).

_____ 'A Magnificent Fungus on the Political Tree: The Growth of University Representation in the United Kingdom, 1832–1950', *History of Universities*, xxiii/1 (2008), 109–86.

Merton, Robert K., 'Three Fragments from a Sociologist's Notebooks: Establishing the Phenomenon, Specified Ignorance, and Strategic Research Materials', *Annual Reviews of Sociology*, xiii (1987), 10–23.

Moody, T.W., 'The Irish Parliament under Elizabeth and James I: A General Survey', *Proceedings of the Royal Irish Academy, Section C*, xlv (1939), 41–81.

_____ and J.C. Beckett, *Queen's Belfast, 1845–1949* (2 vols, 1959).

Moore, R.J., 'The Twilight of the Whigs and the Reform of the Indian Councils, 1886–1892', *Historical Journal*, x (1967), 400–14.

Morpurgo, J.E., *Their Majesties' Royall Colledge: William and Mary in the Seventeenth and Eighteenth Centuries* (Williamsburg, VA, 1976).

Mukherjee, Sumita, ' "Narrow-Majority" and "Bow-and-Agree": Public Attitudes towards the Elections of the First Asian MPs in Britain, Dadabhai Naoroji and Mancherjee Merwanjee Bhownaggree, 1885–1906', *Journal of the Oxford University Historical Society*, ii (2004), 1–20.

Mullinger, James Bass, *The University of Cambridge* (3 vols, Cambridge, 1911).

Newman, Melanie and Rebecca Atwood, 'Students Told: "Terrify Main Parties or be Screwed Over" ', *Times Higher Education*, 22 Apr. 2010, pp. 6–7.

Ogg, Frederic A., 'The British Representation of the People Act', *American Political Science Review*, xii (1918), 498–503.

O'Gorman, Frank, *Voters, Patrons, and Parties: The Unreformed Electoral System of Hanoverian England, 1734–1832* (Oxford, 1989).

Olson, Alison G., 'Eighteenth-Century Colonial Legislatures and their Constituents', *Journal of American History*, lxxix (1992), 543–67.

Owen, Nicholas, 'British Progressives and Civil Society in India, 1905–1914', in *Civil Society in British History: Ideas, Identities, Institutions*, ed. Jose Harris (Oxford, 2003).

Palande, M.R., *Introduction to Indian Administration* (5th edn, Bombay, 1951).

Pargellis, S.M., 'The Procedure of the Virginia House of Burgesses', *William and Mary Quarterly*, 2nd ser., vii (1927), 143–57.

Parliament as an Export, ed. Alan Burns (1966).

Pateriya, P.R., *Provincial Legislatures and the National Movement* (New Delhi, 1991).

Pedersen, Susan, *Eleanor Rathbone and the Politics of Conscience* (New Haven, CT, 2004).

The People's Choice: Electoral Politics in Colonial New South Wales, ed. Michael Hogan, Lesley Muir and Hilary Golder (Sydney, 2007).

Porritt, Annie G., 'The Irish Home Rule Bill', *Political Science Quarterly*, xxviii (1913), 298–319.

Porritt, Edward, 'Barriers against Democracy in the British Electoral System', *Political Science Quarterly*, xxvi (1911), 1–31.

Prest, Wilfred R., *The Inns of Court under Elizabeth I and the Early Stuarts, 1590–1640* (1972).

Pugh, Martin, 'Popular Conservatism in Britain: Continuity and Change, 1880–1987', *Journal of British Studies*, xxvii (1988), 254–82.

Ramanna, Mridula, 'Profiles of English Educated Indians: Early Nineteenth-Century Bombay City', *Economic & Political Weekly*, xxvii (1992), 716–21, 723–4.

Reeves, P.D., B.D. Graham and J.M. Goodman, *A Handbook to Elections in Uttar Pradesh, 1920–1951* (Delhi, 1975).

Reinhardt, William W., *The Legislative Council of the Punjab, 1897–1912* (Durham, NC, 1972).

Re-reading the Constitution: New Narratives in the Political History of England's Long Nineteenth Century, ed. James Vernon (Cambridge, 1996).

Rex, Millicent Barton, 'The University Constituencies in the Recent British Election', *The Journal of Politics*, viii (1946), 201–11.

_____ *University Representation in England, 1604–1690* (1954).

Rosselli, John, *Lord William Bentinck and the British Occupation of Sicily, 1811–1814* (Cambridge, 1956).

Rothblatt, Sheldon, *The Revolution of the Dons: Cambridge and Society in Victorian England* (New York, 1968).

_____ 'The Diversification of Higher Education in England', in *The Transformation of Higher Learning, 1860–1930: Expansion, Diversification, Social Opening, and Professionalizing in England, Germany, Russia, and the United States*, ed. Konrad H. Jarausch (Chicago, IL, 1983).

_____ *The Modern University and Its Discontents: The Fate of Newman's Legacy in Britain and America* (Cambridge, 1997).

_____ *Education's Abiding Moral Dilemma: Merit and Worth in the Cross-Atlantic Democracies, 1800–2006* (Oxford, 2007).

Rubinstein, W.D., 'Education and the Social Origins of British Élites, 1880–1970'. *Past & Present*, no. 112 (1986), 163–207.

Russell, Ben, 'After 10 Years, How Close is Labour to Reforming the House of Lords? The Big Question', *The Independent*, 6 Feb. 2007, p. 30.

Russell, Meg, *Reforming the House of Lords: Lessons from Overseas* (Oxford, 2000).

Sanderson, Michael, *The Universities and British Industry, 1850–1970* (1972).

_____ *Education, Economic Change and Society in England, 1780–1870* (Cambridge, 1995).

Schneider, Fred D., 'The Imperial Factor and the "University Question" in Upper Canada', *Journal of British Studies*, xvii (1977), 82–104.

Scott, Ernest, *A History of the University of Melbourne* (Melbourne, 1936).

Seaman, John T., *A Citizen of the World: The Life of James Bryce* (2006).

Selleck, R.W., *The Shop: The University of Melbourne, 1850–1939* (Melbourne, 2003).

Serle, Geoffrey, 'The Victorian Legislative Council, 1856–1950', *Historical Studies, Australia and New Zealand*, vi (1954), 186–203.

Sewak, Ram, *History of Bihar between the Two World Wars (1919–1939)* (New Delhi, 1985).

Shimmin, A.N., *The University of Leeds: The First Half-Century* (Cambridge, 1954).

Shinn, Christine Helene, *Paying the Piper: The Development of the University Grants Committee, 1919–1946* (1986).

Simms, Marian, *From the Hustings to Harbour Views: Electoral Institutions in New South Wales, 1856–2006* (Sydney, 2006).

Simpson, Renate, *How the PhD Came to Britain: A Century of Struggle for Postgraduate Education* (Guildford, 1983).

Sinha, Mrinalini, *Colonial Masculinity: The 'Manly Englishman' and the 'Effeminate Bengali' in the Late Nineteenth Century* (Manchester, 1995).

_____ 'Britishness, Clubbability, and the Colonial Public Sphere: The Genealogy of an Imperial Institution in Colonial India', *Journal of British Studies*, xl (2001), 489–521.

Smith, F.B., *The Making of the Second Reform Bill* (Cambridge, 1966).

Smith, Janet Adam, *John Buchan: A Biography* (1965).

Southard, Barbara, 'Colonial Politics and Women's Rights: Woman Suffrage Campaigns in Bengal, British India in the 1920s', *Modern Asian Studies*, xxvii (1993), 397–439.

Srinivas, Bobby, 'Patriotism Made Easy!' *The Hitavada*, 16 Nov. 2005.

Sweet, Rosemary, 'Freemen and Independence in English Borough Politics c.1770–1830', *Past & Present*, no. 161 (1998), 84–115.

Thomas, Malcolm I., *A Place of Light and Learning: The University of Queensland's First Seventy-Five Years* (St Lucia, 1985).

Tinker, Hugh, *The Foundations of Local Self-Government in India, Pakistan, and Burma* (1954).

Turney, Clifford, Ursula Bygott and Peter Chippendale, *Australia's First: A History of the University of Sydney, Vol. 1: 1850–1939* (Sydney, 1991).

University and Community: Essays to Mark the Centenary of the Founding of University College Bristol, ed. J.G. McQueen and S.W. Taylor (Bristol, 1976).

The University of London and the World of Learning, 1836–1986, ed. F.M.L. Thompson (1990).

Vella, Andrew P., *The University of Malta: A Bicentenary Memorial* (Malta, 1969).

Vernon, James, *Politics and the People: A Study in English Political Culture, c.1815–1867* (Cambridge, 1993).

Vernon, Keith, *Universities and the State in England, 1850–1939* (2004).

Viswanathan, Gauri, *'Masks of Conquest': Literary Study and British Rule in India* (New York, 1989).

Wallace, Stuart, 'National Identity and the Idea of the University in 19th-Century Scotland', *Higher Education Perspectives*, ii (2006), 125–46.

Ward, W.R., *Georgian Oxford: University Politics in the Eighteenth Century* (Oxford, 1958).

_____ *Victorian Oxford* (1965).

Wheare, Joan, *The Nigerian Legislative Council* (1950).

Williams, J. Gwynn, *A History of the University of Wales, Vol. 2: The University of Wales, 1893–1939* (Cardiff, 1997).

Wright, Raymond, *A People's Counsel: A History of the Parliament of Victoria, 1856–1900* (Melbourne, 1992).

Yasin, Madhvi, 'Lord Dufferin and the Liberalisation of the Provincial Councils', *Journal of Historical Research*, xix (1977), 77–86.

7. Biographical and Other Reference Works

A Catalog of Graduates Who Have Proceeded to Degrees in the University of Dublin, from the Earliest Recorded Commencements to July, 1866, with Supplement to December 16, 1868 (Dublin, 1869).

Dictionary of National Biography, ed. S.P. Sen (4 vols, Calcutta, 1972).

Dod's Parliamentary Companion, 1944 (1944).

Glover, William and Mary Newton Standard, *The Colonial Virginia Register: A List of Governors, Councillors and Other Higher Officials, and Also of Members of the House of Burgesses, and the Revolutionary Conventions of the Colony of Virginia* (Albany, NY, 1902).

History of the Irish Parliament, 1692–1800, ed. E.M. Johnston-Liik (6 vols, Belfast, 2002).

The History of Parliament:

> *The House of Commons, 1690–1715*, ed. Eveline Cruickshanks, Stuart Handley and D.W. Hayton (4 vols, Cambridge, 2002).
>
> *The House of Commons, 1715–1754*, ed. Romney Sedgwick (2 vols, 1970).
>
> *The House of Commons, 1754–1790*, ed. Lewis Namier and John Brooke (3 vols, 1964).
>
> *The House of Commons, 1790–1820*, ed. R.G. Thorne (5 vols, 1986).

Martin, A.W. and P. Wardle, *Members of the Legislative Assembly of New South Wales, 1856–1901* (Canberra, 1959).

Oxford Dictionary of National Biography, ed. Colin Matthew and Brian Harrison (40 vols, Oxford, 2004), online edn, http://www.oxforddnb.com/.

Thacker's Indian Directory (Calcutta).

Thompson, Kathleen and Geoffrey Serle, *A Biographical Register of the Victorian Parliament, 1859–1900* (Canberra, 1972).

Index

Index